Ethel K. Smith Library

Wingate University
Wingate, North Carolina 28174

THE

TROUBLED HEART

OF AFRICA

ALSO BY ROBERT B. EDGERTON

*Like Lions They Fought: The Zulu War and the
Last Black Empire in South Africa*

Mau Mau: An African Crucible

The End of the Asante Empire

*Warriors of the Rising Sun: A History of the
Japanese Military*

Death or Glory: The Legacy of the Crimean War

*Warrior Women: The Amazons of Dahomey and
the Nature of War*

*Hidden Heroism: Black Soldiers in
America's Wars*

Africa's Armies: From Honor to Infamy

Robert B. Edgerton

THE

TROUBLED HEART

OF AFRICA

A History of the Congo

ST. MARTIN'S PRESS ~ NEW YORK

www.stmartins.com

Design by Kathryn Parise

Map by Sharon Belkin

ISBN 0-312-30486-2

First Edition: December 2002

10   9   8   7   6   5   4   3   2   1

Contents

Acknowledgments

I would like to thank staff members of the Royal Geographical Society, London, the Department of History of the Presbyterian Church (USA) in Montreat, North Carolina, the Musée Royal de l' Armée et d'Histoire Militaire in Brussels, and the Charles E. Young Research Library at UCLA, especially its interlibrary loan department. Among the many Africans who helped me try to understand their world, I am especially indebted to Aramu Mundugu, Yovan Chemtai, and Simeon Kioko. I can't possibly thank all of the anthropologists who have helped me, but I am especially grateful to Wally Goldschmidt, Keith Otterbein, and Tom Weisner. For drawing the map, I thank Sharon Belkin. And this book could never have been written without the dedicated research assistance and manuscript preparation of my former graduate student and now Ph.D., R. Jean Cadigan. I have worked with over a score of editors over the years, but none has been as insightful and helpful as Tim Bent. Many thanks. And to Steve Boldt, thanks for a wonderful job of copy editing. Finally, to my anthropologist wife, Karen L. Ito, thank you for making everything worthwhile.

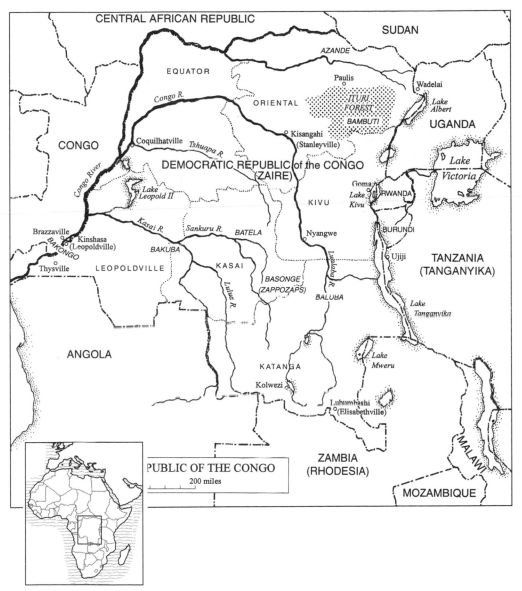

CENTRAL AFRICAN REPUBLIC

SUDAN

AZANDE

EQUATOR

Paulis ○

Wadelai ○

ITURI FOREST

Lake Albert

Congo R.

ORIENTAL

BAMBUTI

UGANDA

CONGO

Coquilhatville ○

Tshuapa R.

○ Kisangahi (Stanleyville)

DEMOCRATIC REPUBLIC of the CONGO (ZAIRE)

Lake Victoria

Congo River

Lake Leopold II

Kasai R.

Sankuru R.

BATELA

KIVU

Goma *Lake Kivu*

RWANDA

Nyangwe

BURUNDI

Brazzaville ○

Kinshasa (Leopoldville)

Lualaba R.

○ Ujiji

TANZANIA (TANGANYIKA)

BAKONGO

BAKUBA

Thysville ○

LEOPOLDVILLE

KASAI

Lulue R.

BASONGE (ZAPPOZAPS)

BALUBA

Lake Tanganvika

ANGOLA

● *Lake Mweru*

KATANGA

Kolwezi ○

Luhumbashi ○ (Elisabethville)

..PUBLIC OF THE CONGO

200 miles

ZAMBIA (RHODESIA)

MALAWI

MOZAMBIQUE

Inset of area

Introduction

Why should the Congo's past interest anyone today? An obvious reason is to try to understand the seemingly endless suffering and endurance of its people. The history of the Congo is one of unremitting evil on the part of its leaders, whether Europeans or Congolese, yet at every stage of this history ordinary people refused to surrender their compassion for one another, their quest for happiness, and their hope for a better future. The racist greed of the many Europeans who exploited the Congolese people for slaves and later for the country's mineral riches is as appalling as the tyranny of the Congolese dictators who followed them. The history of the Congo is one of brutalized people striving not only to remain alive but to create meaningful lives for themselves. During my visits to the eastern Congo, where a volcano recently killed many and left hundreds of thousands homeless, I have never witnessed such widespread misery nor experienced greater human kindness.

And there is the future: a political issue with international ramifications. The Congo is richer in mineral wealth than any other country in Africa. That wealth had previously been stolen by the Congo's leaders and their cronies. But for the past few years, it has been mined by troops from neighboring countries that have engaged in bloody warfare against one another. Millions of Congolese have died as a result of this war, which threatens the stability of the entire continent.

The Congo is hardly the only country in the world to have become known for its troubled history and uncertain future. Bangladesh, El Salvador, Myanmar, North Korea, Russia, Sri Lanka, Sudan, Yugoslavia, and now Afghanistan come readily to mind. But none of these—and probably no other country on earth—can match the Congo. In 1899, Joseph Conrad's famous novella *Heart of Darkness* depicted the Congo as a place of degradation, but long before Conrad's visit and for over a century since his book appeared, the Congo has been the scene of unremitting horrors that have condemned untold millions of people to lives of misery and led to the deaths of millions more.

Will the Congo ever awaken from the nightmare of its history? Though still plagued by deadly strains of malaria, sleeping sickness, yellow fever, and other diseases, it also still has many resources. Although its volcanic mountains, extensive swamplands, and dark, dense forests are not suitable for farming, many parts of the huge country have successfully been brought under intensive cultivation, and its many rivers, including the Congo River—the world's second-longest and deepest—are richly stocked with fish.

Nonetheless, the legacy of exploitation remains a heavy shackle. Once European powers took possession of the Congo, its people were almost perennially hungry, and its mineral wealth enriched only politicians and foreign corporations. Life expectancy has always been short and may today be its shortest ever. Portuguese slave traders inflicted horror on the Congo's population early in the sixteenth century just as Zanzibari Arabs did in the nineteenth century. Slavers were joined by ivory and rubber traders, brutal government officers, soldiers, and cannibals in tyrannizing, torturing, and killing many millions of people—perhaps 10 million during King Leopold II's nearly pathological reign from 1885 to 1908 alone. European and American missionaries and missionary doctors brought some benefits to the Congo, as did the Belgians and other Europeans who settled in the "Belgian Congo" from 1908 to 1960, when political independence came to a population wholly unprepared to rule themselves. Wars exploded across the country. Joseph-Désiré Mobutu seized power in 1965 and held it until 1997, when Laurent-Désiré Kabila was brought to power by troops from Uganda and Rwanda. Kabila was assassinated early in 2001 and was succeeded by his twenty-nine-year-old son, Joseph.

Belgian rule saw the development of modern cities, including the posh metropolitan center of Léopoldville (later Kinshasa) with glass-and-concrete skyscrapers and five-star hotels. It saw the creation of riverine, railroad, and highway transport, airports, schools, and an extensive health-care system. But these were accompanied by deeply entrenched racism and the conscious decision not to provide university education for Congolese. Independence under Mobutu brought outrageous corruption. Mobutu became one of the world's richest men while the country's economy collapsed, democracy vanished, and most people went hungry most of the time. The Congolese people were ill, disillusioned, and without hope.

Yet the earliest European explorers, traders, and missionaries found thriving societies, peopled by well-fed, contented, hard-working, and creative people. Cannibalism existed in some places, but did not become widespread and thoroughly brutal until later, when the Arab-and-European-led ivory, rubber, and slave trades ravaged traditional societies. Before that time, there were kingdoms in the Congo with large towns, elegant houses, clean streets, little crime, fair courts and juries, productive farmers, skilled ironworkers, and remarkably skilled artists whose crafts in wood, metal, and cloth quickly found their way into Europe's museums. The Congo was not paradise, but most of its people led prosperous lives, helped by religious rituals and strong family ties. By the time that Henry Morton Stanley brought the Congo to the world's attention in 1877, most of that good life had disappeared, and by the time Leopold's brutal regime ended three decades later, the Congo had become perhaps the most dreadful place on earth.

Today, its economy remains in ruins. There are no public services. Armed soldiers demand money from anyone thought to have any, and hungry Congolese beg for food on the streets. Since 1997, the Congo has also been the site of a brutal international war. The troops from Uganda and Rwanda that forced Mobutu to flee for his life chose to remain in the eastern Congo, where they amassed riches by mining diamonds, gold, coltan, and other minerals. In return for mineral concessions of their own, Angola, Namibia, and Zambia sent troops to the Congo to aid Joseph Kabila's tottering regime. The resulting warfare has continued to this day, with an estimated death toll of 3 million men, women, and children, many of them victims of disease and famine.

Faced with the threat that this appalling disaster could destabilize all of central Africa, in mid-2001 several African nations came together with the United Nations to organize a peace conference to be attended by all the opposing parties. Due to a lack of adequate funding for all the participants, the first conference, held in Addis Ababa in October, failed, but several countries, led by Nigeria and South Africa, persisted, and a second conference, this time amply funded, began in early 2002, in South Africa. As this is written, the fate of Central Africa, if not all of Africa, hangs in the balance.

THE

TROUBLED HEART

OF AFRICA

1

THE LAND BEYOND
OBSCURITY AND DARKNESS

The Congo that so horrified Joseph Conrad in the 1890s embraced nearly 1 million square miles, an area as large as the United States east of the Mississippi or all of Western Europe. When Europeans first discovered it in the late fifteenth century, it was home to at least 250 different ethnic groups, ranging over fifteen cultural regions as different as the Mbuti Pygmies, who lived by hunting in the Ituri Forest in the eastern Congo, and the prosperous farmers of the Bakongo Kingdom in the west, where cleared fields and large towns once supported well over a million people spread across three hundred square miles.[1] Most of the peoples in the Congo spoke a Bantu language, and although most of these were not mutually intelligible, the first word an infant uttered in all of them was "Mama"—mother— and a dying person's last utterance, too, was often "Mama."[2] There were also people in the northeast of the Congo who spoke Sudanic or Nigritic languages, including the warlike Azande people, who successfully resisted European rule well into the twentieth century.

Large portions of the Congo are open, strikingly beautiful, silver-baobab-tree-dotted savannas of tall, yellow elephant grass that are home to herds of wildlife. Some hilly areas are covered with ten- to twelve-foot-tall grass with edges so sharp that when dry, cut like razors. Other regions, particularly in the east, are steeply mountainous but split by deep valleys where bamboo, tree ferns, huge orchids, lobelias, and other beautiful flowers flourish. The volcanic peaks and glaciers in this eastern region, known as the Mountains of the Moon, are permanently snowcapped and higher than the Alps. Their foothills are black lava, and nearby lakes are jade green or a brilliant blue. These eastern uplands are so cold that they are completely free of both flies and mosquitoes, and the Europeans who later came to live there had to wear sweaters even at midday. But the low-lying regions of the Congo are intensely hot, steamingly humid, and home to multitudes of fleas, centipedes, large grasshoppers with green bodies and scarlet wings, cicadas, cockroaches, bees, ticks, leeches, hornets with a painful sting, little green fireflies, and myriads of beautiful butterflies and dragonflies of all colors. Throughout the low-lying, central Congo basin, there are hordes of flies as large as hornets, and blood-sucking mites, while every evening brings swarms of mosquitoes so voracious they can bite through European clothing.[3]

Large portions of the Congo are permanent swampland, but almost half of the country is covered by a dense, dark tropical forest—"darkness," literally. Within these forests there are lichen- and moss-covered ebony, oak, mahogany, cedar, walnut, and rubber trees, as well as clumps of bamboo all tied together by lianas and flowering vines. Within many of these dark forests there is rarely any sound or movement, and a sickening smell of decaying vegetation pervades the air. Usually, no birds, bats, or monkeys are to be seen, nor whirring insects to be heard. The silence is so profound that when explorers in large caravans first entered these forests, they felt compelled to speak in whispers, and if a monkey chattered, a toucan shrieked, or a tree limb fell, they were visibly startled.

In most of these forests, there are no flowers, but a dark green wall of trees usually rising two hundred feet overhead. The ground is covered with sodden, decaying vegetation that often is several feet deep. European explorers often despaired of cutting their way through these "jungles," as they called them, a Hindi word meaning impenetrable thicket. Yet, in some parts of the Congo, forests such as these have long been cleared, allowing millions of people to farm the now open land. In many of these areas, palm trees flourished, providing both highly valued palm oil and palm wine in return for little effort. Bananas and yams also thrived in these hot, moist regions while older crops such as sorghum and millet would not. And in some parts of these forests there are bats, rats, flying squirrels, civet cats, hairy pigs, monitor lizards six feet long, and even elephants.

Much of the Congo basin is crisscrossed by so many wide, rapidly flowing, mud-brown rivers that together they make up one-sixth of the world's hydroelectric potential. Spanned by hundreds of vine bridges, dotted by over four thousand islands covered with trees, reeds, mangroves, and water hyacinth, most of these rivers have long been traveled by people paddling standing up in long canoes made from hollowed-out tree trunks. The rivers are home to many crabs, shrimp, turtles, hippopotamuses, and crocodiles, while nearby live thousands of pelicans, egrets, ducks, pygmy geese even smaller than ducks, kingfishers with scarlet beaks, five-foot-tall purple herons, sacred ibises, white-tailed flycatchers, scarlet and black weaver birds, and fish-eating eagles. Many people came to live along the banks of these rivers, fishing and farming after they had cleared away the forests atop sandstone cliffs that were sometimes red, sometimes yellow, and even white. But most people did not live along riverbanks; they built their villages in fertile valleys farther inland and walked some distance to pick up water for drinking and bathing. The Congo River itself was not only a rich resource for fish and crustaceans, but it also posed few dangers because it neither flooded nor ran dry. Because the Congo's tributaries come from both north of the equator and south of it, when it is the rainy season in one region, it is dry in the other, maintaining the huge river's even flow year-round.

The Congo's more open forests and grasslands are still home to elephants, giraffes, zebras, buffaloes, lions, leopards, cheetahs, and all manner of antelope, ostriches, and smaller animals, such as rabbit-sized nocturnal tree-hyraxes that emit ear-piercing screams, while carrion-eating hyenas, jackals, and vultures are still seemingly everywhere.[4] But rhinos have never lived there. In some forested areas there are still seemingly millions of monkeys, while in others there are none. In parts of the eastern Congo there are both chimpanzees and gorillas. Pythons, cobras, mambas, puff adders, and other deadly snakes are commonplace as well, as are scorpions, huge, beautiful spiders, and fiercely biting, inch-long red ants. At times, so many black bats can fly overhead that the sky is literally obliterated. People still use machetes or even sticks to knock them out of the air and cook them. Even away from the rivers, hundreds of different sorts of birds live in the Congo, from majestic eagles and hawks to gray parrots with bright scarlet tails, long-winged blue swallows, red-chested cuckoos, thick, gray plovers, and black hornbills.

Despite its location astride the equator, the Congo has dramatically differing seasons. For much of the region, from February to May there is heavy rain and flooding. But, even during the rainy season, it does not rain every day. Some days are dry but the sky is gray and the sun is seldom seen. When rain does fall, it is sometimes so warm that some travelers have likened it to human sweat.[5] However, every two or three days during the late afternoon, a huge purple-black cloud forms in the east. As it moves to the west, the air becomes still and claps of distant thunder grow louder by the minute. As the black, arching cloud finally passes overhead, lightning strikes, thunder crashes, and the wind suddenly roars at sixty or seventy miles an hour, driving torrents of rain almost horizontally, flooding everything for an hour or so before moving on, leaving behind a gentle rain that may continue throughout the night. In Katanga, the Congo's southernmost province, when thunderstorms strike at its four-thousand-foot elevation, spray splashes five or six feet into the air, making it impossible to drive a car.

From May through October the weather is usually dry but cloudy, and it is cold at night with temperatures often falling to fifty degrees Fahrenheit even at lower elevations, and sometimes reaching freezing in Katanga. It can also be so cold during the day that hail the size of hen's eggs has been known to fall for hours and people have to stay inside by a warm fire. October, November, and December are rainy and hot, while January is dry and still hot. Whether humid or dry, although mornings are usually damp and cold, in many areas the midday heat is oppressive.

Whatever the season, diseases continue to be rampant. There are waterborne afflictions such as schistosomiasis, Guinea threadworm, and "river blindness," as well as bouts of malaria, sleeping sickness, dysentery, and yellow fever. Mosquito-borne yellow fever strikes abruptly with a high fever, headache, muscle pain, and violent vomiting. Blood pressure falls, blood oozes from every tissue surface, and the kidneys fail. As recently as 1960–62, yellow fever killed thirty thousand people in Ethiopia. The Congo has also been plagued by tuberculosis, pneumonia, smallpox, influenza, and with the arrival of Europeans and Arabs, syphilis. Until European rule took hold early in the twentieth century, there were wars, too, and both cannibalism and slavery were common although not universal. Nevertheless, the Congo's population was large, perhaps as much as 20 million people, and growing at the time of European contact at the end of the fifteenth century.

The ancestors of these people began to migrate south and west into the Congo basin perhaps five thousand years ago. The first to arrive were light-skinned Pygmies, who lived by hunting and gathering in the Congo's game-rich forests. They were not warlike, but despite their diminutive size they were well able to defend themselves if attacked. Capable of hiding almost to the point of invisibility in their dense forests, they could throw a spear hard enough to pass halfway through a man and could fire their deadly poisoned arrows so rapidly that four could be in the air before the first one struck. Although these little people—even today men average less than four feet six inches in height while the women are smaller still—did not practice any form of horticulture, they knew how to make fire, were skilled metallurgists, had effective medical practitioners, and created a joyous way of life that continues to this day among Pygmy groups.

Sometime around two thousand years ago, much taller, usually but not always darker-skinned Bantu-speaking horticulturalists began to move into the basin, fully settling it by A.D. 1,000. They borrowed much from the Pygmies, who traded dried meat and honey for agricultural products, salt, and iron.[6] Bantu people treated the Pygmies as markedly inferior—"mere animals" they often called them—and in return the Pygmies had little respect for the Bantu people. Yet, in their growing interdependence with farmers, the Pygmies somehow lost their languages. Nevertheless, they were highly successful hunters and gatherers. Pygmy groups routinely gathered nine or ten types of fruit, as many as eight types of snails, thirteen kinds of termites, and over twenty kinds of caterpillars, as well as several kinds of honey and over thirty types of mushrooms. Their nutrition was every bit as good as that of the Bantu farmers, and sometimes better.[7]

Like the Pygmies, Bantu-speaking farmers sometimes hunted,

trapped, and gathered, but they relied mainly on cultivation. Initially dependent on yams, they later adopted imported American plants such as maize, manioc, beans, and tobacco and also came to rely on avocados, sugarcane, pineapples, coconuts, tangerines, peanuts, and especially bananas, which were relatively easy to grow as they required little clearing of forests yet provided a yield ten times that of yams.[8] One large Bantu society, the Bakongo Kingdom, cultivated twelve species of vegetables, a different one becoming ripe each month of the year.[9] These farming people became highly skilled ironworkers, potters, weavers, and artists. The social systems they created were complex yet effective. There was little crime and steady population growth. There were many differences among the hundreds of societies in the Congo. Some had marked social inequality, while others were largely egalitarian; some had complex ceremonials, while others did not; some were fiercely warlike but others avoided conflict whenever possible; and some lived in simple bamboo houses, while others fashioned large wooden homes that were elegantly decorated. Despite warfare and the ravages of tropical disease, their populations grew, their religious beliefs and institutions prospered, and most people's lives appear to have been rewarding.

In the fifth century B.C., Herodotus told of an expedition that sailed south of the Canary Islands, and in the first century A.D., Pliny described an admiral who sailed all the way to Senegal.[10] But no European is known to have ventured into the Congo's "darkness" until 1482, ten years before Columbus sailed to North America. Both dangerous and alluring, Africa south of the Sahara was still thought by Europeans to be the home of one-eyed or two-headed people, among other monsters, as well as ferocious, gigantic animals, including birds large enough to carry away elephants, and ants as big as foxes. It was also thought to be the home of long-lost Prester (Presbyter) John, a Christian king who according to legend possessed a fountain of youth as well as unimaginable wealth from his many gold mines. Thanks to a forged letter from Prester John that reached the pope around A.D. 1165, Europeans became terrified of Africa. The letter not only described his wealth, it warned of Africa's horrible dangers and horrors. Thousands of copies were made and it was widely circulated. Some Europeans hoped to discover Prester John and share in his vast riches. But despite the lure of Prester John's gold and his fountain of youth, Africa's dangers remained terrifying.

South of the Canary Islands off the southern coast of Morocco lay what was known to Europeans as the dreaded Sea of Darkness, where every imaginable horror awaited any European explorer rash enough to enter it—liquid sheets of flame falling from the sky, a boiling ocean, mountainous waves, and deadly whirlpools where Satan lay in wait to kill. Should anyone miraculously survive these deadly terrors, he would be forever lost in the inescapable and even more fearsome Sea of Obscurity, which lay beyond the Sea of Darkness. Yet urged on by their king, who craved the riches of unknown lands as well as the discovery of a passageway to the great wealth of India, dauntless Portuguese ship captains eventually sailed through the Seas of Darkness and Obscurity in such numbers that by the middle of the fifteenth century, fifty of their ships had reached the coast of Guinea. They returned to Portugal with over a thousand African slaves. Arabs had long taken African slaves from Sudan, but these were the first Africans known to be enslaved by Europeans.[11]

All the while, shipbuilders in Lisbon—at the cutting edge of their profession—worked to improve their sailing ships, especially the new *caravel,* a relatively small vessel, only sixty to a hundred feet long, with a broad bow, small stern, three masts bearing cloth and lateen sails, and a crew no larger than fifty or sixty men. By the latter half of the fifteenth century these new ships were able to survive powerful storms and to sail into the wind.

As the years passed, Portuguese caravels sailed progressively farther south down Africa's northwest coast and then east along its south-facing western "slave" and "gold" coast, as it would later be named by British explorers and slave traders. In 1482, an experienced ship captain, Diogo Cão, sailed his caravel farther south than any other European had ever been, well beyond the Sea of Darkness and the Sea of Obscurity, even beyond the equator.

As he sailed south below the equator, still 150 miles from shore, Cão was surprised to see the blue-green ocean slowly turning the color of tea, then dark brown, before, to his amazement, it became covered by plants of all sorts, including large trees. As he approached the shoreline, sailing against a current of nearly ten miles an hour although he was still dozens of miles offshore, he finally saw the seven-mile-wide mouth of a silt-filled river surrounded by several more miles of small streams, sandbanks, and mangroves. The Congo, home to more than five hundred species of fish, some of them over four feet long, was far larger than any river that Cão or any other European had ever seen. It was the second-largest river in the entire world. Only the Amazon carried more water to the sea.

After he had come ashore, Cão somehow managed to ask the Bakongo people who lived along its estuary what the river was called; they answered, "Nzere, the river that swallows all others."[12] Cão misheard the name as Zaire, and the river was known by this name until some years later, when it became known as the Congo, after the Bakongo people to whom Cão had spoken. In the Bantu language spoken by these natives, the prefix *Ba* in *Bakongo* indicates "people of" Kongo. Cão sent four of his sailors to the king of the Bakongo with gifts, giving the men a date beyond which he could not wait for their safe return. Although Cão actually waited well past this deadline, his men did not return. In retaliation, Cão seized four high-ranking Bakongo hostages at gunpoint and sailed home.

Before Cão sailed to Portugal, he erected a five-foot-tall stone pillar topped by an iron cross that he had carried from Portugal—a *padrão*—as an official notification of Portuguese dominion. Carved into the stone by order of Portugal's King John II were these memorable, if immodest, words: "In the year 6681 of the world and in that of 1482 since the birth of our Lord Jesus Christ, the most serene, the most excellent and potent prince, King John II of Portugal did order this land to be discovered and this pillar of stone to be erected by Diogo Cão, an esquire in his household."[13] The pillar stood until the mid-1600s when a Dutch warship shelled it.

Cão sailed back to Africa three years later. He first tried and failed to find a route to India by sailing as far south as he could. He was forced to return to the great river, where he hoped to recover the four men he had left behind. This time he found them. They explained that they had missed the deadline three years before because of language difficulties, then regaled Cão with tales of how well they had been treated, with ample food, comfortable housing, and bevies of attractive young women. Cão then set free his four Bakongo hostages, who had been treated exceptionally well in Portugal, where they had received many indulgences from King John II. They had lived in the royal palace, been taught to speak Portuguese, and exposed to the dazzling wonders of Lisbon. In return for all of this, King John II hoped that when returned to their homeland, they would convince the king of the Bakongo to become an ally of Portugal's.[14] To the amazement of the Bakongo, these four men returned wearing the elegant garments of Portuguese noblemen and had nothing but praise for King John II and the Portuguese. The king of the Bakongo was so impressed that he designated one of those noblemen, a man named Nsaka, as his ambassador to John II. Accompanied by several children of other nobles, Nsaka went to

Portugal with Cão and spent five years in Lisbon. The children were adopted as the godchildren of Portuguese nobility.

After an exchange of gifts and pleasantries with the king of the Bakongo, Cão then sailed one hundred miles up the Congo River until he was stopped by the Yellala Cataract at the Crystal Mountains, a three-hundred-foot-tall waterfall that sent deafening torrents of water crashing down. Cão and his party were awestruck. They managed to climb to the top of the cataract, where Cão engraved an open rock face with the shield of Portugal, a cross, and an inscription reading, "Here arrived the ships of the illustrious King John II of Portugal. Diogo Cão. Pêrc Anes. Pêro de Costa."[15]

Cão left no written record of what he saw, but in 1883, the English adventurer Sir Harry Hamilton Johnston described what he saw from the spot where Cão and his companions must have stood:

> It *was* a grand view . . . we looked down some hundred feet on the giant Congo, leaping over the rocks and dashing itself wrathfully against the imprisoning hills. Several islands bestrewed its stream, one especially remarkable from being a mass of velvet woods. This was called the Island of Pelicans, for numbers of these giant birds used this inaccessible spot as a breeding-place.
>
> Before the first fall took place the river came gliding on so smoothly, with such a glass surface, as if never suspecting the terrible conflict before it, and when at first it met the rocks and the descent it streamed over them almost unresistingly until, exasperated by repeated checks, in the last grand Fall of Yelala [*sic*], it lashed itself into white and roaring fury, and the sound of its anger deafened one's ears, and the sight of its foam dazzled the eyes.[16]

Cão had no means of knowing that for the next two hundred miles upriver, the Congo River is torn by thirty-one powerful cataracts like the one before him. Beyond them lay a large, still pool, twenty-five miles long and sixteen miles wide, containing seventeen islands. Inland from this pool, the river is navigable for one thousand miles, after which there are more dramatic waterfalls. Fed by innumerable rivers and streams, in places the Congo River is an incredible ten miles wide. Though his ships successfully sailed back to Portugal, Cão himself was never again mentioned in written records. It is believed that he died there in the Crystal Mountains.[17]

Six years later, in 1491, in response to a request by Afonso I, the king of the Bakongo, an expedition of Portuguese soldiers, laborers, priests, masons, carpenters, and artisans, many of them accompanied by their wives, arrived at the mouth of the Congo. After a ten-day march of 150 miles along a road that was swept clean by the orders of Afonso I, who also sent food to them each day, they arrived in the capital of the Bakongo people. They were immediately taken to the king, who welcomed them on his handsome ebony throne inlaid with ivory on a raised platform.[18] One by one, the men knelt and kissed his hand before showering him with gifts, including bolts of silk and satin, gold and silver jewelry, and for some obscure reason, a flock of red pigeons. The king welcomed them warmly in a grand, if tumultuous, ceremony. His hospitality may have been sincere; he had, after all, heard such wondrous praise of the Portuguese from the four Bakongo who had spent three years with them. But it may also have reflected his wish to use their muskets to put down a troublesome provincial rebellion. Still, undoubtedly, he was also greatly impressed by Portuguese riches, which he hoped to share.[19] The Portuguese immediately set themselves to building stone churches, schools, and living quarters. As soon as the first church was built, the king was baptized, as were many of his nobles.[20]

King Afonso I maintained an elaborate court at the capital town of San Salvador, located on a cliff top to the southeast of the Congo River. He was surrounded by a host of slaves, pages, and personal attendants, as well as his harem of wives. Special officials such as a chief priest and a royal executioner were also in attendance.[21] Afonso I had a ritual relationship to the land, and as was common in West Africa, no one was permitted to observe a sovereign eating or drinking—he intended to convince his subjects that, unlike mere mortals, he needed no earthly sustenance. The symbols of his high office included that throne with its ivory carvings, a white cap, and a zebra's tail. He exercised supreme judicial power, including the exclusive right to order the death penalty. However, such orders appear to have been rare. Instead, the king spent his days in public discussions. As a later British visitor noted of the Bakongo people, "They take a keen delight in oratory, which may in fact be said to constitute one of their important arts. They talk fluently and employ many metaphorical and flowery expressions. Possessing a natural gift of rude eloquence, it is greatly enhanced in effect by the soft inflections and the harmonious euphony of their language; they reason well and display great aptitude for debate."[22]

The visitors soon learned that in addition to the yams, bananas, and other various fruits and vegetables they cultivated, the Bakongo also raised cattle, goats, and pigs. They used cowrie shells as currency, their value regulated by the royal court, which also collected taxes. The Portuguese were enormously impressed not only by the low rate of crime but by the artistry the Bakongo displayed in smelting iron, forging copper by means of the lost wax process, carving marble into columns and obelisks, weaving cloth, and carving wood and ivory. The ivory impressed them most of all; they soon exported it to Europe in large quantities. The Portuguese were pleased to learn that not only were the Bakongo horrified by the idea of cannibalism, which the Portu-

13

guese believed was practiced by all Africans, but they were also mild-mannered, dignified people who were respectful of their women and children.[23] They were anything but the "naked savages" the Portuguese had expected to find.

The Portuguese priests, who rapidly undertook missionary activities, were, however, appalled by the multiple wives possessed by the Bakongo men who could afford them, but they were unable to end the practice. Nor did they succeed in convincing the Bakongo to destroy their fetishes and idols, or to cease the erotic rituals the priests found so un-Christian. Most important for the course of future events in the Congo, neither Portuguese laymen nor priests were at all horrified by the Bakongo practice of slavery.

The Bakongo had four categories of slaves: persons from other tribes captured in warfare, Bakongo debtors, criminals, and children given away by their families as part of a dowry. Some types of slaves were treated quite well, while others, especially criminals, were not, but all slaves were productive members of society, and some earned their freedom.[24] Even though King Afonso I banished the increasingly meddlesome Portuguese from his kingdom in 1495, only four years after their arrival, they remembered avidly the large numbers of Bakongo slaves, their many useful skills, and the obvious reality that many other valuable people like them could either be purchased or, thanks to Portuguese muskets, captured.

Although their priests had been expelled, a few Portuguese slave buyers continued to arrive in the Congo, particularly after Brazil was "discovered" by the Portuguese in 1500. That new colony's developing mines and coffee plantations cried out for slave labor, and Portuguese of all sorts, including even some of the Roman Catholic priests who had been expelled, rushed back to the Congo to engage in the already immensely profitable slave trade. Located several hundred miles to the north of the Congo

River's estuary, the island of São Tomé played a crucial role in the early days of the slave trade. First sighted by the Portuguese in 1470, it soon after became a colony for exiled Portuguese Jews, expatriates, and criminals, who served their time there while supervising the agricultural labor of thousands of African slaves, many of whom would later be shipped to Brazil. Until well into the 1500s, however, most of the African slaves from the Congo wound up in Portugal itself, not Brazil. In 1535, for example, four thousand to five thousand slaves were sent to Portugal from the Congo, and in several parts of Portugal, Africans made up more than 50 percent of the population.[25] There were illicit sexual relations between Portuguese men and slave women, but African slaves were typically not well treated. Slave owners were not even required to bury dead slaves. Instead, their bodies were thrown into a roadside ditch where dogs ate them.[26]

Meanwhile, more and more heavily armed Portuguese slave traders, inevitably followed by Catholic priests, made their way to the shores of the Congo River, most of them moving inland some sixty miles to Boma on the north bank of the Congo River, a place that was then so hot, swampy, and infested by huge mosquitoes that it was virtually unlivable. Others went to nearby areas in the west of the Congo, where missions and schools were built to "civilize" and baptize the Bakongo people who lived in this region. Many Portuguese traders did not set an exemplary example of Christian civilization. One of these, a ship's captain named Gonsalve Rodrigues, arrived in the court of King Afonso I in 1506, claiming falsely that King Manoel of Portugal had sent him to pick up two missionaries and take them back to Portugal. Hoping to create a positive relationship with King Manoel, Afonso I gave up the missionaries, who were at odds with him in any event, and sent the Portuguese king many expensive gifts and valuable slaves. When sickness broke out aboard ship, Rodrigues heartlessly put the afflicted slaves ashore on a deserted coast to fend for themselves. He also ruthlessly threw overboard slave children, who had little value because of their age, along with at least one older slave who had somehow displeased him. And he kept all the gifts meant for King Manoel for himself.[27]

By this time, King Afonso I had been baptized and was promoting the missionaries' efforts to Christianize the Bakongo, but relations between him and his European visitors remained tense. Portuguese priests simply could not abide polygyny, but those Bakongo men who were wealthy enough to afford multiple wives staunchly refused to give them up. Matters worsened when it became clear to the Bakongo that Church doctrine called only for baptizing slaves, not doing anything to improve the quality of their lives. As far as the priests were concerned, it was quite acceptable for Africans to be taken into slavery as long as they were baptized. The priests' greatest fear was that slaves, or any other Africans, might live as "heathens."[28] More remarkable still, many priests actually joined in the slave trade, explaining that their low salaries forced them to do so.[29]

Afonso I grew disillusioned with his Christian visitors and the increasingly vicious slave trade they were causing to expand. Slavery had become so profitable by the 1530s that some Bakongo were actually selling members of their own family into slavery. In 1540, after King Afonso I had increased his earlier attempts to curtail the slave trade, several Portuguese merchants tried unsuccessfully to kill him during a mass that he attended on Easter Sunday. By the time of his natural death, three years later, his support for the missionaries had ended, and by 1560, almost all of the Catholic missionaries had been made to feel so unwelcome that they returned to Portugal.

In the 1600s, Dutch sea power weakened the grip of Portuguese slave traders in the Congo. Other European traders began to arrive in significant numbers as well. More and more, the remaining Portuguese retreated south into what is now Angola. In 1665, the Bakongo king, Antonio I, assembled an army of some seventy thousand men, led by ten Europeans, and attacked a force of three hundred and sixty Portuguese soldiers plus six or seven thousand warlike Yaga tribesmen, in Angola. The attack failed, and King Antonio I was killed along with one hundred of his Bakongo leaders, precipitating a disorganized and bloody flight by the surviving Bakongo. Pursued into their homeland, they were so shattered that their kingdom would never again regain its former power.

The Angolan victors also took many slaves, aided by Portuguese priests, many of whom lived astonishingly dissolute lives. They drank heavily, kept concubines, took part in pagan ceremonies, and actually charged a fee for administering the sacraments. Some priests were even accused of cannibalism, and one priest was accused of poisoning another.[30] At the same time that these less than Christian actions were taking place, two Catholic priests became the first Europeans to get past the Crystal Mountain's Yellala Cataract and the others behind it on the lower Congo River and actually reach what later became known as Stanley Pool, two hundred miles inland. Their reports were buried in long-forgotten archives.[31] Despite feats like this, as the years passed, the priests' influence, like that of the sober Capuchins—an austere branch of the first order of St. Francis of Assisi—who had followed them, weakened so steadily that by the early 1800s, those Congolese who wore crucifixes viewed them as simply another talisman.

That the Capuchins were anything but enamored of the Bakongo as potential Christians can be seen in these comments made by the Capuchin missionary Antonio de Gaeta in 1669:

Devils by the deformation of their features, devils by the blackness of their bodies, devils in their souls because their wills are always fixed on evil; devils in their thinking, by continually having in mind superstition, witchcraft and sorcery; devils in their speaking, by the great lies they utter; devils in their actions, by so many grave sins which they commit; and finally, devils and more than devils, damned and more than damned, by that bestial pride, that inhuman and barbarous cruelty, which they display all the time and in every action.[32]

French Catholic missionaries, on the other hand, learned to speak Kikongo, generally respected the Bakongo people, and were well received by them in return. However, deadly diseases soon forced the French priests to abandon their work.

While most European missionaries and slave traders stayed near the coast in the far west, a few explored inland. In 1806, two Portuguese mulattoes walked all the way from coastal Angola to Mozambique, spending considerable time during their journey in mineral-rich Katanga in the southernmost part of the Congo, where they were the first non-Africans the inhabitants there had ever seen.[33]

British interest in Central Africa was negligible until 1807, when Britain outlawed slavery and the Royal Navy began to suppress the transatlantic slave trade. Even so, the British expressed no apparent interest in the Congo River until 1814, when two Royal Navy frigates sailed fifty miles up the river to the dismal trading station of Boma. Their officers found little worthy of mention in their reports except the dangers posed by the river's strong current and its "floating islands with trees still erect," as they described the river's debris that they observed floating out to sea.[34] However, their visit must have had an impact on the Foreign Office because, in the following year, the British government not only financed a major expedition to the Congo River but commissioned the first steamship ever built by the Royal Navy to lead it. The ship's construction took much longer than anticipated, so it was replaced by the sailing sloop *Congo*, accompanied by the troopship *Dorothy*, filled with supplies, not soldiers. The two ships set sail from England on February 25, 1815, under the command of Royal Navy captain James Kingston Tuckey, a thin, tall, forty-two-year-old veteran of naval service in the Caribbean, Europe, and India, as well as nine years of captivity in France during the Napoleonic wars. During his captive years, he married an Englishwoman, also a prisoner, and had two sons.

Tuckey was instructed to record as much as possible about the Congo's slave trade, its geography, animal life, minerals, vegetation, climate, and its people's "genius and disposition."[35] To assist him in this daunting mission, Tuckey assembled a crew of fifty-three Europeans including carpenters, blacksmiths, a surgeon, fourteen Royal Marines, an anatomist to study local animals, a gardener from the Royal Gardens at Kew, a self-taught natural historian, and a thirty-one-year-old Norwegian professor of botany with the unlikely name of Smith. Several African seamen sailed with the expedition as well. A kind and courteous man, Tuckey demonstrated a respect for the Congolese people that was remarkable for that time—and would remain so for a century to come—issuing this written order to his crew: "As one of the objects of the expedition is to view and describe manners, it will be highly improper to interrupt, in any matter, the ceremonies of the native, however they may shock humanity or create disgust; and it is equally necessary, in the pursuits of the different Naturalists, to avoid offending the superstitions of the natives in any of their venerated objects."[36]

When Tuckey's ship arrived at the mouth of the Congo on July 5, 1816, the current was slow and he sailed on to Boma without difficulty. There he found seven Portuguese slave ships along with one apparently (from the colors it was flying) Spanish slaver that actually fired a warning shot toward him, then fled. Tuckey ignored the incident and the remaining slave ships and went ashore. He soon concluded that the practice of kidnapping slaves would not exist were it not for the presence of European slave traders, who, he noted with disgust, gave the Congolese only brandy, muskets, and gunpowder in return for slaves.[37] He described the Africans he saw in Boma as "sulky looking vagabonds, dirty, swarming with lice," a product, he wrote, of the shameful Portuguese "civilization" that had given the Congolese nothing but the torn and filthy clothes the people wore. He also met with the Bakongo chief of the Boma area. After an exchange of gifts and pleasantries, the British visitors were offered women, but Tuckey declined their services. Thanks to the unbelievably fortuitous presence of an English-speaking Bakongo member of Tuckey's crew, they learned a great deal about Bakongo culture.

In a story that is truly stranger than fiction, eleven years earlier this same wealthy and powerful Bakongo chief had seen enough of European ships, weapons, and material culture to realize that a European education could vastly improve the life—and the influence—of an African who received one. Choosing one of his favorite sons, who was then about ten years old, he trustingly gave much ivory and other valuables to a British ship captain to take the boy to Britain, to see that he was educated there, then to safely return him to his father. This captain, whose name is unknown, happily accepted the gifts and readily agreed to see to the boy's education, but he sailed not to England but to the Caribbean, where he promptly sold the boy into slavery in St. Kitts. There the boy, who became known as Simmons, learned English as a field hand, and after some eleven years of life as a slave managed to stow away on a British ship and escape to England, where he was immediately set free. Sir H. Popham, the captain of the ship on which Simmons had stowed away, learned about Tuckey's expedition and told Simmons about it. He was taken on as a cook's mate.[38]

As fortune would have it, Simmons's father was still alive when

Tuckey's expedition arrived. The aging chief had faithfully met every British ship that had visited the Boma area for the past eleven years hoping to find his son. When he was finally reunited with his son, he was overjoyed, hugging him passionately as Tuckey and his crew looked on.[39] Tuckey observed that Simmons, dressed in an English jacket and trousers, and proud of his ability to speak English, seemed somewhat embarrassed by his father's ecstasy.[40] If so, the old chief could not restrain himself. He immediately ordered his son treated as a prince, dressing him in a silk coat embroidered with silver, a black glazed hat sporting an enormous grenadier feather, and a silk sash that held a ship's cutlass. Shaded by slaves carrying umbrellas, the young man was carried everywhere in a palanquin, escorted by twenty men with muskets, given every favor, and addressed as Prince Schi.

Simmons, or Prince Schi, continued to interpret for Tuckey as he sailed farther up the Congo past scenery that Tuckey called "as beautiful and not inferior to any on the banks of the Thames."[41] But once beyond the Kikongo language area, Simmons abandoned the expedition, returning to his father and his people. Tuckey was able to sail upriver for 145 miles before he encountered the impassable Yellala Cataract as Cão had done, and like Cão, he was determined to press on. For another fifty miles, he and several of his men struggled ahead, climbing up the steep, rugged, almost perpendicular, quartz-rock-strewn Crystal Mountains, dotted with red boulders, tufts of purple grass, and scrubby thorn trees. However, by early September the terrain had become so formidable, food so scarce, and the Europeans so sick with intense fevers that he had to turn back.

Tuckey and his botanist colleague, Dr. Chetien Smith, left extensive descriptions of the landscape as well as sensitive accounts of the people and their cultures. They, too, reported that they found no cannibalism. However, Smith was concerned about what he saw as the exploitation of women as laborers by "indolent" men.[42] He also concluded that three hundred years of Portuguese missionary work had achieved no significant effect, largely, he believed, because the Catholic missionaries were so intolerant of polygyny that the Congolese ignored them.[43] Tuckey went on to describe the Congolese people as honorable, honest, "extremely hospitable to strangers and always ready to share their pittance, sometimes scanty enough, with the passing stranger."[44]

As the explorers attempted to make their way back to their ships, the onslaught of fever—in all probability yellow fever—worsened, and Tuckey's last journal entry was on September 18, 1816. His last written words were: "Flocks of flamingos going to the south denote the approach of the rains."[45] Although the weather was idyllic throughout their stay in the Congo with the mercury rarely rising over seventy-six degrees Fahrenheit or falling below sixty degrees at night, Tuckey, Smith, and nineteen others of the fifty-six Europeans on the expedition died. The ship's surgeon wrote that most died of a violent fever, but that some, including Tuckey, seemingly died of exhaustion. It is assumed that Prince Schi survived and chose to remain with his father in the Congo, but nothing is known about the remainder of his life.

After the survivors of the Tuckey expedition returned to England, the country's political leaders and traders alike lost interest in the Congo until 1840, when antislavery patrols by the Royal Navy began in earnest in that part of Africa. Previous to that time, the Royal Navy had been restricted to patrols north of the equator. Slave ships could often outsail the Royal Navy ships, and even when the British succeeded in capturing Portuguese slave ships, the result was usually hellish. In 1857, Commander Jason Hunt of the steam sloop *Alecto* captured the slave vessel *Windward,* with 603 slaves on board, chained and packed almost on top of one another. Hunt drove the slave ship toward the the British Colony of St. Helena, but before he could land, 149 of the slaves had died. Many of the others Hunt freed far from home probably died as well.[46]

At the same time, British trading firms set themselves up at Boma, dealing in ivory, copper, and palm oil. It is seldom recognized that, by the 1880s, British trade in the Congo had become extensive, worth £2 million per annum in 1884, compared to £3 million for the far more developed and seemingly richer West African Bights of Benin and Biafra combined.[47] The British government and its traders insisted on their commercial rights in the Congo, where they typically practiced humanitarianism, providing decent wages and living conditions for their employees, and no tolerance for slavery. British and American Protestant missionaries were active as well.[48]

The impact of the European presence—slavers, traders, and missionaries—on most Congolese societies was profound, but some chiefdoms and even one large kingdom remained untouched for centuries. The Bakuba Kingdom (also known as Bushongo) in what became Kasai Province in the east-central Congo was not even seen by a European until 1892, when black American missionary William H. Sheppard was permitted to visit their royal court despite a fiercely enforced prohibition against any foreigner doing so. Sheppard had learned the Kuba language from traders who visited his nearby mission station, and his fluency in it convinced Bakuba king Lukenga that Sheppard was a reincarnated Bakuba. The Bakuba had been so isolated that until Sheppard's arrival they had never seen or even heard a gun.

The kingdom was small, about two-thirds the size of Belgium, and had perhaps 120,000 to 160,000 inhabitants.[49] But for Sheppard, and all other Europeans who would later visit the kingdom, it seemed remarkably complex compared to its African neighbors. Public ceremonies exhibited astonishing pomp—honors, insignia, and pageantry. And its artistic tradition was one of the finest in all of Africa. The Bakuba also had a remarkably sophisticated social system, one with marked differences in wealth and power, ranging from wealthy patricians who were virtually above the law, to peasants and slaves. There was greater social inequality among these people than among any other in Central Africa, yet slaves were well treated, and their offspring always became free people. A few slaves were buried with their deceased patrician masters to serve them in the next world; still, there had never been a slave revolt. Bakuba also had a legal system that was unique to all of Africa in its day. Each person accused of a crime was judged by a jury chosen specifically for that case.[50]

Their religion was intricate as well, boasting a rich variety of gods and a belief in reincarnation, as well as fear of witchcraft and sorcery, a central role for diviners to detect witches, and many cults, ceremonies, and practitioners. There was much grieving for the dead, who were buried in wooden coffins eight feet into the earth. Bakuba men were more involved in clearing fields, harvesting crops, and building granaries than were men in any other Congolese society. Women and girls worked hard as well, tending crops, drawing water, cooking, and caring for the household. The capital city of some ten thousand people was noteworthy for its wide, clean streets, which were tended to early every morning by war captives and convicted criminals. The king's palace included meeting halls where eighteen powerful counselors discussed and sometimes even dictated policy, but as was the case with the Bakongo, the king alone had the power to order an execution. His palace also held storehouses, his harem, and courtyards for public assemblies, all enclosed by a wall nine to ten feet high. The court collected taxes, imposed corvée labor when needed, and maintained a uniformed police force.[51]

The king lived lavishly. Pampered in every way, shown every obeisance, and adorned with jewels and cowrie shells, he was sung to sleep by his wives, who also sang him awake in the morning.[52] The wealthy patricians lived almost as grandly. As anthropologist Jan Vansina wrote:

> The wealthier patricians lived within fenced compounds in lavishly decorated houses having several rooms and sometimes a separate kitchen, with slaves to serve them and perhaps a snake charmer or other performer for after-dinner entertainment. . . . The men's interests among all the patricians revolved around the court, its intrigues and its ceremonies, while the women embroidered raffia cloth, did the shopping and kept house, freed from the hard chores of most other women.[53]

Nothing distinguished the Bakuba more than their artwork. Elegant carvings of wood and ivory were commonplace. Doors and sliding door panels were beautifully carved as well, as were masks, stools, drums, boxes, dishes, and tobacco pipes. There were highly ornamented pots, swords, and metal jewelry. There were also sculptures of people and animals. One that survived to become a museum piece included realistically carved women paddling a canoe filled with boxes of goods. There were elegant gowns of weaving and delicate embroidery. Their cloth was soaked and then beaten until it took on a velvety, silken finish.[54] There were also four life-size ebony statues of former kings that were considered sacred.[55] Bakuba art has been displayed in museums in Europe and the United States for over a century. Several European artists have been influenced by the Bakuba art they have seen in these museums. Art critics have pointed out that Picasso's cubist period owes a great deal to the Bakuba art he saw in an exhibit in Paris in 1907.

As one European visitor after another noted, the peoples of the Congo differed greatly. Some practiced slavery and cannibalism, but others did neither. Some welcomed Europeans, others fled or fought. Some were warlike, others were peaceful. Some welcomed the opportunity to work for the Europeans, others fled to the forests. Perhaps predictably, some European visitors characterized the Congolese people as above all lazy, infantile, unintelligent, ungrateful, and lacking foresight.[56] One Belgium Catholic missionary described them as "laziness incarnate, turning their hands to nothing, becoming drunk, dead drunk . . . whereas the women and slaves, driven with the whip, work pitifully hard."[57] A British Protestant missionary wrote, "The chief characteristics of [the Congolese] people appear to be drunkenness, immorality and cruelty."[58] But other Europeans described the Congolese people they met as intelligent, elegant, courageous, gentle, communicative, gay, and thoughtful.[59] One young British man who spent several years with different peoples in the Congo concluded in a book he wrote: "It has been my experience that the longer one lives with Africans, the more one grows to love them. Prejudices soon vanish. The black skin loses even something of its unpleasant characteristics, for one knows that it covers such a very human heart."[60]

While British firms were setting up trading stations along the Congo coast, followed to a lesser extent by French, Dutch, and other European companies, European exploration continued. In 1848, Hungarian explorer László Magyar, a former lieutenant in the Argentine navy in its wars against Uruguay and the illegitimate son of a Hungarian minor landowner, led a two-month expedition up the Congo River. In his diary he reported that Boma was by then a huge slave market with a large resident population of white slave traders. Tuckey had estimated the annual export of slaves from Boma in 1817 at two thousand; thirty years later, Magyar estimated it at twenty thousand. He was outraged by the inhuman abuses of slaves that he witnessed: "The most heart-rending spectacle is when five- or six-year-old children who followed their manacled parents on the long, pitiful journey, as it were sharing their miserable existence, are torn without pity from the arms of their screaming mothers by the inhuman [slave drivers]."[61] Magyar climbed to the top of the Yellala Cataract, describing it in his diary:

> Then a majestic scene of nature appeared before my eyes. The air was vibrating with the thundering weight of the water, which fell with the speed of lightning. The greenish welter at the base of the fall dissolved into spray, which rose towards heaven, in which the sun transcribed rainbows. An awe-inspiring spectacle, at which an ordinary mortal could only worship his creator in amazement. . . . I could not overcome the depth of the impression this made on me. I watched for a long time sunk into myself.[62]

Magyar then explored farther inland, leaving behind in his diary detailed and insightful portraits of the people he met. Had he translated his diary into a better-known European language such as German, Italian, Portuguese, or Spanish—all of which he spoke and wrote as well—then sent it to the British Royal Geographical Society, he would have become at least as famous as Dr. David Livingstone later did, as we will see. Instead, the diary languished unread in Hungarian, and Magyar remained virtually unknown, though he spent the next five years exploring Angola and South Africa, traversing much of the same territory later described by Livingstone, who refused Magyar's request to meet with him.[63]

After 1853, Magyar lived and explored widely in Central and Southern Africa, marrying the daughter of a chief and also acquiring several slave women as wives, and lots of children. Lacking sponsorship and a source of funding, he could not mount a major exploration of the Congo. He eventually became impoverished and died in 1864 at the age of forty-six. One serious student of Magyar's life believes that he actually starved to death.[64] Unfortunately, most of his letters were lost, and his diary, as I've explained, had little impact, although his observations were keen and insightful and his adventures at least as thrilling as those that made David Livingstone famous during the same period.

In 1857, German geographer-ethnographer Adolf Bastian visited the Congo south of the river's estuary. He wrote warmly of the inhabitants—their great kindness, generosity, and courtesy. But like Magyar, he described an active and brutal Portuguese slave trade. He also reported that Portuguese missionaries publicly flogged Congolese daily. Even women were flogged by the missionaries, who called upon St. Michael and his angels to give them strength. Bastian had little sympathy for the missionaries' attempts to convert the Congolese people to Christianity, saying that all baptism accomplished was to replace tattooing as a ritual practice, and that baptism was an "easily displaceable rite."[65] As Tuckey had noted earlier, Bastian wrote that crosses were to be seen everywhere but that for the Congolese people they were simply another of their many fetishes and had no Christian significance.

The legendary British adventurer Sir Richard F. Burton traveled up the Congo River in 1863, visiting a number of tribal peoples. As was usual in his African travels, Burton described these people as members of "lower races," but his view did not prevent him from consorting with beautiful Somali women, from whom he acquired syphilis. His ardor may have contributed to his conflict with Somali warriors, one of whom drove a spear into his left cheek and out his right one. After his widely published travels in East Africa in the late 1850s that led to many controversies about the source of the Nile, Burton became British consul for West Africa from 1861 to 1864. When he began his trip up the Congo River, he was recovering from a severe bout of malaria but found the cool air near the Yellala cataract "charming, quite a sanitarium." His account of his exploration was preceded by lengthy comments about the Portuguese missionaries' brutal despotism.[66] Like others before him, he noted that while many Congolese people wore crucifixes, "all traces of Christianity had disappeared."[67] Burton was as critical of missionaries as he was of slave traders.

Burton also described the Congo's topography, vegetation, animals, and villages in great and erudite detail, often referring to obscure aspects of African history. But the spirit of Africa still comes through. He was particularly struck by the total silence that night brought—"neither beast, nor bird nor sound of water."[68] He climbed to the top of Yellala Falls, which he measured at 390 feet, and grudgingly declared that it had "a certain beauty and grandeur," but he was unable to travel farther upriver.[69] Because Burton's expedition had not been approved by the British Foreign Office, he had to pay all of its expenses himself. Burton's two-volume book about his travels appeared in 1876. Yet, despite Burton's genius and the power of his writing, not until 1877 did Henry Stanley bring the Congo to the world's attention. As we shall see in the next chapter, Stanley's book in 1877 describing his adventures down the Congo to the sea, opened "The Land Beyond Obscurity" to European rapacity, and a new kind of darkness.

 2

EXPLORING THE CONGO

Despite the activities and writings of all these European traders, missionaries, and explorers, no one brought the Congo to the world's attention until Henry M. Stanley came on the scene. Through his writings and lectures, he discovered the Congo for his Western readers. One might even say that he invented it. By the time the nineteenth century drew to a close, Sir Henry Morton Stanley was one of the best known and most highly honored men in the Western world. By then, most Westerners knew that he had led an expedition to Africa that had located the famous and long "missing" medical missionary Dr. David Livingstone, uttering as he did so the immediately much parodied greeting "Dr. Livingstone, I presume?" That was in 1871. Three years later, Stanley would lead another expedition. Once again he recruited porters in Zanzibar before leaving for mainland Africa. Like Burton, Speke, and other previous British explorers of East Africa, he chose Zanzibar because it had long been the jumping-off place to East Africa, which was at that time under the influence of Zanzibari Arab traders. This time, after exploring both Lake Victoria and Lake Tanganyika, Stanley found the Congo River and determined to follow it to the sea. To achieve this never-before-accomplished feat, he endured a zigzag odyssey of almost mythic proportions over seven thousand miles, lasting 999 days.

Stanley's dramatic two-volume account of this great "adventure," like his earlier book about Livingstone, was an enormous bestseller. It described how his men struggled to overcome forests, diseases, and warlike tribesmen, fighting over thirty major battles against Africans as he made his way west. He also discovered magnificent Congolese scenery, including the turbulent Stanley Falls and the hauntingly beautiful Stanley Pool, as he immodestly named them. That he accomplished the seemingly impossible task of dragging and carrying his boat, the *Lady Alice*, and his canoes past more than thirty crashing cataracts also left readers dazzled. As far as most Westerners were concerned, Stanley "discovered" the Congo, and they sympathized with the pain of his ordeal. Near the end of his journey he wrote this in his diary: "I have publicly expressed a desire to die by a quick sharp death, which I think would be a mercy compared to what I endure daily. I am vexed each day by thieves, liars and unconquerable laziness. . . . Weeks are passing swiftly away and goods are diminishing until we have but little left, and at the rate we are going six weeks will suffice to bring us at death's door from starvation."[1]

A few years later, he would return to the Congo to supervise the construction of a road through the Crystal Mountains around the river's cataracts, a feat that required dynamiting and smashing so much rock that he became known as *Bula Matari*—"the rock smasher."[2] He also had his men carry portions of steamships around the rapids so that they could be assembled on the navigable waters beyond. The road was completed in 1884. And in 1886, despite years of fighting against the malaria and dysentery that had plagued him throughout his African journeys, with his hair long since gone thoroughly white, the forty-five-year-old

Stanley would lead yet another large expedition into the Congo, this one from the Atlantic coast up the river to save Emin Pasha, an intellectual German doctor. Thanks to the famed British general Charles Gordon, who ruled Sudan from Khartoum, Emin had become the governor of the southernmost province in the Sudan only to be driven to the Ugandan border by rebellious Mahdist armies that were determined to spread Islamic rule and drive out all forms of foreign influence. Followers of their religious leader, the Mahdi, beheaded General Gordon, then moved south toward Emin Pasha. As the world waited, Stanley's expedition endured almost three more years of terrible trials before, as Stanley put it, he "saved" Emin Pasha, who in reality had no desire to be rescued and strenuously resisted Stanley's heavy-handed efforts to dislodge him from the people he believed that he was sworn to serve. Stanley's admirers were not advised of this embarrassing fact when Stanley wrote about saving Emin.

By this time, Stanley's articles, books, and speaking tours had made him far richer than any other travel writer of his time—and perhaps of any time since as well. Early in 1890, Queen Victoria offered him a knighthood, an honor he had to decline because, unknown to most of his admirers, he was by then a U.S. citizen, something he had chosen as a means of protecting the royalties earned by his books published in the United States. Henry Morton Stanley was emphatically not born into this world of gentility, wealth, and fame. His mother, Betsy Parry, was an unmarried, nineteen-year-old housemaid from rural north Wales. His birth registry in the town of Denbigh for January 28, 1841, reads "John Rowlands, Bastard." It is likely that his real father was a married local barrister who paid Rowlands, a notorious wastrel and drunkard, to give the child his name. In any event, Stanley's mother, who would have three more illegitimate children before eventually marrying, gave the child to her father, with whom he lived for the first five years of his life. Soon after his grandfather died, the boy was cruelly dragged away by a relative to a Welsh workhouse, where, one month after his sixth birthday, he was imprisoned with some seventy other children and young adults who had likewise been abandoned.

Stanley's writings later described his treatment there as brutal. He does appear to have been beaten at times during his early years of confinement, as were many of the other children. The food was barely edible, there was flogging, and every day ended with bedtime at eight and began at six the next morning. Some of the inmates were prostitutes waiting to give birth, others were younger girls learning that trade, and there were boys and young men from many backgrounds. Some were homosexual, all were poor and abandoned. Like the other young children there, John Rowlands shared a bed with an older boy, so sexual abuse was also likely.[3] Though he spoke only Welsh when he entered the English-speaking workhouse, records show him to have been a good student, even such a favored one that he eventually became known as a "teacher's pet."[4]

Being a favored student was small consolation for the young boy. He suffered acutely from the shame of illegitimacy and abandonment by his mother, who later spent several weeks in the workhouse herself along with two of her other illegitimate children. Rowlands did not at first recognize her, and even after he learned who she was, she ignored him. The father, or his alleged father, John Rowlands, also ignored him. When Stanley later sought out this prosperous Welsh farmer, the man coldly rejected him. At the age of fifteen, Rowlands either escaped from the workhouse, as he claimed or, as seems more likely, was simply released, living first with an aunt and uncle, then eventually finding employment in Liverpool.

At the age of sixteen, he was delivering a package from a butcher's shop where he worked in Liverpool to the U.S. merchant ship *Windemere*, then in port. The ship's captain, David

Hardinge, looked over the five-foot-five-inch but husky, 170-pound teenager and offered him $5 a month along with the gift of some seafaring clothing if he would sign on as a cabin boy. Rowlands jumped at the chance. After a severe bout of seasickness during the early days of the ship's seven-week return trip to New Orleans, John Rowlands discovered not only that he would serve as a common deckhand, rather than a privileged cabin boy, but that discipline was brutal. He must also have experienced sexual abuse, a practice common aboard merchant ships of that time.

It was hardly surprising that young Rowlands jumped ship in New Orleans or that he found this vibrant, cosmopolitan city exciting. While looking for a job, he met a cotton broker named Stanley who not only hired him as his "boy," but apparently lavished him with so much affection and caring that Rowlands took the man's name for his own and later wrote that he thought of him as his father. In his autobiography, Stanley wrote that after two years together, the elder Stanley, who was English, not American, left young Stanley and New Orleans behind for a trip to Havana, where he died soon after. In reality, the elder Stanley continued to live in New Orleans until his death in 1878, as did his wife, who Stanley insisted had died of yellow fever in 1860. Whatever had happened to distance young Stanley from his adopted father and mother was apparently so painful that the young man had to invent these deaths to explain their loss. It is known that the elder Stanley had sent Rowlands, then calling himself J. Rollins, to learn the business of rural storekeeping from a friend in Cypress Bend, Arkansas. Still searching for an identity, young Rowlands, Rollins, or Stanley experimented with middle names as well—Morley, Morelake, Moreland. The one thing that was clear was that he soon came to dislike the rural South.

When the Civil War broke out, as happened soon after, Stanley made no attempt to volunteer for military service until shamed into it by a girl he had fallen for. He then became Private Henry Stanley of the Dixie Greys of the Arkansas Volunteers. He served for nine dreary months of miserable camp life, drilling and trying to recover from the ravages of dysentery, typhus, and malaria, which struck many of the men, before taking part in the battle of Shiloh, one of the bloodiest of the war. Stanley was appalled by the human destruction he saw: "I was beginning to know the real truth! Man was born for slaughter," he wrote in his memoirs.[5] Later in his life he would confirm this apocalyptic vision of mankind more than once.

After twelve hours of battle, Stanley was part of an advancing skirmish line when he heard an officer call out his name and admonish him "to move briskly forward." Embarrassed, he moved forward too briskly and soon found himself surrounded by Union soldiers. He next found himself one of three thousand Confederate prisoners in a former cattle yard on the outskirts of Chicago, a terrible, makeshift prison where filth, hunger, and disease were rampant. He endured these conditions for six weeks before, along with some others, gaining his freedom by enlisting in the Illinois Light Infantry of the Union Army. Before reaching the battlefields of Virginia, however, he collapsed with dysentery so intense that doctors at a military hospital at Harpers Ferry despaired of curing him and discharged him to civilian life. He had no money, no prospects, and still no middle name. Had he not been taken in and cared for by a local farm family that found him wandering and desperately ill, he might not have survived.

After recovering, Stanley worked briefly, then took a ship back to England and from there visited Wales, where he found his mother, now married with two legitimate children. Although shabbily dressed and destitute, Stanley was sure that his newfound manliness and battle experience would win her over. They did not. "I was told that 'I was a disgrace to them in the eyes of their neighbours, and they desired me to leave as speedily as possible.' "⁶ After allowing him to stay only a single night, his mother gave her son a shilling and said, "Never come back to me unless you come better dressed and in better circumstances than you seem to be in now."⁷

Brokenhearted, Stanley signed on several merchant ships, including one that he deserted in Barcelona (he fancifully wrote that the ship was wrecked and he had to swim ashore naked), before once more making his way to America, working as a deckhand.⁸ After working for a time in Brooklyn, he inexplicably enlisted in the Union Navy, serving as a ship's clerk on the USS *Minnesota,* a frigate that actually saw combat bombarding Confederate forts on the coast of North Carolina. Stanley became one of very few men to have seen combat on both sides of the American Civil War. Soon after this battle ended, Stanley deserted again, jumping ship in New England and going briefly to New York before heading West, where he met a freelance reporter, and the two young men shared several adventures involving Plains Indians before heading off on an abortive trip around the world.

That trip took Stanley to Turkey, where he was robbed, nearly killed, and proved himself a liar of truly monumental proportions. He also behaved abusively toward the young journalist who traveled with him.⁹ When Stanley and this young man presented themselves at the American embassy in Constantinople, hungry and destitute, they were housed and fed. The next day, the American minister, Edward Jay Morris, lent Stanley $600. Stanley gave Morris a note for the same amount in the name of his "father"— a man he declared lived in New York City. Of course, neither the man nor the address existed.¹⁰

Throughout his life Stanley was ravenous for respect and recognition. He returned to Wales in the uniform of a Turkish navy officer he had purchased, which he described to others as that of a U.S. navy ensign. Calling himself Ensign John Rowlands, he first visited his old workhouse, lecturing the children about the virtues of the education he had received there. He then visited his mother, who was so impressed by her dapper naval-officer son that she had him stay with her over Christmas and New Year's. No one noticed that the brass buttons of this uniform bore Ottoman crescents and stars, not the U.S. rope and anchor. After leaving Wales, he returned to the United States and once again headed West, this time to publish exciting if heavily embellished stories about Plains Indian warfare under the name Henry Stanley.[11] Despite his Welsh accent, which became especially obvious when he became emotional, he insisted that he was American born and bred.

In 1867, Stanley visited New York, where he convinced James Gordon Bennett Jr., the ruthlessly ambitious, young editor in chief of the *New York Herald,* to hire him as a correspondent. Bennett had read Stanley's adventurous reports from the West and had been impressed. Stanley was sent to cover the punitive campaign being waged by the British against the emperor of Abyssinia, a clearly deranged individual who had been holding some British diplomats and their families hostage in response to what he imagined was an insult by Queen Victoria. Through good luck, and a bribe to a telegraph operator, Stanley scooped all other competing reporters by being the first to send a dispatch describing the decisive victory of the British forces led by General Sir Robert Napier, which brought about the emperor's suicide and the safe return of all the hostages. No sooner had Stanley's story been sent than the trans-Mediterranean cable snapped. All of the other correspondents' stories, as well as the official British army report of the expedition, had to be carried to England onboard a ship. Stanley had still not settled on his middle name, but his career as a journalist and a world traveler had begun.

Soon after, Bennett would finance Stanley's expedition to find Livingstone.

In 1813, David Livingstone was born into a Scottish family so poor that by the age of ten he was compelled to work as a mill hand every day except Sunday from 6 A.M. to 8 P.M. From eight to ten each evening he attended school, then read until he fell asleep. Livingstone became a cotton spinner at nineteen, making enough money to pay his way through medical training and become a minister as well. Drawn to Africa by its mystique and his missionary zeal, from 1852 to 1855 he crossed Southern Africa from west to east, discovering Victoria Falls and publishing a book, *Missionary Travels and Researches in South Africa,* which sold so well that he became independently wealthy. Now seen as more an explorer than a missionary, he was funded by the British government and the Royal Geographical Society to map the Zambezi region and evaluate its mineral and agricultural potential. This exploration lasted from 1858 to 1863 and led to another bestseller. In 1866, at the age of fifty-two—his mournful face with its bushy mustache and long sideburns now familiar to most Britons—Livingstone returned to Africa to seek the source of the Nile. Then he disappeared.

When Stanley set out to find him, Livingstone had not been seen by a European for three years. A letter printed in the *Times* of London reported that he had been killed and eaten by cannibals. Neither Bennett nor Stanley were deterred by this possibility, nor by the fact that Stanley had no experience as an explorer, had never led any sort of expedition, and had never set foot in sub-Saharan Africa. Stanley arrived in Zanzibar in January 1871, where with Bennett's ample funds (Bennett was the son of a Scottish millionaire) he bought over six tons of supplies, including silver goblets, champagne, Persian carpets for his tent, a portable bathtub, and Fortnum and Mason hampers filled with

pâté de foie gras and other delicacies. He also hired an interpreter, two young British seamen, 192 porters, and a fifty-year-
old man named Bombay, the same caravan master who had
earlier led expeditions by Burton and Speke. Stanley was obviously unaware that Speke had become so annoyed with Bombay
that he had knocked out three of the man's front teeth.[12]

Despite foul weather, the hostility of African tribesmen—some
of whom were cannibals—dangerous fevers, and dysentery, which
reduced his weight from 180 pounds to 130 after thirty-eight days
on the march, Stanley pressed on.[13] He had decided not to be a
kind and gentle caravan leader but to rely instead on the "whip
and slave chain" approach. He ordered that porters too sick to
carry their loads be flogged and, on one terrible occasion, ordered that his chief Palestinian Arab interpreter, a boy named
Selim, be brutally flogged because he had taken some sugar to
ease his fever brought on by smallpox. Stanley permitted no one
but himself to touch the sugar supply.[14] Despite this brutality, the
small, frail, teenaged Selim somehow remained loyal. And so
would a young African slave named Kalulu, who was given to Stanley by an Arab merchant in Tabora, Tanzania. Only seven or eight
years old, Kalulu was described by Stanley as "diligent, smart, and
frisky . . . I have but to express a wish and it is gratified. He is a
perfect Mercury, though a marvelously black one."[15] In no time,
Kalulu became Stanley's trusted page, his "chief butler" as he
described him, and his gun bearer. His porters, however, continued to plague Stanley: "They are faithless, lying, thievish, indolent knaves, who only teach a man to despise himself for his folly
in attempting a grand work with such miserable slaves."[16]

Determined not only to make rapid progress but to suffer no
indignity at the hands of African tribespeople, whom he described as "troublesome and ungrateful," Stanley took a direct
route toward Lake Victoria rather than following safer but more
indirect well-traveled Arab slave-trading routes. In doing so, he

met African tribes that had never before seen a white man. When men of one such tribe stared at him in open amazement, he became so annoyed that he struck one man with a donkey whip. It took all of Selim's tact and charm to prevent bloodshed.[17] But when Stanley encountered Mirambo, the famed and feared war leader of the Nyamwezi, whose territory Stanley had to cross, he was enchanted by him:

> Throughout all my travels in Africa I have not yet met such disinterested kindness as I have received from the great bandit Mirambo. He had 15,000 muskets with him, all handled by desperate fellows, but the minute their chief embraced me all the savages clapped their hands, and hailed me as a brother of their chief. . . . He is tall, large chested and a very fine specimen of a well-made man. . . . He is as quiet as a lamb in conversation, rather harmless looking than otherwise, but in war the skulls which line the road to his gates reveal too terribly the ardour which animates him.[18]

After 236 days of marching, Stanley found Livingstone in the town of Ujiji on the eastern shore of Lake Tanganyika and uttered his famous greeting. Most Europeans who spent time with Livingstone in Africa found him distant and difficult at best, but Stanley spent four months with the missionary physician, learning to revere him as the father he had never had. Livingstone grew fond of Stanley as well. Both men were Celts, not Englishmen, very short, and looked down upon by upper-class Englishmen, literally and figuratively. They were also brought closer together after Livingstone told Stanley about his son, who had enlisted in the Union army under an assumed name and been killed near Richmond, Virginia, where Stanley had collapsed with dysentery. The two men came to be so fond of one another that when Livingstone declined to leave his work in Africa, and Stanley had to return to Zanzibar, their parting was emotional. Both men sobbed.

When Stanley returned to Zanzibar, his once black hair was flecked with gray. Stanley's many public speeches about his discovery of Livingstone—followed by his articles and his bestselling book *How I Found Livingstone,* published in 1872—made him the target of derision by the many disbelieving members of the British Royal Geographical Society. Eventually, however, his achievement was accepted and even applauded, due in large measure to Queen Victoria's letter thanking him for relieving her and her subjects of their concern for Livingstone. She also sent him a valuable gold snuff box encrusted in jewels. Privately, however, Victoria derided him as an "ugly little man with a strong American twang."[19] All that his safari to find Livingstone had taught Stanley about the Congo was that Livingstone had spent time at a town called Nyangwe on the Lualaba River in the eastern Congo, where he had witnessed Arab slavers slaughtering hundreds of people at a market. But it was not antislavery fervor that would soon send Stanley to the Congo. It was his zeal for adventure and public acclaim. And before Stanley would begin his Congo adventure, a British naval officer would precede him.

Verney Lovett Cameron, son of a Scottish clergyman and a young officer in the British Royal Navy, had served in the Napier-led British campaign in Abyssinia in 1868 that had launched Stanley's career as a reporter (though they never met). He had also served as senior lieutenant on the HMS *Star* on the east coast of Africa when the Royal Navy had attempted, without much success, to suppress the Arab slave trade. The suffering of slaves that he witnessed in Arab dhows sickened him. He hoped that he would be able to do more to end this "inhuman traffic," as he called it. Cameron was also fascinated by Burton's adventures in Africa and volunteered to the Royal Geographical Society to once again make contact with Dr. Livingstone. His offer was accepted, and he was funded in 1872, the same year that Stanley's book appeared. Cameron was only twenty-eight, three years younger than Stanley. His close friend and former messmate, naval surgeon Dr. W. E. Dillon, was appointed to accompany him. Later, Cecil Murphy, a lieutenant in the Royal Artillery, and Robert Moffat, a nephew of Livingstone's, also joined the expedition. A young South African, Moffat sold his sugar plantation in Natal— all that he owned—to finance his part in the expedition. Cameron would spend three years and five months "on the tramp," as he called it, in Africa, first searching for Livingstone, then trying to make his way across the Congo to the Atlantic.

Even the shrewd and ruthless Stanley had had difficulties organizing an expedition in Zanzibar, and the gentlemanly Cameron and Dillon were no match for the crafty Zanzibari Arabs, who foisted off the dregs of the island on their expedition. Because Cameron was under orders from London to "press on with all possible speed," he felt that he could not delay until more experienced porters became available. He even hired as headman the aging, drunken, sly, and unreliable Bombay, who had previously served in the same role for Speke and Stanley.[20] Despite all the urgency, it was almost three months before the expedition was ready to march inland with 35 soldiers, 192 porters, and scores of cooks, servants, and gunbearers. Each of the soldiers was outfitted in a red patrol jacket, red fez, white shirt, and cummerbund. The expedition had a portable India-rubber boat as well as twenty-two donkeys, three dogs—including Cameron's favorite, a large mutt named Leo—and the wives of some of the soldiers and porters. Some of the more senior Arabs even had slaves with them. Cameron complained that the porters straggled, were lazy, and stole "unceasingly," making progress a daily nightmare.[21]

The caravan slowly moved inland across Tanzania, its progress slowed by the necessity of paying tribute to each chief whose territory they entered, and of recruiting new porters to replace those that regularly deserted. These new men had to be paid one-half of their wages in advance and be well fed even though most of them deserted after a few days. The caravan was also slowed by the severe malarial fevers suffered by the four Europeans. During one severe bout, Cameron was so delirious that he complained to Dr. Dillon that the leg of a grand piano was on top of one of his two heads. On other feverish occasions, he mistook anthills for his tent and believed that he was twenty different people. Young Moffat was so badly stricken by fever that he died.

Before the caravan reached Lake Tanganyika, a bearer delivered a letter that both Cameron and Dillon were too delirious from malaria to read. It took some time for the bearer to explain to them that his "master," Dr. Livingstone, was dead. Dillon and Murphy decided to accompany Livingstone's body to the coast. After much deliberation, Cameron chose to continue Livingstone's unfinished exploration in the Congo by retracing his steps to the Lualaba River, which Livingstone thought was the Congo, then following it to the sea. At this time Africa was an "unknown" continent. The drive to explore it gripped Cameron just as it had Livingstone and so many others. Cameron sadly bade his European comrades farewell, literally saying, "Westward ho!" Dillon soon after accidentally shot himself to death while in the grip of a malarial delirium. Murphy returned to the coast to continue his military service.

Cameron marched west, still accompanied by a large retinue, whom he often described in insightful and witty terms. He was particularly amused by one of his guides who ordinarily wore only a loincloth, but also possessed a European umbrella, which he insisted on twirling overhead as he marched. When rain fell, he would strip off his loincloth, fold it neatly, then place it on top of his head. Cameron could not help exploding with laughter, as he put it, as this totally naked, umbrella-toting man led the caravan forward.[22] Cameron was also amused by his cook named Sambo, who preferred to cook everything in castor oil, with diarrhea being the predictable result. They passed through remarkably varied terrain, from beautiful green savannas that reminded Cameron of well-tended English parks, to mountains and dense forests. Cameron's dog, Leo, proved worthy of his name. Some Africans on the expedition said he was a match for any two lions. Unfortunately, snakes were a greater threat than lions, and one day Leo was carried to Cameron so badly poisoned that he could barely lick Cameron's hand and wag his tail once before dying. Cameron was distraught after the death of his beloved dog, who had been constantly by his side for a year, but did his best to carry on, transferring some of his affection to a female goat he named Dinah that slept at the foot of his bed and came running when he called her name, amazing onlookers.[23] He was terribly upset when Dinah was stolen and never returned.

Cameron was far more interested in the African natives he met than Stanley had been, judging from his largely cursory and condemnatory accounts of them. Cameron deftly describes the varied peoples he encountered—their customs, clothing, hairstyles, and houses. These latter in particular he found of great interest, from long, rectangular homes along a neatly swept street, to some on stilts in the middle of a lake, and tall, conically thatched-roof homes with elegantly carved wooden doors. In some places, men wore aprons of antelope skin; in others, long cloth robes; and in a few places, nothing at all. Some men wore their hair plastered with clay; others sported complex hairstyles including elegant carvings. In one society, women had their hair combed out into two huge cascading bundles that draped over each side of a complex basket framing their faces.[24] However, in some places hairstyles were seemingly neglected altogether. His two-volume book, *Across Africa,* is a cornucopia of his beautiful and informative drawings of sights such as these.

Like other explorers who traversed the Congo, Cameron met people who conformed to the Europeans' worst suspicions by being openly cannibalistic. Some described human flesh as the tastiest food on earth, adding that men tasted better than women. Yet, in one such tribe, Cameron was surprised to discover, people were very affectionate to one another.[25] He was also surprised to find such a diversity of emotional styles and cultural practices as he marched—or was carried when ill—from one tribe to the next on his way toward the Atlantic.

In August 1874, Cameron finally reached the town of Nyangwe on the Lualaba River. It was here that Livingstone had mistakenly theorized that he had found the source of the Congo River, but because he could not obtain canoes had pursued his explorations no further. Intending to carry on for Livingstone, Cameron offered everything he could think of to acquire canoes, but, just as Livingstone had experienced, weeks passed and no canoes were forthcoming. Cameron was repeatedly told that what he had to offer for canoes was of no value. The only things the local people would trade their canoes for were slaves. As described in Cameron's book, the notorious Arab slave trader Tippu Tip then appeared, all six foot two of him, elegantly dressed and something of a dandy according to Cameron. Tippu Tip was the leader of the Arab slave traders whose base of operations was at Nyangwe. Tippu Tip was charming to Cameron, and no doubt a deal exchanging slaves for canoes could have been struck had Cameron been willing. But he was not willing, and without canoes, like Livingstone, he had to abandon his plan to follow the Congo to the sea. Cameron wrote nothing about his thoughts on this dilemma in *Across Africa.* Years later, however, when Stanley criticized Cameron for abandoning the Lualaba River exploration exactly where Livingstone had, Cameron retorted that had he been willing to connive with Tippu Tip and the slave trade as Stanley had done, he could have descended the Congo just as Stanley did, only earlier.[26] However, Cameron neglected to mention that he had accepted Tippu Tip's generous offer of two of his men to guide him as he marched through the southern Congo and Angola toward the coast. We will further examine Tippu Tip's role in the ivory and slave trade and its impact on cannibalism in the next chapter.

Abandoning his hope of canoeing down the Congo River, Cameron took the advice of Tippu Tip and set off for the coast by land. Again he described fascinating African peoples and beautiful scenery. He was especially captivated by the country of the Baluba (he called them Bailuba) people, who lived in a highland region he described as a

> glimpse of paradise. . . . Neither poet, with all the wealth of word-imagery, nor painter with almost supernatural genius, could by pen or pencil do full justice to the country of Bailuba.
>
> In the foreground were glades in the woodland, varied with knolls crowned by groves of large, English-looking trees, sheltering villages with yellow thatched roofs; shambas, or plantations, with the fresh green of young crops and bright red of newly hoed ground in vivid contrast, and running streams flashing in the sunlight; whilst in the far distance were mountains of endless and pleasing variety of form, gradually fading away until they blended with the blue of the sky. Overhead there drifted fleecy white clouds; and the hum of bees, the bleating of goats, and the crowing of cocks broke the stillness of the air.[27]

Not exactly the vision of "darkest Africa" that Joseph Conrad and others would hauntingly evoke, but Cameron was not the only visitor to the Congo to admire its beauty.

Cameron moved on to the west of Baluba, where he met some friendly Portuguese settlers before crossing the mountains he had admired from afar. Food became increasingly scarce, and although wiry and remarkably hardy, Cameron suffered painfully from a bleeding mouth and swollen tongue caused by scurvy. His men were near starvation. Desperate to find food, he sent a written message to the coast. Then he and his men staggered forward as best they could. Near the end of their endurance, they were met by a man with a basket of food and a message in English welcoming them to the Portuguese seaside town of Benguela. It was November, 1875.

With treatment from a Portuguese doctor, Cameron survived his painful and dangerous bout of scurvy that caused his mouth to bleed and his body to erupt in blue, black, and green blotches. Once he recovered, he then sent his men back to Zanzibar by sea while he sailed on another ship to England, arriving there on April 21, 1876, to be met by his mother, who had long before given him up for dead.[28] The British foreign office promptly rejected his claim that the Congo become a British protectorate—for one thing, about half of his route had been through Portuguese Angola, not the Congo—seeing little value in such a claim and fearing Portuguese objections. Nevertheless, he was created a Companion of the Bath, promoted to the rank of commander, awarded an honorary doctorate at Oxford, and given the Founder's Medal by the Royal Geographical Society. Cameron became a director of several trading companies with African interests, always insisting that the welfare of Africans had to be assured. He also wrote popular adventure stories for boys' magazines before he died in a tragic hunting accident in 1894 when a horse he was trying to mount bolted and he suffered a deadly head injury. He was forty-nine.

Across Africa, Cameron's two-volume account of his travels across the Congo and Angola, appeared in 1877, the same year that Stanley succeeded in following the Congo River all the way to the Atlantic coast. Stanley's achievement immediately eclipsed that of Cameron. By any standard, it was an amazing accomplishment, one that he dedicated to the memory of Livingstone but also used to vindicate himself in the eyes of his critics, many of whom continued to see him as an egomaniac. After leaving Livingstone, Stanley had marched back to Bagamoyo on the coast of Tanzania, then sailed first to Zanzibar and next to the Seychelles, always cared for attentively by Selim and Kalulu. Leaving the Palestinian Selim behind in Cairo with thanks and severance pay, Stanley took Kalulu with him to Marseilles, where he purchased up-to-date European clothing for himself and the boy, then took the train to Paris. At first terrified by the sudden darkness of train tunnels, Kalulu came to love the train ride and charmed several passengers. After Paris, Stanley went to London, where Kalulu acquired a page's outfit, before setting out for New York. Servant and master were inseparable. Kalulu served Stanley's many needs while improving his own English. Stanley actually wrote a novel based on the premise of Kalulu as an African prince. The novel was never published. There were many rumors about their relationship, including homosexual accusations.

From New York, where Stanley met with Bennett and his publishers, Stanley and Kalulu returned to London, where Stanley left the boy in the care of an English schoolteacher who taught him to read and write English, while Stanley sailed to the Gold Coast of West Africa, where he spent four months being paid to cover Wolseley's campaign against the Asante for Bennett's *New York Herald.* Stanley also published a book about the campaign

for Harper's in 1874. Before the war began with three famous
regiments of regular British troops marching against King Kofi
Kakari's poorly armed militia, Stanley cut to the core of the issue:
"King Coffee [Kofi] is too rich a neighbor to be left alone with
his riches, with his tons of gold dust and accumulations of wealth
to himself."[29] When the combat began, Stanley put himself in the
thick of the fighting, blazing away with his rifle without a trace
of apprehension. He would soon do the same in East and Central
Africa.

Stanley returned to London from the Gold Coast just in time
to serve as a pallbearer at Livingstone's funeral. Kalulu walked
behind the coffin in a new gray suit. Stanley wrote in his diary
that he was determined to complete the exploration of the Lualaba River that Livingstone had begun and, moreover, to resolve
all of the vexing questions about the source of the Nile raised by
Burton, Speke, Grant, and Baker that so fascinated public interest. He swore first to explore the Great Lakes region in East
Africa, then to follow the Lualaba wherever it took him. To finance this ambitious exploration, Stanley first turned to London's *Daily Telegraph,* whose editor, Edwin Arnold, was a member
of the Royal Geographical Society but nevertheless a strong pro-
ponent of Stanley's. Arnold readily agreed to help. Stanley then
telegraphed Bennett at the *Herald,* asking if he would split the
cost with Arnold. Stanley estimated that it would cost $60,000—
an enormous sum in those days. Twenty-four hours later, Bennett
replied with a single word: "Yes."

After a brief trip to New York to see Bennett and his publishers at Harper and Brothers, Stanley returned to London, where
he spent two months at the posh Langham Hotel reading more
than 130 books about Africa and studying every map of the continent he could lay his hands on. And after both the *Daily Telegraph* and *New York Herald* announced the expedition, he sorted
through more than twelve hundred letters from men eager to

join him. The letters came not only from Britain and the United States but from throughout Europe. In addition to three generals and five colonels, the aspirants included junior officers as well as midshipmen, engineers, mechanics, and even spirit mediums. Some claimed to know Africa well; others professed special skills, such as making the caravan invisible or causing the African "savages" to fall asleep. One man offered to poison them, "thereby making it unnecessary to shoot them."[30] In the end, Stanley rejected all of these applicants, choosing instead three young Englishmen, two sailor-fishermen from Kent, Edward and Francis Pocock, and a desk clerk at the Langham Hotel named Frederick Barker. All three would be suitably loyal and subservient, Stanley no doubt assumed. He also acquired five dogs, including two purebred mastiffs, one of which would die of heat exhaustion on the first day of marching, and all the rest soon after.[31] Kalulu would again serve as his personal attendant and gunbearer.

Stanley also commissioned the construction of a forty-foot-long boat built of Spanish cedar in five detachable sections of about 280 pounds each. Stanley named the boat *Lady Alice,* after Alice Pike, the seventeen-year-old daughter of an American whiskey millionaire whom he had met while she was visiting London. Hopelessly smitten, Stanley poured out his love for her and she responded in kind. Stanley recorded in his journal, "She has shown undying fidelity to me and our parting was very tender."[32] After exchanging kisses with Stanley, Alice promised to marry him, "so help me God."[33] Before he left for Zanzibar, they signed a marriage pact, pledging to be faithful to one another and to be married upon Stanley's return from Africa, which he promised would take place in two years. In reality, he would be away nearly three years, but Stanley's delay was not what led young Alice to break her vow. She married another man within a year of Stanley's departure.

Once in Zanzibar, Stanley recruited porters and soldiers, including some of the same Arabs who had accompanied him in his search for Livingstone. Although he had chosen to travel as lightly as possible, he took eight tons of trade goods, arms, ammunition, food, living utensils, and of course, the *Lady Alice*. In addition to the 270 porters, the expedition included several chiefs, plus their thirty-six wives and ten children.

Stanley pushed his expedition so hard that he reached Lake Victoria, after a 720-mile march from Bagamoyo, in only 103 days. However, only 166 of the 356 people who had begun the march survived. One who died was Edward Pocock, who succumbed to fever while still in Tanzania. After a week's rest, Stanley recruited over a hundred new porters, assembled the *Lady Alice*, and with eleven picked men set out to circumnavigate the lake, the second largest in the world. He proved that Speke had been right when he posited that it was one body of water. He also became so friendly with Mutesa, the king of Buganda, that he briefly joined his forces in a war Mutesa was waging with his neighbors in Uganda, then went crocodile hunting with him for sport. Stanley was very taken with Mutesa, whom he described as intelligent, dignified, and so admirable that "I think I see in him the light that shall lighten the darkness of this benighted region."[34]

When a young French colonel, Linant de Bellefonds, arrived at Mutesa's court, sent there by General Gordon at Khartoum to carry out a reconnaissance mission, Stanley felt challenged and left to continue his journey around Lake Victoria.[35] When he stopped on Bumbire Island, he was immediately surrounded by hundreds of spear-waving warriors, who stole his oars. He barely escaped with his men's lives but managed to sail successfully back to his base camp, where he learned that Fred Barker—the former desk clerk—had died. Very ill himself, Stanley abandoned his original plan to sail back to Buganda, then trek to the northwest to explore Lake Albert. Instead, as soon as his fever abated somewhat, he moved south to Lake Tanganyika, then crossed over it to march to the Lualaba River. But as his caravan passed by Bumbire Island again, he decided to confront the natives who had so rudely threatened him earlier. When their chief offended him by refusing to discuss matters, Stanley ordered his men to open fire, killing thirty or forty Africans and wounding hundreds more, many of whom staggered away no doubt later to die of their wounds. When news of this massacre appeared in the *Herald* and *Daily Telegraph,* many people were horrified by Stanley's apparent eagerness to shoot Africans. Richard Burton, himself a critic of almost everything African, sniffed that Stanley "still shoots Negroes as if they were monkeys," and a British missionary suggested that Stanley should be sent back to Bumbire and "hanged as other murderers are."[36]

On May 27, 1876, after a grueling four-month march, Stanley reached Ujiji on Lake Tanganyika, where he had earlier met Livingstone. By then, he had traveled nearly thirty-five hundred miles and had been in Africa for seventeen months. He was disappointed to find no mail from Alice waiting for him in Ujiji. He could not know that, by then, Alice was four months pregnant. After pouring out his love to Alice in a letter, he swallowed his heartache and sailed Lake Tanganyika's coast for fifty-one days, eventually deciding that it had no outlet to the north that could feed either Lake Albert or the Nile, shattering Burton's long-cherished theory. After some further delay, including a one-day desertion by Kalulu, who was apparently reluctant to leave his native Tanzania, Stanley and 140 followers crossed the lake and began to march through immense tropical forests across the Congo in search of the Lualaba.

The forests were so dark that Stanley could not see to take notes. The undergrowth was deep and soggy with dew and rain that had soaked fallen branches and leaves, turning the earth into a clayey paste. The men slogged forward, slipping, falling, cursing, their clothing drenched. Suffocated by the forest's intense miasma, exhausted by hacking their way through the undergrowth, and unnerved by its silence, the caravan slowly slogged its way ahead, watched by small, white-necked monkeys. There were also huge pythons, deadly puff adders, and thousands of biting red ants, mosquitoes, and enormous, biting flies. When Stanley finally reached the market town of Nyangwe on the Lualaba, his men were in such bad condition that he had to order a week's rest. It was October 17, 1876. Later that month, one of Stanley's Arab soldiers accidentally shot Kalulu in the leg. He recovered, and Stanley's affection for the now thirteen- or fourteen-year-old boy intensified.

Eager as Stanley was to follow the river to the ocean, he learned that nothing had changed since Livingstone's and Cameron's attempts. There were no canoes to be had. Tippu Tip was still there, however, and after much negotiation he agreed to accompany Stanley downriver for sixty days as a military escort in return for a fee that Stanley recalled as being $5,000, but that Tippu Tip insisted was $7,000. Tippu Tip also insisted that the money did not matter to him, and that he had chosen to help Stanley for other reasons.[37] On November 5, 1876, Stanley set off, led by Tippu Tip's four hundred men, two hundred of them soldiers, as well as twenty women from his harem. Lacking canoes, the caravan was forced to slog its way through the wet, dark, fetid forest along the river while Stanley's men carried the *Lady Alice*. The air was so heavy that even breathing was difficult. As before, the column was quickly exhausted and demoralized. At one point, while they slowly pressed on, the formerly silent forest suddenly erupted—armies of parrots screamed, hippopotamuses thundered, and there were so many insects that the entire forest seemed to vibrate.[38]

After ten days of their ordeal cutting their way through the almost impenetrable forest, Tippu Tip had had enough. He went to Stanley and told him that the forest's foul air was killing his people. Complaining that he had never before tried to travel through the Congo's forests, he said that the journey was insufferable. Declaring that the forests were made for pagans, monkeys, and beasts, he said that he would go no farther. It took two hours of Stanley's most impassioned oratory to convince Tippu Tip to stay on. To ease matters a little, Stanley ordered the *Lady Alice* to be launched, and the expedition found some damaged canoes that they were able to repair, but the party was soon attacked by screaming warriors, who were mowed down by the modern Sniders and Winchesters of Stanley's men, sheltered as they were behind a fortified stockade. Bodies were soon piled everywhere between the stockade and the forest, yet the fighting continued for three days, with more Africans attacking the stockade from all sides, and eight hundred more attacking from canoes in the river. Stanley's badly outnumbered and exhausted men were on the point of collapse when Tippu Tip's land party, which had gone on ahead, suddenly returned and routed the attackers.[39] This attack was followed by thirty-one others, including one by two thousand men in fifty-four large canoes, and another that lasted for five hours along a ten-mile stretch of the river.[40] The African warriors would sometimes shout their intention to eat Stanley and his men: "Meat! Meat! We shall have plenty of meat!"[41] We cannot know for certain, but these tribesmen probably fought so hard because they believed that Stanley's men had come to capture slaves.

Not long after one of these final attacks took place, smallpox killed many of Tippu Tip's people, including his favorite concubine.[42] Tippu Tip again declared that he would go no farther. Unable to change the Arab's mind this time, Stanley convinced him to stay a few days to celebrate, of all things, Christmas. Tippu Tip's Muslims joined Stanley's "pagans" in a few days of feasting, dancing, and racing both in canoes and on foot. The highlight was a three-hundred-yard match race between Tippu Tip and Frank Pocock. Although Tippu Tip was over forty and no longer thin, he easily beat the athletic, young Pocock to the finish line.[43]

Before Tippu Tip's people left, Stanley had luckily found twenty-two canoes, enough to carry his entire force. He loaded 149 men, women, and children, two donkeys, two goats, and a sheep into the canoes, which he gave names such as *Telegraph*, *Herald*, *Livingstone*, *London Town*, *America*, and of course, *Stanley*. On January 4, 1877, they reached the first of the seven cataracts at a place he would name Stanley Falls. For the next three weeks, his party struggled to carry and drag their canoes and the *Lady Alice* around these falls.

For the next thousand miles the river—ten miles wide in places—proved navigable, but the attacks by tribesmen continued. As his party came closer to the coast, they encountered angry Africans armed with muskets acquired from the European slave trade. Fortunately for Stanley's people, these muskets were so poorly maintained that they did little damage. When Stanley finally and with great relief reached the placid waters of Stanley Pool, the local people were no longer hostile and he was only four hundred miles from the coast. However, many deadly cataracts still stood between him and his goal. Most of the cataracts were completely impassable. The canoes, each weighing upward of three tons, and his boat had to be portaged around them. Pulling the canoes over rollers or branches, pushing, tugging, and lifting, his increasingly exhausted, near-starved men somehow struggled on despite deluges of rain and the knife-sharp rocks that tore their feet. Some chose to risk their lives by traveling close to cataracts in canoes. On March 17, 1877, Kalulu was one of several men aboard the seventy-five-foot-long canoe *Crocodile* when it was swept over the Rocky Island Falls, drowning all of them. Stanley was profoundly depressed, writing in his diary, "My heart aches sorely."[44] He later renamed the cataract the Kalulu Falls. Soon after, Frank Pocock decided to shoot one set of rapids rather than portage. He, too, was drowned, a loss that pained Stanley deeply, almost as deeply as that of Kalulu. When at last Stanley reached the powerful Yellala Cataract, which had stopped Tuckey when he had tried to ascend the river in 1816, Stanley decided to march overland toward Boma, said to be only five days away. He left the *Lady Alice* behind, as he said, honorably "consigned to her resting place . . . to bleach and to rot to dust!"[45]

For three days, what remained of Stanley's party struggled painfully on across the rugged Crystal Mountains.[46] On the fourth day, when they were finally too weak from hunger to go on, Stanley wrote letters in English, French, and Spanish, pleading with anyone who might receive them in Boma for food. He and his 115 men, women, and children were in "a state of imminent starvation," he wrote, identifying himself as "the person that discovered Livingstone in 1871." Four men of his caravan volunteered to carry the letters, and two men from a nearby village offered to guide them. Because Boma was by then only a day away, the response was rapid. A caravan soon arrived with enough food to feed all members of Stanley's caravan, as well as a basket for him containing every European delicacy one might imagine—from plum pudding to salmon, sardines, loaves of bread, butter, jam, tea, coffee, sugar, ale, sherry, port wine, and champagne. Stanley was a celebrity!

After reviving themselves with this feast, Stanley and his men— he was carried against his wishes, he later wrote—made it to Boma, exactly 999 days after he had begun his journey. After being grandly feted by the eighteen Europeans in Boma, a Portuguese warship took Stanley and his party to better quarters in Luanda, located to the south on the coast of Angola. There he stayed with Portuguese army major Alexandre de Serpa Pinto, who had himself been planning to ascend the Congo River to its source. After talking to Stanley, Serpa Pinto now changed his planned exploration and caravaned to the southwest across Angola and Botswana to Pretoria, a journey similar to the one taken earlier by Livingstone.[47] During the 1880s, the German explorer Major Hermann von Wissmann twice led caravans across the Congo from the west all the way to the coast of Tanzania. And fifty years before Stanley's trek, two slave traders of African-Portuguese ancestry, Pedro Baptista and Anastario José, made at least one round-trip from the west coast of Central Africa to the east coast and back again. Unlike Stanley and von Wissmann, however, they did not write a book about their achievements.[48] Despite the heroism and success of these expeditions and the one by Cameron, only Stanley captured the Western world's attention.

Many of Stanley's people now were openly dispirited, with no expectation for their futures and no belief that Stanley would pay them as promised. Some died in Luanda, bereft of hope. But Stanley did not abandon the survivors. Stanley's people were overjoyed when instead of leaving all of them on the west coast and going directly to England as he was invited to do, he insisted on finding a ship that would carry all of them home to Zanzibar. He did so aboard the British warship the HMS *Industry*. There was a stopover in Cape Town, where Stanley arranged for his Zanzibaris to be treated as favored tourists, who greatly enjoyed the sights of this, the first European city they had seen, as well as a thrilling ride on a railroad train. In late November 1877, the ship arrived in Zanzibar, where the surviving members of Stanley's epic journey rushed ashore, to kneel and kiss the beach of their homeland. There were eighty-nine people in all, including thirteen women, and three infants born on the trek.[49]

For his part, Stanley rushed ashore hoping to find word from Alice. And he did find a letter there waiting for him—to his horror: "I have done," she wrote, "what millions of women have done before me, not been true to my promise." He also received an eighteen-month-old newspaper clipping announcing her marriage to an American railroad heir. Shattered by the news, Stanley nevertheless saw to it that his people received a profitable end to their adventure. He not only paid each of his Zanzibaris what was owed them, he sought out the relatives of those who had died, to pay them as well. When he finally boarded a ship to return to Britain, many of his former porters and soldiers rushed to the dock to bid him farewell. What he did with the photograph of Alice that he had carried with him throughout his journey, carefully wrapped in oilskin, is not known.

The stories that Stanley had sent from Boma, Cape Town, and Zanzibar had been published months before his return to Europe in January 1878. Everywhere he went, he received a hero's welcome. Heads of state vied for his attention. The U.S. Congress gave him a vote of thanks. Even Burton, Baker, and Cameron praised him. Sick and exhausted, his hair so gray that he seemed to have aged twenty years, Stanley turned away from most of the praise and the pomp and focused on writing a book about his travels. His two-volume account of his amazing journey, *Through the Dark Continent*, was published later that same year. He also found some time to relax in Paris and Switzerland.

But his passion remained the Congo. He was convinced that the Congo River would be the "grand highway" of commerce to Central Africa, and he urged the British to claim it as their own. More aware than anyone else that the two hundred miles of cataracts in the Crystal Mountains were a barrier to commerce, he proposed to build first a road, then a railroad, through and around the mountains to connect the thousand miles of navigable river behind Stanley Pool with the sea. Trading stations would spring up and trade would flourish. Like Cameron before him, Stanley, despite his appeals, could not interest the British government or British financiers in "opening up" the Congo. No other European country saw a political or military advantage to seizing the Congo either. French, Portuguese, and British traders carried on as before—without any governmental framework for their commerce and with no funding for either a road or a railroad. This remained the case until 1885, when King Leopold II of Belgium made the country his personal fiefdom, a remarkable coup and a fascinating episode in world history that I will examine in the next chapter.

What mattered for the future of the Congo was the willingness of the world to cede control of that huge space in Central Africa to Leopold, who had always insisted that it was his mission to civilize the people of that vast land. For example, in a speech made in 1876, he declared, "To bring civilization to the only part of this globe where it has not penetrated, to pierce the darkness that envelopes entire populations—is, I dare say, a crusade worthy of this age of progress."[50] Leopold decided to retain none other than Stanley to build the road that would open the Congo—not to civilization, as Leopold so often insisted, but to vast profits for him from ivory, rubber, and mining, along with the deaths of millions of Congolese that followed soon after.

Given a five-year contract and a salary, Stanley proposed to build a road around the cataracts, then carry disassembled steamboats to Stanley Pool, where they would be reassembled so that river trade could be carried out with trading stations in the interior. After the road had been completed, he would blast a path for a railroad line through the granite of the Crystal Mountains. All of these arrangements were carried out in the utmost secrecy. Stanley had been hard at work on his road-building scheme for over six months before his French rival for staking a claim over the Congo, Count and French naval officer Pierre Savorgnan de Brazza, had any idea what was under way. Brazza, who was the seventh son of an Italian count, was born Pietro Paulo Francesco Camillo Savorgnan di Brazza, but after serving in the French navy—a boyhood dream—he changed it to Pierre Savorgnan de Brazza.[51]

Stanley began his task of road building on August 14, 1879. His crew included Belgians, Americans, Britons, Frenchmen, and other Europeans, some of whom were engineers. Many proved to be largely useless because they were so frequently ill and needed luxury items—food, medications, equipment—that were difficult to come by. The backbone of the work brigade consisted of over one hundred locally recruited African workmen and sixty-eight Zanzibaris Stanley had recruited on his way to the Congo. These numbers would multiply rapidly as months passed. Before he could begin construction, Stanley had first to convince local African chiefs to sell him the rights to a twenty-square-mile area for a base camp, as well as the right of way through their territory for the road and the railroad. As we will see in more detail in chapter 4, he did all this at bargain-basement prices, typically using sleight-of-hand tricks to convince chiefs of his superhuman powers.[52] In case a show of force was helpful—and it often was— he had a thousand men armed with repeating rifles, twelve Krupp cannons, and four machine guns.

Actual road construction began on October 1, 1879, when, as a large crowd of workmen and natives looked on, he took a sledgehammer away from an African who had been trying unsuccessfully to crack a granite rock. Aiming at a cleft in the rock, Stanley shattered it with a single blow. There was a loud shout of approval from the crowd. Then and there he was crowned *Bula Matari*, the "rock smasher."

Ten hours a day, six days a week, the grueling work went on. Forests had to be cleared, mountains cut away, ravines bridged, and mangrove swamps drained. The work went slowly; disease struck down many of the workers; there were incessant quarrels. Leopold became increasingly concerned, especially after he learned that Brazza was pushing toward Stanley Pool to claim it for France. On November 7, 1880, Brazza and fifteen Gabonese sailors, armed with Winchester repeating rifles, appeared in Stanley's camp, where they were coolly but politely welcomed. Thanks to his prior negotiations and extraordinarily friendly relations with local African chiefs, Brazza would single-handedly provide the basis for France's future sovereignty over the north bank of Stanley Pool, where the city of Brazzaville would eventually be built and the country of what is now Congo-Brazzaville would take shape. Stanley took no immediate action to thwart Brazza. Leopold was furious.

By the end of 1881, the road from the Atlantic coast to Stanley Pool had been completed, and several boats had been hauled to the pool and launched. Leopoldville was built directly across the pool from Brazza's fort. The Congo River was now a navigable waterway that stretched east for one thousand miles. By May of 1885, after a short trip back to Europe, Stanley began to build more trading stations farther east. To his surprise and mounting horror, he found large stretches of formerly heavily peopled land totally devastated—crops destroyed, houses burned to the ground, no one to be found. Stunned, Stanley finally located some Africans who told him what had happened—Tippu Tip and his Arab slavers had followed Stanley's footsteps down the Congo to ravage villages that had never before been targets of the slave trade.

A few days later, Stanley came upon one of Tippu Tip's camps and, despite his years of personal brutality on the march, including the liberal use of the lash and chains, was shocked to see so many women and children in chains, most of them covered by their own feces and urine. The smell was so terrible he referred to the slave camp as a human kennel. Stanley counted 2,300 slaves in this one camp, the product of raids on 118 villages, during which, as far as he could ascertain, at least 4,000 other Africans had been killed.[53] His journal records his agonized speculation about how many adults had been killed to capture a single small child who would be useless as a slave for many years. It also contained this angry entry about the Arabs: "What a pity I did not bring up one of the Krupps. I could then have annihilated the camp."[54]

Stanley completed the road in 1884 and returned to Europe with detailed plans for the railroad he had hoped would have been under way years earlier. Leopold had been awarded the "Congo Free State" during the Berlin Conference of 1884–85, but he lacked the funds to implement Stanley's railroad until 1887, when private Belgian investors led by Major General and wealthy entrepreneur Albert Thys came forward. Leopold had promised the Belgian people that the Congo Free State would cost them nothing. In 1887, however, he requested a loan of 10 million francs to help with the construction of the railroad, and in 1890, he asked for another 25 million francs. Both loans were overwhelmingly approved by the Belgian parliament.[55] Soon after the money came forward, sixty thousand men, from Liberians to Chinese, labored on this difficult engineering project only made possible by the road Stanley had built. Many were Africans who had been dragged there in chains, were fed little, and paid nothing. Untold thousands died. Joseph Conrad was horrified to see not only workmen in chains, but what he called a "grove of death" where hundreds of men lay dead or dying, callously abandoned to their fate.[56]

The railway was finally completed in March 1898. A trip to Leopoldville that had required a twenty-day march along Stanley's road now took only two days in well-ventilated comfort. How many men died to achieve this result is unknown, but the number of Africans who died in the first two years alone has been estimated at four thousand. Close to two hundred Europeans died as well.[57] Many of the workers soon found conditions so appalling that they mutinied, and some escaped from the Congo.

Of the five hundred and forty Chinese hired to work on the railroad, three hundred died or deserted. Some of the deserters tried to walk back to China by following the sun and were later found alive five hundred miles inland.[58]

As we will see in chapter 3, under the guise of bringing Christian civilization to the Congo Free State, Leopold organized a system of trade as brutal as anything ever conceived by Arab slave traders. He himself was a major financial beneficiary until international outrage finally forced him to give the Congo to Belgium in 1908. But before that transfer could take place, Stanley would once again return to that ever more brutalized land, and with him would come new contributions to its "darkness."

In 1885, the same year that the Congo Free State was created, the Mahdists of the Sudan rose against Egyptian rule, beheading Sudan's governor, British general Charles Gordon in Khartoum and embattling Emin Pasha, the progressive governor of Equatoria, Sudan's most southerly province. Emin had brought peace and prosperity to this previously troubled region since 1876, when he was first sent there by the Egyptian government as a medical officer. A few years later he became its governor and was promoted to the rank of pasha. By the summer of 1886, Emin Pasha had found refuge from the Mahdists in Wadelai, located on the Nile, near the Ugandan border north of Lake Albert. He managed to get a letter out through Zanzibar describing his flight from the Mahdists and their continuing advance toward Wadelai. Furious about Gordon's decapitation by "Muslim hordes"—not to mention the Mahdist demands that Queen Victoria go to Sudan, submit to Mahdist rule, and convert to Islam— ordinary Britons donated tens of thousands of pounds sterling, while all manner of British officers volunteered to lead the rescue mission to save Emin Pasha, a short, slight, very nearsighted German who was born Eduard Carl Oscar Theodor Schnitzer in 1840.

Described by most historians as a Jew, Schnitzer had in fact been baptized as a Protestant. If he had any Jewish ancestry, he never mentioned it.[59] When his beloved Abyssinian wife died in 1887, in his grief he requested a Bible.[60] He sometimes told his Arab superiors and even General Gordon that he was a Muslim, but gave little evidence of devotion to that faith, beyond taking the name Emin, meaning "the faithful one." He was trained as a medical doctor in Germany, but due to a technicality involving registering as a physician, he could not practice there. An accomplished linguist and botanist, Schnitzer could speak Albanian, German, French, English, Italian, Greek, Turkish, Arabic, and several African languages. Frustrated by German red tape, he went to Albania, a part of the Ottoman Empire, where he was able to practice medicine. After a brief return trip to Germany, Schnitzer moved to Khartoum, where he again practiced medicine and met General Gordon. After the Mahdist rising and the death of Gordon, Emin Pasha's red fez, thick spectacles, and dark, bushy beard became familiar to readers of British newspapers, who were warned that he might well meet the same fate as Gordon.[61]

The British government chose Stanley to lead the rescue effort. King Leopold, who still had Stanley under salary, saw much useful publicity in such a rescue mission. He also had territorial designs on Equatoria. He agreed to permit Stanley to lead the rescue and even offered to make his steamships on the Congo available. Not only did Leopold want Stanley to "save" Emin Pasha, he wanted him to offer Emin the governorship of a province in the Congo Free State. Although it was obvious to many that the shortest and easiest route to Emin Pasha, near the Uganda-Sudan border, was from Zanzibar across East Africa, Leopold insisted that Stanley lead his rescue mission up the Congo from the Atlantic. Stanley agreed, in part because he believed he could proceed most of the way by steamship, but also because he feared that his Zanzibari porters and soldiers might desert if they were attacked in Uganda or Rwanda but could not easily do so in the faraway Congo.[62] At the request of the *Herald*'s Bennett, Stanley ludicrously led his mission while carrying the flag of the New York Yacht Club.[63]

In January 1887, Stanley set off on his last, and in many respects most difficult, African adventure up the Congo River. Despite possessing a modern six-hundred-round-per-minute Maxim machine gun, Stanley needed almost as much time to go up the Congo to bring out Emin Pasha as it had earlier taken him to go down it—nearly three years. At least four hundred members of his party of eleven Europeans and six hundred and fifty Africans died from food shortages, diseases, and attacks by hostile tribesmen. There were multiple desertions, violent mutinies, and shocking brutalities that went beyond even Stanley's experience.

The expedition began in Zanzibar, where Stanley once again recruited porters and soldiers. He also signed a contract with none other than Tippu Tip, who agreed to provide porters for the overland portion of the journey from Stanley Falls to Sudan. Before Stanley left Zanzibar, he sent Emin Pasha a letter by a native courier informing him that he was on his way and bringing ammunition for rifles, official letters from Egypt, and much mail from friends and advisers.[64] When Stanley sailed from Zanzibar to Boma, his ship carried 623 Zanzibaris, 61 Arabs, 62 Sudanese, 12 Somalis, 9 Europeans, 3 interpreters, and Tippu Tip—along with 35 of his wives.[65]

While Tippu Tip steamed up the river to recruit carriers, Stanley unloaded his ninety thousand pounds of stores that included one hundred thousand rounds of ammunition for the Remington rifles used by Emin Pasha's men, not to mention forty loads of the choicest provisions from Fortnum and Masons and nine fully equipped medicine chests.[66] Stanley prepared seven hundred loads of sixty-five pounds each, but could locate only 170 porters. Hoping to find Tippu Tip farther into the interior of the Congo, Stanley pressed ahead on foot, leaving the seven hundred loads, most of the porters, and six Europeans behind as his "rear guard." As the first European to traverse it, he and his men struggled terribly through the Ituri Forest, some days working from dawn to dark to cut a path no more than four hundred yards long. Some of his men were killed by the poisoned arrows of Pygmies, whose territory they had invaded. Finally, they found Tippu Tip, who again promised to provide six hundred porters. However, he was unable to recruit them, and meanwhile Stanley's rear guard waited. Many of its porters died of starvation and disease, and all six of its Europeans fell dangerously ill with malaria and dysentery.

The first of Stanley's European officers to reach Emin Pasha was A.J.M. Jephson, a British gentleman who actually shelled out £1,000—a princely sum—for the right to join Stanley's expedition.[67] Soon after the journey began, Stanley wrote that Jephson "is supposed to be effeminate" but "is actually fierce when roused."[68] Indeed, Jephson later proved himself to be an intrepid man who earned the Zanzibari nickname of "cheetah" because he was so fast and aggressive, often winning foot races against all manner of Africans while Stanley's caravan was encamped.[69] Jephson found Emin in Wadelai, with an army of fifteen hundred men. Most were Sudanese, but fifty were Egyptian officers, who treated the Sudanese as scum, earning their profound hatred.[70]

Jephson traveled with Emin some seventy-five miles north, down the Nile, to inspect the impressive military station of Dukilé, a place with imposing brick housing for its well-uniformed officers, soldiers, and civil servants along with a mosque, steamer wharves, engineering shops, and gardens. Enclosed by tall earthworks and a moat, the station proved to be invulnerable when the Mahdists later attacked it. However, when Emin and Jephson arrived, rebellious soldiers, furious with their Egyptian officers, held them prisoner for three months before finally allowing them to leave. Emin and Jephson were soon forced to flee farther south in such haste that Emin had to leave behind all his scientific equipment, books, and notes as well as four large boxes filled with rare stuffed birds intended for the British Museum.[71] He also had to abandon his enormous stash of ivory, the estimated value of which was well over £100,000 (or well over $1 million today).

When Stanley finally reached Emin Pasha on Lake Albert, he produced three bottles of champagne he had carried hidden in a long sock buried deep in one of his trunks.[72] Emin greeted Stanley warmly, but immediately made it quite clear that he had no desire to be "rescued." Refusing to abandon the thousands of Sudanese who trusted him, he said, "I am now asked to give up everything, to abandon everything, and go away. That was not my idea of Stanley's expedition and its purpose."[73] He not only treasured his role as governor of Equatoria, he did not want to give up his scientific activities, especially collecting birds. To compound Stanley's embarrassment, Emin turned out to be so well provisioned that he was able to feed Stanley's emaciated survivors for a month, also providing them with clothes and shoes. After weeks of futile attempts at persuasion, Stanley finally left Emin and returned to his rear guard, whom he had abandoned to their own devices—without carriers or regular sources of food—for fourteen months, from June 1887 to August 1888. He hoped to return with them and their supplies to Emin, to change his mind.

He soon learned that the conduct of the British leaders of his so-called rear column had been appalling. Stanley later said that two of his officers had done things "too horrible to describe in all their barbarity—things which were they fully described would make an Englishman's blood boil and his cheeks flush with shame."[74] One was the commander of the rear column, Major Edmund Barttelot of the Seventh Fusiliers, a gentleman whose wealthy father was a baronet and MP. Barttelot had previously served bravely in Afghanistan and Sudan. The other was James Sligo Jameson, a wealthy big-game hunter and amateur naturalist who, like Jephson, had paid £1,000 to join Stanley's expedition.

A Syrian interpreter, Assad Farran, swore an affidavit before Belgian officers that Jameson had purchased a slave girl from Arab traders in order to satisfy his intellectual curiosity about cannibalism. Former British sergeant William Bonny of the Army Medical Department, whom Stanley described as a "staid and observing man," and Barttelot himself described as "rough and slow" but "steady, honest, and sure," confirmed Farran's accusation.[75] Bonny, who competently provided medical care for the "rear guard" and had done his best to control Barttelot's increasingly brutal temper, wrote to the *Times* of London that Jameson had made six sketches of what had happened while Farran and others looked on.[76] First, the girl is shown tied by one hand to an African holding a knife in his right hand. He is then shown stabbing her, her blood spurting out. Then the girl is shown being carved up, natives scrambling for pieces and cooking them. And finally, the feast itself is pictured as the girl is eaten.

Jameson's diary reported a version of the event that made him seem both innocent and horrified. During a conversation with Tippu Tip, who described African cannibalism that he had witnessed, Jameson

told him that people at home generally believed that these were only "travellers' tales," as they are called in our country, or, in other words, lies. He then said something to an Arab called Ali, seated next to him, who turned round to me and said, "Give me a bit of cloth, and see." I sent my boy for six handkerchiefs, thinking it was all a joke, and that they were not in earnest, but presently a man appeared, leading a young girl of about ten years old by the hand, and I then witnessed the most horribly sickening sight I am ever likely to see in my life. He plunged a knife quickly into her breast twice, and she fell on her face, turning over on her side. Three men then ran forward, and began to cut up the body of the girl; finally her head was cut off, and not a particle remained, each man taking his piece away down to the river to wash it. The most extraordinary thing was that the girl never uttered a sound, nor struggled, until she fell. Until the last moment, I could not believe that they were in earnest. I have heard many stories of this kind since I have been in this country, but never could believe them, and I never would have been such a beast as to witness this, but I could not bring myself to believe that it was anything save a ruse to get money out of me, until the last moment.

. . . When I went home I tried to make some small sketches of the scene while still fresh in my memory, not that it is ever likely to fade from it. No one here seemed to be in the least astonished at it.[77]

However, Bonny wrote to the *Times* of London that Jameson had admitted to him that he had known the girl would be killed and had calmly sketched the scenes while they were taking place.[78] Stanley later said that he was horrified to learn from Bonny that Jameson, who had died of disease soon after the cannibalistic act took place, had seemed to take pride in being the only European to have witnessed such a cannibalistic act, and that he enjoyed showing others his sketches.[79]

The second case involved Major Barttelot, who made no secret that he loathed Africans, kicking, beating, and whipping them on many occasions. One member of the expedition said, "He had an intense hatred of anything in the shape of a black man."[80] Although only five feet four inches tall, Barttelot was tough and wiry with a violent temper.[81] Bonny described one instance in which Barttelot ordered John Henry, a mission-educated Zanzibari, who was so hungry that he stole Barttelot's pistol and traded it for food, to be whipped by four large Sudanese porters, each of whom would deliver seventy-five lashes. Bonny wrote, "This scene was the most horrible I ever saw. Mortification set in, the man's flesh fell off in pieces to the ground, and his body swelled to twice its ordinary size. Within twenty-four hours, John Henry died."[82]

Barttelot seemingly became demented during the fourteen months Stanley was away, perhaps because his many bouts with malarial fevers deepened his loathing of Africans. He savagely bit a woman on the cheek for no apparent reason, often struck porters, and became obsessed with poisoning, both fearing for his own life and threatening to poison others.[83] Furious because a Zanzibari "headman" refused his demands for extra porters, Barttelot kicked his servant boy so savagely that the boy later died. It took all that Bonny could do to prevent Africans who saw this senseless attack from killing Barttelot, and later that evening after a bullet was fired into the hut that Bonny and Barttelot shared, Barttelot seized the man he thought guilty of firing it, stabbed him thirty times with a steel-tipped staff he always carried, then beat the "man's brains out before the eyes of all in the village."[84] Bonny was only able to save Barttelot by knocking him down himself, apparently convincing the Africans that he would punish him. That night, guns were fired all over the village as an expression of rage against Barttelot. The following morning, Barttelot rushed out of his hut with a revolver in hand and began frenziedly kicking and beating a woman who had annoyed him by beating a drum. The woman's husband shot him to death. Stanley would later write that no court in England would have convicted the husband, but he had nevertheless been tried and shot by members of the rear guard.[85]

Some have argued that Joseph Conrad used the story of Stanley's rear column as his inspiration for *Heart of Darkness*, with either Barttelot or Jameson serving as the model for Kurtz.[86] Conrad's most authoritative biographer insists that Kurtz was based on "the behavior of a great many Europeans in Africa," not just Jameson or Barttelot.[87]

After the horrors he discovered among his rear guard, Stanley took those porters still able to march and made yet another exhausting and deadly return trip to Emin Pasha, arriving in March 1889, after six months of trekking. It took him over a month to convince Emin Pasha to accompany him to the eastern coast, and when he did, it was literally at gunpoint. Emin Pasha's men had only 40 guns while Stanley's force had 294 rifles and often brandished them. After weeks of being unable to persuade Emin to join him, Stanley ordered his armed men to confront Emin's followers, saying that those who wished to follow Emin to the coast had to stand behind him. The others should stand aside. All chose to follow Emin, who to avoid bloodshed consented to leave. With Stanley's guns still very much in evidence, Stanley's 360 people were joined by Emin's 600, 380 of whom were women and children. One of these children was Emin's beautiful six-year-old daughter, Ferida, whose Abyssinian mother had died two years earlier.[88] The resourceful Jephson designed a hammock for the child to be carried in and sometimes carried her on his back. After reaching Zanzibar, she was sent to Germany, where she lived out her life. She was lastingly grateful to Jephson for his kindness to her.[89]

The march to the coast of Tanzania was long and painful. Not one day passed when one of the four Europeans was not down with a high fever, often reaching 105 or 106 degrees. Emin Pasha was often ill as well, as were his Egyptian officers, dressed in spotless white uniforms. Emin proved to be even more indifferent to the well-being of his people than Stanley was to his, and he also displayed a nasty temper.[90] According to a British officer in Stanley's force, Emin Pasha and Stanley "hate each other to an extent almost incredible."[91] By the time the caravan neared the coast in early December 1889, over half of Emin Pasha's followers had died. The survivors were met by the explorer Major Hermann von Wissmann, who was now the military governor of Tanganyika, Germany's most recent African colony.

On horses provided by von Wissmann, Stanley and Emin Pasha arrived in Bagamoyo to a tumultuous welcome. A brass band from a German navy warship played "God Save the Queen," and a telegram of congratulations from Kaiser Wilhelm awaited. A sumptuous champagne lunch was followed later that evening by a lavish dinner in a two-story building. Emin Pasha drank so much champagne that he became noticeably tipsy. The badly nearsighted man stepped out a low window, mistaking it for a door, and fell over fifteen feet to the pavement below, fracturing the base of his skull and two ribs. Had his fall not been broken by the slanting roof of a lean-to shed, he would have been killed.[92] As it was, it was twenty days before blood stopped flowing from his ears, and months before his broken ribs healed.[93] Stanley was forced to return to Europe without him.

In 1890, at the age of forty-nine, Stanley, a world-famous celebrity, married for the first time. His bride was Dorothy Tennant, a well-known, handsome, upper-class British portrait painter who claimed descent from Cromwell and whose widowed mother (with whom, though thirty-nine, Dorothy still shared a bedroom) was a grande dame of Victorian London. Stanley had asked Dorothy to marry him four years earlier, but unsure of her feelings for him she had declined. Only after his return from the three-year-long Emin Pasha adventure did she agree to the marriage. Their wedding was the society event of its day. As word of the impending marriage spread, the prices for her paintings rose dramatically, Queen Victoria gave her a locket studded with thirty-eight diamonds, and Thomas Edison sent the newlyweds one of his new phonographs. Although Stanley still had some vocal detractors, the cream of British society crowded into Westminster Abbey for the wedding ceremony, and King Leopold II of Belgium—a cousin of Queen Victoria's—sent Count d'Aarche to serve as Stanley's best man.

Stanley suffered such a severe bout of gastrointestinal pain—a reminder of his ordeals in the American Civil War and his years in Africa—that he had to sit through much of the ceremony and could not attend the wedding reception at all. Soon after his honeymoon, to which he invited his male assistant, Stanley was well enough to continue his speaking tours, was elected to Parliament, where he served one term as a backbencher, and after renouncing his U.S. citizenship in 1895, was duly knighted. His wealth and his fame were so great that when he, along with Dorothy, made a speaking tour of the United States and Canada, they did so in an elegant private railroad car equipped with a grand piano. Once again, he was accompanied by his young assistant and Dorothy by her mother. We do not know if their marriage was ever consummated.

While Stanley was marrying and traveling, Emin Pasha somehow recovered. He joined the German Colonial Service, and although half-blind as a result of his fall, two years later he led an expedition toward Uganda, which the Germans hoped to claim as their colony. Still an avid collector, he preserved many insects, birds, and plants as he traveled, but his caravan suffered terribly from smallpox, and eventually he altered his course to take him into the Ituri Forest of the Congo. Before doing so, however, Emin asked the Arab commander of this region, Sultan Kiponge, for a letter permitting his expedition to march through. Kiponge agreed. In October 1892, as Emin's column struggled through the Ituri Forest, he was befriended by Arab slavers who were just beginning a campaign to drive the Europeans out of the Congo. Soon after Emin Pasha's friendly welcome, however, another letter written by Sultan Kiponge was delivered to the Arabs. It ordered his death.[94]

After his armed men were sent away on a ruse, Emin Pasha was seized. When he protested that he had written permission from Sultan Kiponge to continue his journey, the second letter from Kiponge was shown to him. According to the later confession of one of the men who killed him, after reading it Emin Pasha drew a long breath, then said, "Well, you may kill me, but don't think that I am the only white man in this country. There are many others who will be willing to avenge my death: and let me tell you that in less than two years from now there won't be an Arab left in the entire country held by your people."[95] While five men held him, another calmly cut his throat. The Arabs removed his boots and clothing, then left his naked, headless body in the bush to be eaten by animals.

By the time Stanley left Africa for good, the Congo had fallen under the personal control of King Leopold II of Belgium. It would be difficult for anyone to present a greater contrast to Stanley than Leopold. Very tall, with an immense beard, Leopold possessed a regal presence, was an eloquent speaker, and often acted out his lust for women. He had long coveted a foreign colony, and his eyes had fallen on the Congo, which became his in 1885. Emin Pasha's death marked the start of a war by Arab traders and their African allies aimed at driving Leopold's traders and soldiers out of the Congo once and for all. King Leopold's forces won, and before his reign ended in 1908, Leopold's policies inflicted unimaginable horrors on the native peoples of the Congo.

3

CONQUERING THE CONGO

When Leopold II assumed the throne of Belgium in 1865, his position was anything but enviable. Surrounded by powerful neighbors, Prussia and France, and independent only after its revolt against Holland, Belgium had a tiny population of only about 5 million, divided between the largely Dutch-speaking Flemings in the north and the much more affluent, French-speaking Walloons in the south. Most of the Flemings were devout Catholics, while many Walloons were openly anticlerical. The Flemings worked hard but were badly impoverished. However, thanks to rich coal deposits in Wallonia, and the development of steam power, before the end of the nineteenth century, Belgium led the world in railroad construction, with projects in places as far away as Russia, China, Egypt, and Argentina. This industry in turn stimulated coal mining, ironworking engineering, and the construction of machinery, steam engines, cable cars, and tramways to such an extent that by the time Leopold's dream of achieving an overseas empire was realized, Belgium was one of the most economically advanced countries in the world, with some of the world's most powerful banks. It was, however, hardly the world's most advanced democracy. Some Belgian men did not even possess the franchise until 1919, and as late as 1910, 37 percent of the population was illiterate.[1] And when Leopold acquired the Congo Free State in 1885, Belgium was tensely divided between Catholics and socialists, farmers and townspeople, and workers and employers.

Belgium had no history as a colonial power, having come into being as an independent state only as recently as 1831. It did not even possess a navy. Its small army consisted of Flemings officered by Walloons. Undeterred, the wily, ambitious, and ruthless Leopold had dreams of an empire that would empower and enrich his tiny, vulnerable nation. He explored various possibilities of acquiring colonies in several parts of the world including China, North Borneo, and the Pacific. He actually tried at one point to purchase the Philippines from Spain, but failed. In 1876, when he learned about Cameron's report of the great natural wealth of the Congo, which he had just traversed, Leopold decided to "find out discreetly whether there may be something doing in Africa."[2] Both France and Portugal had made claims to the Congo, but Germany, England, and America opposed them, not wishing to see any great colonial power become even more powerful. Widely seen at the time as a philanthropist, not a colonialist, Leopold seemed a far safer alternative. On April 30, 1885, the Berlin Conference, devoted to the peaceful partitioning of those parts of Africa not yet claimed by a European power, accorded him personal control of the Congo. Attended by Austro-Hungary, Belgium, Britain, Denmark, France, Holland, Italy, Norway, Portugal, Russia, Spain, Sweden, Turkey, and the United States, along with host Germany, the conference also appeased France by giving her Brazzaville and the territory north of the Congo, and Portugal by awarding her Angola to the south.

At this time, more French, British, Dutch, German, and Scandinavian traders were in the Congo than Belgians. The Belgian people opposed colonialism, and Belgium had no African ties, no businesses there, no contacts, no history of involvement. Yet it was Leopold, rather than the head of any European trading or mining company, who had several years earlier paid Stanley to build the road that opened the Congo River to navigation beyond the cataracts. And it was Leopold—a man who proved so unscrupulous that later even Cecil Rhodes was appalled—who convinced thirteen European powers and the United States at the Berlin Conference that he would improve the moral and material condition of the Congolese and, moreover, put an end to slave trading. More privately, Leopold spoke rapturously of the Congo in terms of new markets, new revenues, and "an outlet for surplus production of men, things and ideas."[3] To dramatize his declared intent to set free the Africans in the Congo, he gave the territory the name Congo Free State.

As Leopold's officers of his newly blessed Congo Free State attempted to move into the vastness of the central and eastern Congo, they were aided beyond measure by the industrious, entrepreneurial Bangala people, but suffered from disease and the absence of roads, health care, and supply depots. Also, as they slogged inland, they encountered not only Africans but Arabs. While the Portuguese were trading for slaves in the western Congo and sometimes a bit farther into the interior, the eastern Congo had fallen prey to white-robed Arab slavers, who not only traded for slaves and ivory, but also stole them at the point of a gun. They also sometimes armed African tribesmen to capture slaves for them.[4] The result was misery and death for millions of Congolese, and a life of slavery for hundreds of thousands more. A few years later, a savage war would be fought to determine whether Arabs or King Leopold's forces would control the Congo's riches.

For as long as there have been written records, Arabs have taken black Africans as slaves.[5] Arabs often enslaved other peoples as well, including Turks, Ukrainians, and some Westerners, including British and American sailors. From 1580 to 1680, nearly 1 mil-

79

lion Christian slaves were taken in chains to the Maghreb, an Arab state that included most of North Africa, where they were forced to kiss the feet of their masters and quickly move out of the path of any oncoming Muslim.[6] Centuries earlier, even more slaves had been taken from East Africa to the Tigris-Euphrates delta in Iraq— so many that when they eventually seized Arab weapons and revolted, they killed thousands and threatened Baghdad itself before their rebellion was finally crushed in A.D. 883.[7] Because Africans lacked firearms, they continued to be especially vulnerable to Arab slave raids. Due to its proximity to the Arab world, the north of Africa was targeted by slave raiders for centuries, and to this day, armed Arab raiders still regularly carry away Africans as slaves in Mauritania and Sudan.

As early as the tenth century A.D., there were Arab settlements along the east coast of Africa. Many of these were lost to the Portuguese after their discovery of the Cape route to the riches of the Indies brought more and more Portuguese warships to the region. But by the beginning of the nineteenth century, Africa's east coast had been reconquered by the imams of Muscat. For the next hundred years, Arab slaving influence was centered on the islands of Zanzibar and Pemba, off the northern coast of Tanzania. There is little evidence to suggest that Arabs raided very far into East Africa for slaves until somewhat later in the nineteenth century, when Pemba became a highly profitable clove plantation worked by African slaves. At about the same time, armed Arab slave caravans first began to move into East Africa, and later into Central Africa, in an ever-widening search for ivory and slaves.

These early expeditions relied on Zanzibari Africans as soldiers and porters, and when these men returned to Zanzibar, some of them became part of a new culture—Africans imbued with a belief in Islam and a sense of their superiority to "pagan" Africans in East and Central Africa. These "black Arabs," many of them dark-skinned "Afro-Arabs," grew wealthy from their trade in ivory and slaves, returning to Zanzibar to marry and enjoy a life of prosperous comfort alongside "white" Arabs. By 1830, thirty Arabs remained in Tabora, 450 miles inland from the coast of Tanzania. Some lived lavishly in nearby Unyanyembé, while by 1840 many others reigned over the booming trading center of Ujiji on the east coast of Lake Tanganyika, where Stanley had found Livingstone. Still others like Tippu Tip settled in Nyangwe on the Lualaba River in the Congo, where both Livingstone and Cameron had tried but failed to obtain canoes. At the time, it was said that "all roads led to Nyangwe," for it was one of the largest markets in Africa. The trade routes that led to Nyangwe and the other trade centers were heavily traveled by large cara-vans and were reasonably safe. The route from Bagamoyo on the coast of Tanzania to Tabora and then on to Ujiji was safely fol-lowed by Burton, Speke, Livingstone, Cameron, and Stanley. The road from Ujiji to Nyangwe was also heavily traveled.

In towns like these, as well as Stanleyville itself—where many other Arabs settled under the blood-red flag of the sultan of Zanzibar—Arab slave traders spoke Swahili, dressed in spotless, ankle-length white robes, and lived sumptuously, served by their concubines, slaves, and retainers. They feasted on delicacies from Zanzibar, gambled, and grew ever wealthier as their large, heavily armed caravans marched off to capture slaves and trade for ivory in the eastern Congo. When Stanley reached Tabora in 1871, it was a town of five thousand people, many of them Arabs, living with their servants and harems in impressive luxury. With their Persian carpets and luxurious bedding, they awaited regular ship-ments from Zanzibar of spices, tea, coffee, curries, sardines, salmon, brandy, and wine, among other delicacies.[8]

This area was not only agriculturally rich, as the Arabs at Ny-angwe soon discovered, it was also blessed with a wealth of rubber vines that would become highly prized during the latter part of the nineteenth century when the demand for tires, hoses, and other rubber products was growing around much of the world. Although decreasing in numbers with every passing year, large herds of elephants also still roamed in the eastern Congo, their ivory highly sought after by buyers in Zanzibar, who sold it for large profits around the world. Ivory was in huge demand for knife handles, billiard balls, and piano keys, as well as for women's jewelry, especially in India, where the bulk of the ivory was sold. Arabs were also in control of the trade in the diamond and gold fields of the northeast Congo, but had far less influence in the copper-rich region of Katanga to the south.

Huge herds of elephants roamed the Congo before Arabs from Zanzibar, heavily armed with Western rifles, moved into the area, enslaving humans and exporting ivory. The Congolese traditionally hunted elephants for their flesh and fat, not their tusks. They sometimes used tusks to decorate graves and build cattle pens and stockades, as well as to fashion decorative posts. They also carved ivory into war horns, axes, bracelets, religious idols, mallets for beating bark cloth, chopping blocks, pestles, and mortars. But the same objects could also be made of wood, preferably ebony. Ivory had no intrinsic value for the Congolese. After an elephant's body had been cut up for its meat, its tusks were often simply abandoned.

In search of the flesh and fat of the hundreds of thousands of elephants that once roamed the Congo, the Congolese developed a number of effective hunting techniques. Sometimes, dozens of hunters would surround a lone elephant, filling it with spears until it resembled a pin cushion and bled to death. They would also attach a spear to a huge beam that was suspended overhead in the forest until an elephant stumbled over a trip-vine, sending the several-hundred-pound weapon plunging deeply into its neck. Poisoned arrows were also used, and so were all sorts of cleverly disguised pits for an elephant to fall into and be impaled on sharp stakes. One of the most widely used methods was hamstringing.

A brave hunter armed with a razor-sharp spear or machete would rush an unwary elephant from behind and sever one of its Achilles tendons, leaving it helpless to defend itself against hunters, who could safely throw spears at the immobilized creature. Sometimes, fires were set to kill by suffocation; heavy matting was used as a net; or elephants were caught by snares attached to logs too heavy even for an elephant to drag very far.[9]

Arabs with firearms changed all that. They initially came peacefully, paying tribute to Congolese chiefs and respecting their authority and cultural beliefs. They bartered cloth, jewelry, mirrors, and other Western goods for the ivory and slaves that they coveted. They not only built their own slaving stations, but forged alliances with powerful chiefs, often providing firearms in return for loyal service. The amounts of ivory they took back to Zanzibar were astonishing. Cameron met one caravan carrying what he estimated at fifteen tons of ivory, and he saw many other caravans with hundreds of large tusks. One caravan that Stanley met near Stanley Falls had two thousand large tusks of ivory. Some of this ivory was the product of peaceful trading, but most was taken in deadly raids that left entire villages in ruins. When Stanley went upriver to rescue Emin Pasha, he described the destruction that Arab slave raids had brought to the eastern Congo. He found mile after mile of burned and devastated villages; the bodies of dead men were seen everywhere, both ashore and afloat. In one Arab camp, he found twenty-three hundred slaves, not a single adult male among them. All the related men had been killed.[10]

A young Englishman whom Stanley hired to set up a station deep in the interior of the Congo wrote the following moving account of Arab ivory and slave raiding:

How the refined possessor of a delicately carved ivory toilet set, fan, or buttonhook would recoil with horror, were it possible to see the blood-stained panorama of destruction to hu-

83

man life, relentless cruelty, and remorseless barbarism daily and hourly enacted to obtain the precious substance so highly prized, but purchased so dearly with human life. Slavery and its attendant cruelties play a part subservient to ivory; there is no attempt on the part of the Arabs to purchase the ivory from the elephant hunters of the far interior. They steal it. A band of Arabs and their followers learn of a village in which some of the occupants have ivory. During the night the native settlement is surrounded by these fiends, and at the earliest streaks of dawn some of the grass thatched roofs are fired and a few guns discharged to throw the village into a state of consternation. The natives, frightened by the unusual noise, emerge from their huts only to fall into the hands of their persecutors. Some of the older men are shot, in order to intimidate the others, and any who resist meet with instant and violent death. All the captives are securely shackled with heavy iron chains and wooden forks to prevent their escape, and the Arabs then open negotiations with the remainder of the tribe, and return the enslaved captives in exchange for ivory. Often it happens that there is not enough ivory to redeem all those who have been captured; in that case the Arabs carry off the remaining slaves and exchange them with some foreign tribe for ivory, or as subjects for human sacrifice in connection with some tribal ceremony, or even to supply a cannibal orgie. Some of the stronger are retained as carriers for the stolen ivory, and a few of the women enter the harems of the slavers."[11]

By the 1880s, the entire region of Kasai, Kivu, and Orientale of the eastern Congo was under the dominion of Tippu Tip, the same Arab who had met and helped Livingstone, Cameron, and Stanley. Other Arab traders raided in this same area as well as farther to the northeast in Orientale Province, but Tippu Tip was the dominant trader. His men not only raided widely to capture slaves and steal ivory, they taxed virtually every Congolese village, built roads and forts, and developed large plantations. Failure to pay Tippu Tip's taxes led to deadly military assaults with the enslavement of anyone who could be captured, followed by the destruction of the village. Often, however, Tippu Tip merely armed African chiefs to collect ivory and slaves for him. All of the territory exploited by Zanzibari Arabs lay within the treaty frontiers of what became King Leopold II's Congo Free State in 1885. To Leopold and his many Free State administrators, traders, corporation executives, and soldiers, it was unthinkable that all the wealth of the eastern Congo should flow east to Zanzibar rather than west to them. War was inevitable.

A British officer who took part in the war of 1892–93 that eventually drove the Arabs out of this land of plenty marveled at the wealth and beauty of the land around Nyangwe. Like others before him, he said that it reminded him of England; there was nothing like it anywhere else in the Congo. He credited the Arabs with its development, including its rich fields of rice, maize, and cotton, but he was not aware that Arabs had also introduced mango, orange, and avocado trees into the Congo, as well as beans, onions, garlic, and tomatoes. He added, however, that the Arabs' slave raids had so completely destroyed food supplies in the area that many peoples of this region, such as the Malela, had been transformed into "perhaps the most inveterate cannibals on the face of the globe."[12] For their part, the Malela were delighted by their diet of human flesh, describing it as "saltish in flavour, and requiring little condiment."[13] Unfortunately for their neighbors, their search for human flesh led to widespread slaughter.

The Arab War of 1892–93 would vastly intensify cannibalism, and so would the tactics of Leopold's Free State administrators, who would soon after the war's end launch their ruthless quest for rubber. Most Europeans in the Congo believed that cannibalism was universal throughout the region, but in reality the nature and extent of cannibalism in the Congo varied enormously. Some tribes, including large and powerful ones like the Bakongo, decried the practice and refused to engage in it for any reason. But the Basongye, or Zappo Zaps as they were often known, sold slaves to their neighbors knowing that they would be eaten; they also ate their own dead.[14] Soon after the end of the Arab War, they would work for the Free State and spread cannibalistic terror across the Congo. Other societies such as the Baluba, for example, ate the hearts of virtuous or brave people to gain their strength, but they also ate the bodies of criminals and slaves to prevent them from doing evil to their masters or haunting them.[15]

In some Congolese societies, people ate human flesh only occasionally to mark a particularly significant ritual occasion, but in other societies in the Congo, perhaps even a majority by the late nineteenth century, people ate human flesh whenever they could, saying that it was far tastier than other meat and, perhaps surprisingly, that male human flesh tasted better than female. Persons to be eaten often had both of their arms and legs broken and were made to sit up to their necks in a stream for three days, a practice said to make their flesh more tender, before they were killed and cooked.[16] Teeth filed to sharp points were widely thought by Europeans to be the mark of cannibals, but in some societies whose people actually were cannibals, teeth were not filed at all, and in others that did not practice cannibalism, people nevertheless filed their teeth to sharp points. As Sydney L. Hinde noted during the Arab War, the Batetela were such devoted cannibals that children actually killed and ate their parents "at the first sign of their decrepitude," but they did not file their teeth.[17]

Many European travelers exaggerated the prevalence of cannibalism everywhere in Africa, but the practice was undoubtedly widespread in the Congo, as it was in many parts of the Pacific, and

North and South America. In 1907, the Bankutu people were seen by a European traveler to hunt people for food as other Congolese hunted animals. They served human flesh in "little rolls like bacon."[18] As late as 1923, American traveler Hermann Norden reported that cannibalism was commonplace. One Congolese man reprovingly scolded him for not eating some human flesh when he was offered it: "You know the flesh of man tastes better than the flesh of a goat."[19] A Belgian companion of Norden's admitted that he had probably been served human flesh and had eaten it unknowingly. In 1925, Hungarian anthropologist Emil Torday reported an encounter with a Muyanzi man who boasted about cooking human brains with a pinch of salt and red peppers, then dipping his bread in it. "Then he would smack his lips and run away like an imp."[20] Missionary and explorer A. L. Lloyd reported that when a European told a Congolese Bangwa tribesperson that eating human flesh was a "degrading habit," the man answered, "Why degraded? You people eat sheep and cows and fowls, which are all animals of a far lower order, and we eat man, who is great and above all; it is *you* who are degraded."[21]

And, as we saw in chapter 2, the gentlemanly British naturalist James S. Jameson apparently purchased a ten-year-old girl, then sketched what happened as she was killed and her body was butchered, then cooked, and finally eaten.[22] While in the Congo, Livingstone saw human parts being cooked with bananas, and many other Europeans reported seeing cooked human remains lying around abandoned fires. British captain and medical officer Sydney L. Hinde, who would take part in the Free State's war with the Arabs in 1892–93, reported an incident in which a Basongo chief asked a Belgian officer to hand him a knife, which he immediately used behind the officer's tent to cut the throat of a little slave girl he owned. He was cooking her when soldiers seized him.[23] British adventurer Herbert E. Ward once asked a group of Congo tribespeople whether they ate human flesh. Their immediate answer was "Yes, don't you?"[24] Later, Ward witnessed cannibalism on numerous occasions and was often offered human flesh to eat. He recalled an occasion when a young Bangala slave was killed. Soon after, the chief's son, a boy of sixteen or so, "nonchalantly" said, "That slave boy was very good eating—he was nice and fat."[25] The Arab slavers did not invent cannibalism in the Congo and their defeat in 1893 did not end it. But their brutal raids forced some societies to rely on human flesh to survive.

Herbert Ward's experiences in the Congo during the late nineteenth century were almost as remarkable as his life itself, because despite serving for a time as an official in Leopold's immensely cruel Congo Free State, he epitomized kindness and compassion for Africans. He would also become a brilliant sculptor. The firstborn son of well-to-do English parents who had high expectations for him, Ward won prizes for drawing at school and became a talented gymnast, while reading every travel and adventure book he could lay his hands on. He dropped out of school in 1878 at the age of fifteen, informing his sculptor father that he intended to explore the world's more remote regions. His father not only refused to support Ward's vagabond travel scheme, he threatened to disinherit the boy and apparently actually did so.[26]

Penniless, except for a few pounds his father had reluctantly given him, Ward sailed in steerage to New Zealand, where he lived with the Maoris for a year. He spent the next three years exploring Australia, supporting himself by working as a stock rider, a miner, and a star performer on the horizontal bar in a Melbourne circus.[27] He then shipped out as an able-bodied seaman to San Francisco and finally home to England. This trip around first the Horn and then the Cape took seven long months. By no means cured of his wanderlust, Ward next took a job with a British trading company among the Dayak headhunters of Borneo. A near-fatal bout of malaria cut short this adventure after less than a year. Back in England, through a friend, he obtained an interview with Henry M. Stanley, in which he asked for a position under Stanley in Leopold's new Congo Free State.[28]

Stanley obliged Ward, who soon received a complicated Belgian contract that offered him only a pittance of pay but much ludicrous advice regarding dress and decorum, including the necessity of providing himself with a mountain climber's alpenstock. Ward signed it nevertheless. By the time he arrived in the Congo, agents of the Free State had made contact with over one hundred previously unknown African societies, founded over forty stations, launched five steamers on the Congo River, and laid claim to much of the western and central Congo. Ward's first fifteen months of service were with the Bakongo, whom he came to like, before moving on to the Bolobo, whom he described as "cruel" people who enjoyed killing and eating their slaves.

He next took command of a fortified station among the Bangala, who may have been cannibals but were nevertheless capable of great affection for one another. He described one touching scene in which a young husband carried his exhausted wife across a raging river while the girl clung to him with "every mark of confidence and affection."[29] He also met the Oupoto people, whose women of all ages were stark naked, something that was quite rare in the Congo.[30] He later served with Stanley's rear guard on his long campaign to save Emin Pasha, but was not in the camp when Barttelot was killed or Jameson sketched the cannibalized girl.

Ward's duties often brought him to the brink of armed violence against Congolese people, but he somehow always stopped short of shooting anyone. Instead, he often doctored sick and wounded Congolese as best he could and somehow managed to produce a host of detailed, almost photographic, sketches of different tribal people, their homes, and their environment. More remarkable still, after he left the Congo and married an American woman, he moved to Paris, where, following in his father's footsteps, he began to study sculpting, eventually producing dozens of bronze statues, many of them life-size, of Congolese men and women. Crafted in dazzling, photographic detail, these bronzes have been considered such works of art that they have won much international acclaim and have been exhibited at the Smithsonian Institution since 1921. Most recently, they were on exhibit in the Getty Museum in Los Angeles.[31]

Ward's bronze sculptures leave no doubt about his respect for the Congolese people, and in his 1910 book, *A Voice from the Congo,* he explains his reasons for crafting them: "I have endeavoured to convey the spirit of something that is deep within me— a fellow feeling for the Central African natives. They are not the altogether degraded race that one might infer by reading instances of their brutality and cannibalism. They are a people whose development has been temporarily arrested by adversity. They are very human: they are often cruel but they are often kind."[32]

After serving in the rear guard of the Stanley expedition to save Emin Pasha, Ward left the Congo in 1889, and not long after, the Free State he had so loyally served found itself at war against the Zanzibari Arab traders. Determined to have the Congo's wealth for themselves, the Free State administrators were determined to drive the Arab slavers and ivory traders out of the Congo, but before they could take any action, Tippu Tip's son, Sefu, beat them to the punch, leading ten thousand men in an attack against the Belgians in an attempt to drive *them* out of the Congo. Tippu Tip was the symbol of Arab slavery and the spiritual leader of the Arab resistance to the Congo Free State. Born Hamed bin Muhammed bin Juma Rajad el Murjebi, Tippu Tip was known to Europeans and many Africans by that nickname, which he said meant "the gatherer together of wealth." He also said that the name was meant to imitate the sound of his men's guns, *tip-u-tip-u-tip*.[33] But most people who knew him were convinced that the name came from his eyes, which blinked rapidly and constantly.[34] His father was a partly African-Arab from Zanzibar. There is some disagreement about the race of Tippu Tip's mother, but the Murjebi family records described her as a white Arab named Bint Habib bin Bushar.[35] She once wrote a letter in which she wondered, "How could a son of mine be so dark?"[36] Whatever his mother's concern, his father was especially affectionate to the boy, raising him as an Arab. Tippu Tip learned Arabic and studied the Koran, but he also became fluent in KiSwahili, the lingua franca of Zanzibar and the coast of East Africa. Both his father and grandfather were slave traders, and he was eager to follow in their footsteps.

Thanks to Tippu Tip's autobiography, published in 1903, the availability of unpublished Murjebi family letters and papers in Zanzibar, and the work of several biographers, much is known about his life and his feelings.[37] He insisted on joining his father's slave caravans in Tanzania while still a teenager, marching along with the porters and soldiers, refusing to be carried or to ride on a donkey. As he would throughout his life, he chose this way of demonstrating his strength, endurance, and humility. Under the blood-red flag of the sultan of Zanzibar, some of these caravans included four thousand men, at least a thousand of whom had muskets. There were also many concubines and children, but legitimate wives, such as Tippu Tip's mother, remained at home in Zanzibar. High-ranking Arab slavers enjoyed the meals and other services provided them by the numerous concubines; ordinary porters and soldiers had no concubines and ate only a single meal each day, usually a thick porridge of maize or millet with some vegetables added. Meat was seldom available, and when it was, only men were served. Women and children rarely, if ever, tasted meat on such an expedition.[38]

Caravans like these sometimes seized thousands of slaves in a single raid, tying them together by their necks, often with six-foot-long poles, and forcing them to carry tusks of ivory. They were whipped for the slightest reason, leaving their bodies covered with open wounds that were quickly covered by flies.[39] Subject to diseases, such as malaria, smallpox, and yellow fever, and fed so little that they were desperately undernourished, those too weak to go on were usually killed, although a few Arab slavers dropped them at mission stations.[40] Women who became too weak to carry both their baby and ivory saw the baby killed. As one slaver put it, "We spear the child and make her burden lighter. Ivory first, child afterwards!"[41] It was not unusual for four out of every five slaves taken in the Congo to die before reaching Zanzibar. Despite this terrible attrition, at least fifty thousand and perhaps one hundred thousand slaves from the Congo reached that island each year.

Those who survived were made ready for sale by being thoroughly bathed, then greased with palm oil so that their bodies glistened. Pretty young women suitable for purchase as concubines were wrapped in colorful clothing and adorned with gold jewelry (which was removed after they had been sold). Healthy young boys were also in demand, often for homosexual relations with Arab men, a practice that was both widespread and socially accepted.[42] Tippu Tip was enormously successful in this trade, but was also said to have actually been less cruel than many slavers. For one thing, he could not abide the practice of castration to produce eunuchs to preside over harems.

When Henry Stanley met Tippu Tip in 1876, he guessed his age at forty-four, and he may have been correct. Like most Arabs in Zanzibar at that time, Tippu Tip did not know his actual age. Photographs show him with dark skin and a curly, white beard, wearing a spotless white turban and robe, a curved dagger with splendid silver filigree in a silk sash, and delicately embossed leather sandals on his feet. He had distinctly African facial features, with sparkling white teeth, but the whites of his eyes were slightly yellow. He always displayed elegant manners to Europeans. "With the air of a well-bred Arab, and almost courtier-like in his manner, he welcomed me," Stanley wrote. Stanley soon concluded that Tippu Tip was the most remarkable man he had met among all the Arabs, coastal people, and "half-castes" in Africa.[43] Tippu Tip emphatically did not reciprocate this esteem. Although Tippu Tip had liked both Cameron and Livingstone, he detested Stanley, accusing him of being a congenital liar, a man without honor, one who did not keep his word, and a worse slave driver to his own men than any Arab slave driver.[44]

Long before he met Stanley, Tippu Tip had proven himself a ruthless slave driver at the head of thousands of armed Zanzibari-African "Arabs" and African porters, most of them from the loyal Nyamwezi people in Tanzania. He was perfectly willing to use brute force to seize slaves or caches of ivory when he located them, but he was also adept at playing one Congolese chief off against another. He often obtained great riches in slaves and ivory without firing a shot. But, when force was needed, he did not hesitate to slaughter all who opposed him. Most chiefs in the eastern Congo soon learned to give him slaves and ivory to ensure safety from his raids. Others were provided with muskets and powder to enable them to capture slaves—and also to make them dependent on him for resupplies of powder. By the time Tippu Tip met Livingstone in 1867 and Cameron in 1874, he was enormously wealthy. As we have seen, he and his men also accompanied Stanley part of the way down the Congo River before Tippu Tip changed his mind and abandoned Stanley to his fate.

Nevertheless, soon after the founding of the Congo Free State, Henry Stanley invited Tippu Tip to move many of his armed men to Stanley Falls, where the Arab leader was asked to establish his headquarters as King Leopold's governor for the region, and to end slavery there. Surprisingly and without explanation, Tippu

Tip agreed. However, the Free State also set up another fortified station nearby, although it was much smaller than Tippu Tip's in Stanley Falls. In 1886, while Tippu Tip was in Zanzibar, his men attacked the other Free State station because its commander, Walter Deane, a British captain, had allegedly stolen an Arab officer's slave woman for his own sexual pleasure. Deane insisted that he had only given refuge to this slave woman because she had been so badly beaten by her Arab master and had refused to return her to him against her will.[45]

Led by Captain Deane and a Belgian lieutenant named Dubois, the fort was manned by eighty Hausas (at that time a generic term for Nigerians) and sixty local militiamen. After a fierce four-day siege, the fort's African defenders ran short of ammunition and asked Deane for permission to flee into the forest. When he refused, they all promptly deserted. After a brief pause to destroy anything of value to the Arabs, Deane and Dubois had no choice but to follow. Despite Deane's valiant efforts to save him, Dubois, who could not swim, drowned while attempting to cross a river. Deane survived thirty days of being hunted in the forest before he was luckily found by a Free State captain, who brought him to Herbert Ward. Ward nursed Deane back to health, but soon after Deane was back on his feet, he was killed by an elephant he was hunting.[46]

When Leopold's men made no military response to this Arab attack, Tippu Tip not only strengthened his Zanzibari forces in the Congo, being joined by his son Sefu—a long-bearded, Caucasian-appearing man—and his nephew Raschid, along with other sometimes competitive Arab slave captains such Nyongo Luteta ("Bitter as Bile"), Bwana Nziga ("The Locust"), Rumaliza ("The Finisher"), and Muinyi Mohara ("The Destroyer"). Mohara was the man who had enforced Kiponge's order of Emin Pasha's execution.[47] Tippu Tip was also joined by several chiefs of powerful African societies, most importantly Gongo Lutete. Lutete had been a slave to Arabs as a child, but his bravery had won him his freedom. Athletic, handsome, and light-skinned, he now had a large following of well-armed Batetela and Bakussu people who would willingly fight with him for Arab mastery of the Congo.

As we saw in chapter 1, the contest for the Congo's riches was not limited to Arab slavers and Leopold's men. The Portuguese had maintained a presence along the coast of the Congo and Angola since the fifteenth century, and many Portuguese slave traders had moved inland, where they continued to treat slaves so brutally that foreigners were unfailingly shocked. When the British government turned down Stanley's invitation to make the Congo its protectorate, some people believed that it had done so because it supported the Portuguese claim to sovereignty. Others, including Leopold, were convinced that France, through the efforts of Pierre Savorgnan de Brazza, was conspiring with Portugal to partition the Congo between them. As we have seen, Brazza had already claimed the land north of Stanley Pool for France, and the city of Brazzaville would grow there across the Pool from Leopoldville on its south bank, only sixteen miles away. Thanks to his adroit dissembling as a champion of civilization, Christianity, and African welfare, by 1885 Leopold was able to establish the Congo Free State, maintained by a military force of European-led Africans, some of whom were actually slaves.[48] In 1892, these men in the Force Publique (People's Army), as it was known, would begin to battle the Arabs for control of the Congo.

As early as 1885, men from the Bangala ethnic group provided elite troops for the Force. One Free State officer described the Bangala as "one of the best gifted races in the Congo in every respect—well built, strong, stocky, and very solid, intelligent and very courageous." Another added that they are "by unanimous consent, the finest people on the [Congo] river—athletic, intelligent, manly, energetic, and fearless to a degree."[49] The first ten men from the Congo to become Force Publique recruits were Bangala; by 1890, seven hundred Bangala tribesmen were in the Force.

In 1888, when the Congo Free State established its armed forces, the Force Publique was officered by Belgians, Scandinavians, and Italians, but almost all of its soldiers were Africans recruited from outside the Congo. There were many Hausas and other British West Africans, as well as Somalis, Egyptians, Ethiopians, and several hundred Xhosa from Natal.[50] There were even some eight hundred Zanzibaris.[51] Later, the Force would rely principally on Congolese natives. A few of these men were volunteers, but most were the product of Free State levies on various Congolese chiefs, who typically turned over slaves or social outcasts for such service. Most were chained while they were marched to their place of service far from their home, where, after some minimal training, they would serve for twelve years as soldiers and laborers. Women were forcibly recruited as well, but were given no training or education. Their role was to produce food and tend to the needs of the male soldiers.[52] Soldiers were allowed to marry, to till a patch of land, and in addition to being fed by the Force, they were paid a token wage. As late as 1912, the Force actually paid to attract young women into service as wives of soldiers.[53]

The whites who colonized the Free State came from throughout Europe. Until 1885, two-thirds of them were not Belgians, many of them being Britons, Germans, and Swedes; there were even a few Americans. By 1904, Belgians had become the majority. Of the 2,469 whites in the Free State at that time, 1,442 were Belgian, 230 Italian, 133 British, 119 Dutch, 108 Swedish, 98 Portuguese, 85 Swiss, 71 German, 48 French, 40 American, 31 Danish, 19 Russian, 19 Luxembourgers, and 26 others including Austrians, Australians, Spanish, Greeks, Turks, Argentinians, Brazilians, and Romanians.[54] Many were Free State administrators or officers in the Force Publique, but most were traders, miners, or businessmen and their families. Not all were involved in the brutal ivory and rubber trade. By 1898, for example, they had planted over 4 million coffee, cocoa, and tobacco plants.

The Force Publique would grow to almost twenty thousand men by 1898, but when the Arabs began their attacks early in 1892, only twelve European officers commanded some three thousand African soldiers, most of whom were Hausas, disciplined and brave men but appallingly bad shots.[55] Fortunately for these regular soldiers, they were supported by thousands of well-armed tribesmen from friendly Congolese chiefdoms. By 1893, the Force Publique had grown to almost eight thousand men, armed with modern breech-loading rifles that fired brass cartridges, not the loose-powder muzzle-loaders—so useless in the rain—that most Arabs and their African allies relied on.[56] The Force also possessed powerful Krupp cannons. Against this force, over five hundred Zanzibari Arab officers were at the head of many thousands of Congolese, such as the men led well and courageously by Gongo Lutete.[57] Gongo Lutete's men always marched following a group of drummers and with their muskets held muzzle-forward across their right shoulders.[58]

The best account of the war of 1892–93 has been provided by Sidney L. Hinde, a British captain and medical officer who served with the Congo Free State forces.[59] Although recruited as a doctor, Hinde fought bravely in a number of battles and was highly decorated for his actions. Force Publique officer Michaux, who fought with Hinde under Dhanis, also describes the fighting in detail and sometimes characterizes the ethnic groups he encountered. He found the people of the lower Congo "degenerate," but portrayed the Sankuru people to the north as strong, beautiful, intelligent, and "sound of mind."[60]

This Congo conflict was virtually a civil war with large bodies of Africans armed with modern breech-loading rifles, old muskets, as well as spears and bows and arrows, fighting for both sides, sometimes changing their allegiance as the fighting wore on. Gongo Lutete, for example, began the war on the side of the Arabs, but after a defeat early in 1892, and angry that the Arabs had not paid him for his services or the ivory he had provided them, he negotiated a transfer of his allegiance to the Free State forces, whom he served loyally well into 1893, when he was accused of planning to betray them as well and was summarily executed. Hinde respected Gongo Lutete and believed that he had been wrongfully accused and executed without an adequate trial.[61]

The Arabs began their assault on the Free State by killing all European members of a peaceful trading caravan, including its leader, Arthur Hodister. Hodister was a black-bearded British ivory trader who spoke fluent Swahili, dressed in a spotless white robe, wore a turban, and was attended to by elegant slaves—including a huge harem of concubines—as he charmed one African leader after another. While Hodister was peacefully carrying on his trade, ably assisted by several other Europeans, a Belgian caravan led by thirty-seven-year-old Captain Guillaume Van Kerckhoven was taking ivory by force, often shooting Arabs who interfered with him. Van Kerckhoven, accompanied by fourteen white officers and a thousand African soldiers armed by Leopold with breech-loading Albini rifles and fifty thousand rounds of ammunition, had marched into Arab-held territory and virtually declared war on them. Arab leader Mohara alone lost 1.5 million francs worth of ivory to him before Van Kerckhoven was accidentally shot and killed by his gunbearer.[62]

Sefu was so enraged by Van Kerckhoven's actions that he seized two Free State agents, Lieutenant Lippens and Sergeant de Bruyne. Both men were later killed, cut into strips, and eaten, though not by Sefu's orders. Their hands and feet were sent to

Mohara in Nyangwe. Hodister and three of his European assistants were also killed and then eaten by the order of another Arab leader, Nserera, who happily received the heads of the four men. Hodister's two young children and their mother were spared and cared for by Mohara. Soon after, one of Hodister's agents at his headquarters at Ribu Ribu on the Lualaba River had an argument with Nserera, who ordered that he be slowly flogged to death. A Belgian Free State agent escaped Nserera's wrath by fleeing into the bush but was soon after captured and made to suffer the same agonizing death.[63] Emboldened by all this—as well as the murder of Emin Pasha—Sefu was by October 1892 in command of over ten thousand armed and so far victorious men. He was so infuriated about Gongo Lutete's defection that he sent a message to the Force Publique saying that if they did not surrender Lutete or at least send him his severed head—then leave the Congo—his army would drive all the way to Leopoldville.[64]

The Force Publique refused Sefu's demand, methodically retreating and fighting rearguard actions while Sefu's pursuing army was slowed by wide rivers and a lack of canoes. Soon Congo Free State reinforcements arrived, and fierce, protracted, and bloody battles took place across the eastern Congo. One Force Publique officer described Arabs fleeing from one battle with their feet literally "bathed in blood."[65] There is no reliable count of casualties on either side of the almost two-year conflict that followed, but Hinde reports that while his Free State forces suffered heavy losses, before the fighting ended the Arab loss "was immensely greater . . . estimated at seventy thousand men."[66] Most of the dead were Africans, not Afro-Arabs. While this death toll may seem inflated, in one documented battle six hundred dead Afro-Arabs were counted on the battlefield, and another two thousand to three thousand were estimated to have been killed when they tried to escape by swimming across a river under heavy gunfire.[67] Scores of battles appear to have been as deadly as this one.[68] Several European officers in the Force noted with a mixture of horror and approval that because Congolese on both sides of such battles cooked and ate all of the dead and wounded, burial parties were unnecessary and diseases were kept under control. Cannibalism was so routine that one Force Publique officer admitted he had become quite "blasé" about it.[69]

The Congo Free State forces were led by Commandant (later Baron) Francis Dhanis, a Belgian officer whose father had been the Belgian consul in London and whose mother was Irish. Although educated in Belgium, Dhanis spoke French with a slight British accent. According to Hinde, Dhanis not only displayed great courage and tactical skill in combat but also a keen understanding of how to campaign in the densely forested world of the Congo. Hinde described one of Dhanis's caravans with four hundred soldiers and eighteen hundred others. Amazingly, it campaigned throughout the Congo for seven months marching single file along perilous ten-inch-wide paths up and down slippery hills and across bogs, without losing a single man to sickness or desertion despite moving through districts so ravaged by Arab slave traders that no food of any kind could be found.[70]

Behind this unprecedented success was Dhanis's decision to encourage every soldier under his command to take along his wife, or wives, and even a slave or servant. As a result, the soldiers carried only their weapons and military gear while the women and slaves carried supplies and sufficient amounts of food to tide the caravan over during long periods.[71] The women and servants also set up camp every evening and did all the cooking and cleaning up. Moreover, Dhanis forbade his men to disturb any African villagers who were not openly at war with him. Because they were accompanied by their wives, his men did not usually molest local women. As a result, Dhanis's force did not face open hostilities as they campaigned, although Arab forces often planted poisoned stakes and arrows along their route.

Dhanis was a rarity among Force Publique officers, most of whom were former noncommissioned officers who had left the Belgian army under a cloud.[72] There were a few brave and honorable men, such as Captain de Wouters, a six-foot-five-inch-tall Belgian known as "the heron" to the Arabs, but there were also renegade French, Greek, and Romanian officers. Their troops were ragged, but these officers "swaggered about the camps and stations radiant in gold lace."[73] They also enforced their own kind of justice. One, for example, hanged an English trader named Stokes, who was accused of selling weapons to Arabs, without a trial, and inflicted hideous torture on Afro-Arab prisoners. One of his favorite practices was to force a bound prisoner to sit in the midday sun with a human leg tied around his neck. Photographs document this practice—as well as other kinds of torture.[74] A British officer who left the Seventh Fusiliers to serve in the Force Publique was appalled by the conduct of many of his fellow officers, calling the Free State "totally immoral" and complaining that profits were all that mattered to people there.[75]

The fighting raged throughout 1893, with thousands of turbaned Arabs displaying such "desperate valor," according to Captain Hinde, who repeatedly fought against them,[76] that the Force Publique was often stalemated and sometimes defeated. This was all the more remarkable because the men in the Force were armed with modern breech-loading rifles, including repeating Winchesters, and even some machine guns, while with a few exceptions the Africans who fought for the Arabs had only old muzzle-loading muskets. The Force also had Krupp artillery pieces that could fire canister as well as explosive shells. The Arabs overcame this inequality in weaponry through their incredible skills in constructing forts. When on campaign, an Arab force used its many slaves to cut down trees and saplings from twelve to fifteen feet in length, and up to six feet in diameter. When camp was reached, these logs were driven into the ground to form a small palisade for officers inside a much larger one manned by soldiers. A moat was then dug outside the larger palisade, with the dirt from the excavation used to reinforce the barricade. Pits were dug and covered with wood for shelter during artillery bombardments. Even large-bore Krupp cannons could do little damage.[77]

As the fighting wore on, more Free State officers, NCOs, and regular troops arrived, along with men from other parts of Africa, including one brave sergeant from heavily Americanized Liberia who spoke English with what Hinde called an "American twang."[78] About him and another English-speaker from Sierra Leone, Hinde wrote, "They succeeded during the Campaign in successfully accomplishing the most daring exploits possible for anyone to undertake. After a day's fighting they habitually got their men together, and followed the retreating enemy far into the night. How they came out alive from some of their undertakings was always a marvel to us."[79] The Arabs were reinforced, too, with new men from Zanzibar. Unlike his father, Sefu was arrogant and insolent to Europeans, and his emissaries reflected his animosity. He also dealt cruelly with any Europeans who fell into his hands. Perhaps because the combat took place in the remote eastern regions of the Congo, it attracted virtually no attention from European countries or America. Not one foreign journalist was sent to cover the fighting, not even from Belgium.

By early 1893, Free State forces had driven Arab forces out of the large market town of Nyangwe, after a fierce, six-week artillery siege and a fire that left only one of the town's thousand or so buildings standing. Ferocious hand-to-hand fighting finally ended the battle. At least a thousand Arabs were killed—then smoked and eaten. One of the Arabs killed was the by then notorious Mohara. Like virtually all war captives, he was promptly eaten, by Gongo Lutete's men. Hodister's two young children, who had been held prisoner in the town but were cared for by

Mohara, were set free. Soon after Nyangwe fell, Dhanis's men also took Kasongo, a walled Arab stronghold farther to the north that was home to sixty thousand people. The Free State attack on Kasongo was so sudden and unexpected that the defenders fled in panic, leaving the invaders in possession of a beautiful town filled with unimaginable luxuries. There were large houses, each of which contained a bathroom with an efficient overhead shower, as well as a separate toilet room. Even common soldiers found themselves sleeping on satin and silk mattresses in elegantly carved wooden beds under silk mosquito curtains. In addition to huge stores of ivory, guns, and ammunition, the Force Publique troops delightedly took possession of long-forgotten luxuries such as candles, sugar, matches, and silver and glass goblets and decanters.[80] According to Hinde, the town's granaries were filled with "enormous quantities" of rice, coffee, maize, and other food; the huge gardens were "luxurious and well planted; and oranges, both sweet and bitter, guavas, pomegranates, pineapples, and bananas abounded at every turn."[81] There were also many cattle and donkeys.

Even the well-born Hinde was stunned by Kasongo's riches. The Arabs who had lived in Kasongo had enjoyed a life of opulence that few Europeans in Africa could hope to match. One of those Arabs was Tippu Tip, who had lived there in a splendid two-story house built around a courtyard. Dhanis's force included twenty thousand Congolese auxiliaries, whom, despite his best efforts, he could not control. They not only ate captives, they pillaged and burned everything, including Tippu Tip's house.[82] Before this destruction took place, however, Force officers recovered Emin Pasha's diary and two of his European decorations.

Tippu Tip did not take an active part in the war. He was so badly stricken by a fever in 1890 that he had to spend months in bed in Bagamoyo, a town on Tanzania's coast whose name meant "lay down the burdens of your heart."[83] When he recovered somewhat, he was still too weak to walk any distance and, for the first time in his life, had to ride a donkey. And the burdens of his heart grew as he had to return to Zanzibar, where he anxiously awaited news of the fighting against the Free State that was being led by his son, Sefu, and other Arab leaders.

With buglers blaring on both sides, battle followed battle, with casualties high on both sides, but the Arabs were suffering the worst of the losses and steadily being driven east. The last major battle took place on October 20, 1893, just to the west of Lake Tanganyika. The battle was a stalemate, but Sefu was killed, as were many of his other relatives and friends. Tippu Tip could not forgive himself for not being able to fight alongside his oldest and most beloved son, who was about thirty-four when he died.[84] Men of the Force Publique also captured and executed two more Arabs who were implicated in ordering the death of Emin Pasha, including Kiponge.[85] By January 1894, the fighting ended with the Free State in command of the eastern Congo. Despite the intensity of the fighting, only sixteen Force Publique officers and noncommissioned officers died in the war, six of them of disease.[86]

Tippu Tip not only lost his dominion over the eastern Congo, but also a fortune in ivory and supplies, as well as twenty thousand muskets and tons of ammunition.[87] Despite these losses, however, Tippu Tip remained a wealthy man with large estates, houses, and valuables of all sorts in Zanzibar. He lived out his remaining years there, dying of malaria at about age seventy in 1905, one year after Stanley's death at the age of sixty-three. Tippu Tip was much beloved by his wives, concubines, and children.

While Tippu Tip and Stanley were living out the last decade of their lives, Leopold's soldiers and administrators were hard at work attempting to solidify their control over the war-torn Congo. After Dhanis's forces had captured Nyangwe and moved on to Kasongo, the task of rebuilding Nyangwe fell to Belgian Force Publique junior officer Émile Lémery, who was also expected to maintain peace in the area, provide work for freed slaves, organize river transport, collect ivory and rubber, protect Arab children whose fathers had been killed, and act as judge and jury. It was a Herculean task, but as we learn in his memoirs, he loved it: *"Vive le Congo,* there is nothing like it! We have liberty, independence and life with wide horizons. Here you are free and no more a slave of society. . . . I hope that later on they [the Congolese] will be grateful for all the efforts I have made here for the good of the State. . . . Here one is everything! Warrior, diplomat, *trader!!* Why not? Whatever they say, I am here for the good of the State . . . and all the means I use are permissible if they are honest."[88] Lémery neglected to mention that he was provided with dozens of "Arab" concubines for his pleasure.[89]

Like so many Free State officers, Lémery was expected to rule wisely, well, and profitably despite his youth, lack of knowledge of local languages, and his inexperience as an administrator. Many thought only of profit and quick escape from the growing horrors of the Congo, but some worked hard and a few were remarkably talented. Although about two-thirds of the Free State administrators were Belgian, by 1908 ninety-two were Swiss, sixty-nine were Swedes, and fifty-seven were Italians. In addition to Danes, Norwegians, Dutchmen, and Luxembourgers, there were Finns, Frenchmen, Russians, and a Bulgarian, an Austrian, and an Argentinian. By that time, however, there were no Americans or Britons.[90] Most of these men not only lacked a working knowledge of the languages of the people they sought to rule, some were barely able to speak French, the lingua franca. Language skills were only one problem the administrators of the Free State had to cope with. In 1890, their death rate from disease was 15 percent per year, and even those who survived were often disabled by fevers and dysentery.[91]

However, even the lowliest state administrator, typically a man of little education, received a lavish consignment of foodstuffs each quarter, including, as we learn from Viscount Mountmorres,

> a bottle of red wine a day, a plentiful supply of flour, of cake, of plain biscuits and dessert biscuits, sardines, pâtés and potted meats of various kinds (foie gras, pheasant, larks, etc.), preserved tinned meats, bacon, marmalade, jams, pickles, sauces, condiments, preserved soup, tea, coffee, butter of two qualities for cooking and table purposes, sugar, rice, preserved fruits and vegetables both dried and tinned, candles, matches, soap, milk . . . whilst all that is sent is of the best quality obtainable. The pâtés came from Fischer's of Strasbourg, the marmalade from England, the jams and preserved fruits from St. James, Paris, the table butter from the Danish Creamery Co.[92]

The duties of these men included not only collecting rubber and ivory and maintaining law and order, but military action as well. In 1895, for example, thousands of well-armed Batetela tribesmen who had fought with the Force Publique rebelled after their leader, Gongo Lutete, was executed by the Belgians for alleged treachery. It was five years before their bloody uprising was finally suppressed. In 1897, a column of Force Publique Congolese turned on Major Dhanis's white officers, killing most of them and making off with hundreds of rifles and much ammunition.[93] Indeed, throughout the 1890s, Congolese rebels armed themselves and fought back against the Force Publique and its Congolese tribal allies. In December 1893, just as the war with the Afro-Arab slavers was winding down, a local chief named Nzansu killed a notoriously brutal Belgian state agent named E. A. Rommel and disrupted traffic along the slave route to Stanley Pool. Nzansu's men fought pitched battles against the Belgians for eight months, then continued a sporadic war for almost five more years. Despite the savagery of the fighting, Nzansu was kind to two Swedish missionaries in the area, saying that unlike the officers of the Free State, they were friends of the Congolese people.[94] There is no record of what became of Nzansu.

Other rebellions broke out when Congolese soldiers could no longer stand the brutality of their Force Publique white officers. That brutality was widespread, and fighting spread across the Kasai and much of the far-eastern Congo. So many disaffected Force Publique soldiers deserted to fight against the Belgians that they marched under their own red-and-white flag. A French priest mistakenly walked into one such rebel camp. When he realized his mistake, he feared for his life only to discover that they treated him as a friend and fed him well. After thanking him for the many kindnesses he had shown to Congolese people, they told him about the atrocities committed by their white officers, including one in which an officer shot sixty of his soldiers because they would not work on Sunday. After spending a few days with the rebels as an honored guest, the priest was set free to go his own way.[95] Another rebel group fought until 1900, when they crossed into German Rwanda and Burundi, where, after giving up their weapons, they were allowed to settle. A few Arab forces in the far-eastern Congo continued to resist the Free State until 1900, as did the Azande tribesmen of the extreme northeast.

Despite Lémery's enthusiasm, with the defeat of the Arabs many of King Leopold's officials did not serve the Congolese people at all. Instead, they enslaved people throughout much of the Congo, killing literally millions who did not provide enough ivory or rubber, an appalling atrocity that the world had not yet discovered. However, the Belgian officers of the Force Publique sometimes showed great concern for the welfare of Africans. Commandant Dhanis, for example, ordered that peaceful African tribesmen not be harmed, and that their possessions be respected by his Free State forces, whom he required to pay for all food they received. His officers, such as Hinde, were often concerned about the health of Congolese Africans, administering smallpox vaccinations and sometimes other medical care. Although many Africans who fought as Dhanis's allies were slaves, they had been enslaved by other Africans who led them into battle, not Force Publique officers.

While some Free State officials were exploiting Congolese and others tried to care for them, a constant concern of these Europeans was cannibalism. It was not simply the eating of human flesh that repelled them, but that so many people were murdered expressly so that others might feast upon their bodies. Early in the 1600s, Englishman Andrew Battell escaped the Portuguese who had enslaved him, to spend sixteen months among the Jaga people near the Congo's Atlantic coast. He reported that they preferred human flesh to their own cattle.[96] Later, as we have seen, healthy children were stabbed to death to provide a feast for their owners, and men were known to help sick coworkers "die," then smoke their body parts for later consumption. Six Bangala men on the *Stanley,* a thirty-ton, stern-wheel steamer, were suspected by the ship's captain of killing two crewmen who fell ill. They pleaded innocence, but smoked human body parts were found hidden in their lockers.[97] Some men showed no restraint in their appetite for human flesh. When one of Gongo Lutete's wives was killed in battle, his own men ate her. Enraged, Lutete ordered these men killed the next day and eaten.[98] None of the Europeans were surprised that Africans on both sides of the war with the Arabs routinely cooked and ate not only the dead they found on the battlefield, but the wounded as well.

On one occasion, some of Dhanis's African allies deserted. When their destination was discovered, Dhanis demanded their return. The chief of that area said that of the thirty-eight deserters, only one had not been eaten, a small boy-servant of

Hinde's who was protected by a friend in the village. Hinde noted that the boy's accounts of what he had seen "were quite sickening."[99] The smoking of human flesh to preserve it was so widespread that Europeans who were often starved for meat would not buy smoked meat for sale in a market because they believed it was likely to be human flesh. Tribespeople throughout the region freely discussed their preferences for certain human body parts over others. As recently as 1950, a Belgian administrator was served a meal of "porcupine meat" that he found remarkably delicious. Not until he had finished was he told that the meat came from a young girl.[100]

In addition to their disgust over cannibalism, or perhaps as a corollary to it, some Europeans developed a fixed belief that Africans were lazy and childlike. One British visitor wrote, "There is something so eminently childish in the Negro's character. . . . In the people of Zanzibar you find men of thought and reflection, whom you may use as counsellors and confidants; men who are really capable of zealous service, of disinterested affection, and to whom (unlike Africans) gratitude is a concept neither foreign to their intelligence nor their tongue."[101]

However, other Europeans emphasized the many admirable qualities of Africans, describing men and women alike in several Congolese societies in the most positive terms possible. Baluba women were said to be graceful, lively, gay, and industrious. Men in several societies were said to be intelligent, trustworthy, compassionate, and wise. As we have already seen, the Bangala were called "intelligent, manly, energetic and fearless."[102] And love was found to exist, not only among parents and children but among husbands and wives. During a battle against Arab forces, Hinde was moved to tears when he came across a woman he knew cradling her dead husband's head in her lap and sobbing. She ignored the bullets flying only a few inches over her head.

After most of the Arab slavers were driven out of the Congo

by 1894, King Leopold's traders stepped up their already highly profitable practice of trading trinkets of little value for ivory and rubber. Villagers were then taxed by Leopold. Failure to pay led to a death sentence. Traders taxed villagers, too, and ruled viciously. Even a relatively compassionate trader such as twenty-three-year-old, part-French, part-Belgian Raoul de Prémorel took brutal actions against Africans. De Prémorel was granted a trading site in Kasai where, in return for rubber and ivory, he traded copper wire, salt, and brightly painted, cheaply made muskets that were useless in the rainy season, and of little value even when the weather was dry. He had over three hundred men "under contract" to him, and although he was reluctant to use force himself, he allowed his supervising Africans to inflict up to twenty-five lashes with a deadly sharp hippopotamus-hide *cicotte* on anyone who failed to bring in enough ivory or rubber.[103]

On one occasion, de Prémorel saw his Liberian cook raising a large butcher knife in apparent readiness to stab one of de Prémorel's European trading partners. De Prémorel seized the man's wrist, disarming him, and the man fell to his knees pleading for mercy. De Prémorel gave the man two choices: to take his punishment then and there and leave in the morning, or to be shipped to a Free State police post where he would no doubt have been condemned to work in a chain gang. Choosing de Prémorel's justice, the cook had his arms tied to a cross-beam on the ceiling so that only his toes touched the floor.

> "You must stay there until morning," I said. "A sentry will stand guard that no one shall turn you loose. At the roll-call at six o'clock when all of the *factorie* report for duty, we will cut you down."
>
> So I left the poor wretch. All night long he hung there, sometimes begging for mercy, sometimes in a kind of swoon. All night long his faithful wife did what she could to alleviate

his suffering. She brought him drink and food, she rubbed his aching legs, she washed his face and body with cold water, but better than all else, she stood by him, encouraging and attempting as best she could to keep him alive. At last when the morning came and my men cut him down, he dropped unconscious in a heap on the ground. . . .

I felt then I was doing my duty, but now sometimes in my sleep I think I am the poor devil and half a hundred black fiends are dancing over about me. I wake up with a great start and I find myself covered with a cold sweat. Sometimes, I think it is I who have suffered most in the years that have passed since that night.[104]

Though others may have shared de Prémorel's sense of guilt, few Free State traders left any evidence that they felt similar self-reproach for their brutal actions. In fact, in many parts of the Congo basin, civilian traders and Force Publique officers used mind-boggling violence to ensure that villagers produced the expected quota of rubber or ivory. Force Publique troops were sometimes used to enforce the traders' demands, whipping and shooting at will, and cutting off the right hand of any person who had not provided sufficient booty. Officers of the Free State also paid heavily armed men from the cannibalistic Basongye tribe to enforce their trading policies. Known as Zappo Zaps after the sound of their rifles, and led by a man with filed teeth (who was said to be seven feet tall), whenever a village failed to produce enough rubber, these men would attack, raping and eating their victims before cutting off their hands.[105] As we will see in the next chapter, an American missionary who witnessed one such attack reported that twenty-two people had been eaten, and he saw a pile of eighty-one amputated hands.[106]

A Free State official casually explained to a missionary that whenever a troop of African soldiers, often known as forest guards, were sent out to collect rubber from Congolese villages, their commander was issued a certain number of cartridges. He had to return each bullet that was not fired, and for each one that was fired, he had to produce a right hand. Bullets were not needed to kill small children, who were simply clubbed to death with rifle butts.[107] The only blessing for the people of the Congo was that rubber vines did not grow everywhere—rubber was plentiful in the central, north-central, and far-western portions of the country, but were absent in the eastern, northeastern, and southern areas. Officially sponsored brutality took place in those areas for other reasons, but it was less intense, less frequent, and less deadly.

While traders, government officials, and soldiers of the Free State were inflicting incredible atrocities on the people of the Congo, all the while railing about their depravity because many of them ate human flesh, many missionaries took up stations in the Congo, and as we shall next see, these men and women played a very different role in the life of the Congo Free State. Today, we reel in horror when we read of the eight hundred thousand or more Tutsi savagely killed in the Rwandan genocide in 1994. But Adam Hochschild, the principal biographer of King Leopold, believes that his regime killed 10 million Congolese.[108]

The Congo River, in an undated photograph, giving a feeling for the density of vegetation.

King D. Alvaro VI of the Congo (1636–1641), receiving a Dutch ambassador. Engraving by O. Dapper (*Description de l'Afrique*, Amsterdam, 1686).

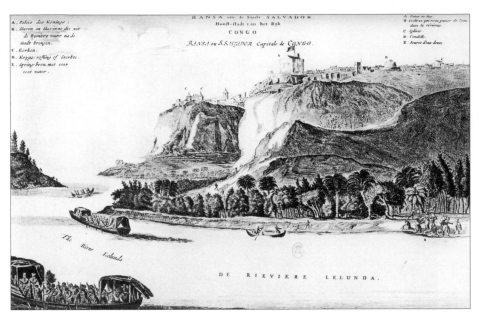

The town of São Salvador. Engraving by O. Dapper (*Description de l'Afrique*, Amsterdam, 1686).

H. M. Stanley with Kalulu, 1877 (courtesy of the Royal Geographic Society).

Alice Pike at age seventeen, c. 1874 (courtesy of the Alice Pike Barney Papers, Smithsonian Institution Archives).

Herbert Ward with Stanley's Rear Column, from *My Life With Stanley's Rear Guard* (1891).

James S. Jameson from *With Stanley's Rear Column* (1890).

Major E. M. Barttelot, 1890.

George Washington Williams, 1874 (courtesy of the Moorland-Spingarn Research Center, Howard University, Washington, D.C.).

Reverend William H. Sheppard, 1891 (courtesy of the Presbyterian
Historical Society, Presbyterian Church [U.S.A.], Montreat,
North Carolina).

King Leopold II of Belgium
(1835–1909), circa 1900
(Bettmann/CORBIS).

Sefu and Tippu Tip in the 1880s, from *Pioneering on the Congo* (1885).

Emin Pasha in 1890,
from *Travels in Africa*.

The severed hands ordered by King Leopold's men, circa 1890
(courtesy of Anti-Slavery International).

Patrice Lumumba arriving in Belgium for a conference, 1960 (courtesy of
Hulton-Deutsch Collection/CORBIS).

President Ronald Reagan bidding farewell to President Mobuto Sese Seko
of Zaire after talks at the White House, 1983 (courtesy of
Bettmann/CORBIS).

Congolese army soldiers stand guard
next to a portrait of slain president
Laurent Kabila, January 22, 2001,
after his body was returned to the
capital, Kinshasa (courtesy of Reuters
NewMedia Inc./CORBIS).

 4

SAVING THE CONGO

Christian missionaries led the way in bringing the brutality of King Leopold's men to the world's attention. David Livingstone is the best-known African missionary, but he was not the first to evangelize there nor was he the most successful in converting Africans to Christianity. We have already encountered the Portuguese and Italian Capuchin missionaries who were in the Congo during the 1500s, all of whom were Roman Catholic, but they soon lost influence and were eventually outnumbered by Protestants. Protestant missionaries had established themselves in West and South Africa as early as 1737, but they did not become active in the Congo until 1878, only seven years before Leopold took control. To maintain themselves, most sought support from their congregations, including donations of money, by portraying the Africans they had come to "save" as uncivilized, debauched, ignorant, diseased, naked, and benighted. Fortunately, they promised, through Christianity, Africans' salvation was near at hand. By 1840, Baptists, Congregationalists, Methodists, Episcopalians, and Presbyterians had all established missions in Africa. There were Mormons, too, along with Seventh Day Adventists and Jehovah's Witnesses.

Surprisingly, more than three decades later, some parts of East and Central Africa had no Christian missionary presence. During the first leg of Henry Stanley's 1875 exploration through Uganda on his way toward the Congo River, he responded to Bagandan king Mutesa's expressed interest in Christianity by sending out a letter that would appear in the *London Daily Telegraph* in 1875 making this plea: "Oh, that some missionary would come here! Here is your opportunity. Embrace it!" Many soon did so, before long leading to actual Protestant-Catholic warfare in Uganda, but others created new missions throughout East and Central Africa, including the Congo, where black American missionaries would be among the first to embrace the opportunity Stanley had evoked. As early as 1820, some black American missionaries wrote about their experiences in Africa, some doing so positively and poignantly, but by about 1880, all of the missionary societies these black evangelists belonged to had declared Africans to be naturally inferior people whose only hope was to be taught Christianity primarily by their superiors—white people.[1] These missionaries, Catholics as well as Protestants, almost all of whom were white, made positive contributions to Africa. Yet the greatest irony is that even more so than European traders, soldiers, or administrators, they perpetuated the portrayal of Africans as savages, writing again and again about African cannibalism, lust, depravity, and the "forces of darkness."[2]

Nowhere were missionaries in Africa more appalled by these "forces of darkness" than in the Congo. An example can be taken from Swedish missionaries, who were sent to the Congo by the Covenant Church of Sweden, a Protestant mission. Theirs are representative of the attitudes and actions of late-nineteenth-century European missionaries. Scandinavians made up 16 percent of the European population of the Congo, in part because Belgium, which had no navy or merchant fleet, had long relied on Scandinavian sailors, many of whom moved to the Congo.

Other Scandinavians who settled in the Congo were traders. But there were dozens of Swedish missionaries as well, most of whom initially proselytized in the Bakongo, the first kingdom to be encountered by European visitors. Some of these missionaries thought the Bakongo people were intelligent, and almost all admired the complexities of the Bakongo language, but most insisted that these "savages" were cowardly, cruel, thievish, ungrateful, lying, and selfish.[3] Although some Swedish missionaries, like their British and American counterparts, ransomed slave children, whom they then freed, raising them as Christians, their goal was not the conversion of Africans to Christianity. As one Swedish missionary put it, "Our *foremost* aim, is not to convert the Congo to God, but our *great* and *splendeous* [*sic*] aim is to *glorify* God."[4] Conversion to Christianity was a desirable byproduct of this glorification, but only a byproduct.

While the Swedish Protestants devoted themselves to God's glorification, they fervently attacked Bakongo culture. As noted earlier, the Bakongo Kingdom was admired by many European visitors, who approved of their rejection of cannibalism and their gentle manner, but the missionaries did not agree. Forming themselves into temperance societies, they did all they could to end the drinking of palm wine, the most common form of alcohol, and refused to drink alcohol themselves—unlike the Catholic missionaries, who drank heavily and did not object to Africans drinking palm wine. As Swedish historian Sigbert Axelson has noted, the Swedish missionaries denounced polygyny and jewelry as un-Christ-like sins. Dancing was "lewd, lascivious and sinful," as was the drumming and singing that accompanied dances. Idols were intolerable, tattooing was evil, and so were all of the other ways in which people decorated their bodies—filing or drilling teeth, decorating ears or noses, wearing bells or anklets, or sporting elaborate hairstyles. Of course, painting various parts of the body was sinful, as was women's practice of exposing their breasts.[5] The Protestants also deplored "ordeals" in which a person accused of a crime was made to swallow poison. If guilty, he or she would die; if the accused survived, it was proof of innocence. The missionaries had good reason to rail against these poison ordeals. In some cases, the native doctor who administered the poison altered its potency based on his own assessment of the accused's guilt or innocence. Some also took bribes to change the strength of the poison.[6]

For the Swedish missionaries, the glorification of God required banning local cultural practices. Very little had changed. Three centuries earlier, Portuguese Catholic priests had taken a similar view of African culture in the 1500s, and those Catholic missionaries who remained in the Congo in the 1880s, many of them Italian priests sent there at King Leopold's request, still did. To a lesser extent, so did the many British Baptist missionaries who went there led by the Reverend George Grenfell.[7] The Americans proved to be somewhat more tolerant.

The first American missionaries to go to the Congo came from a seemingly unlikely source, the Southern Presbyterian Church, where blacks were restricted to seats in church galleries or to racially segregated services. This church had recently embraced a "back-to-Africa" policy for America's former slaves. To further that goal it would send several black missionaries to the Congo, where they served with great devotion to the Congolese people even though they did not bring about a "back-to-Africa" movement of former American slaves. One of the first two of these, the Reverend Mr. William Sheppard, would stay twenty years and contribute as much as any one person to the destruction of King Leopold's tyrannical and bloody rule. William H. Sheppard was born in Waynesboro, Virginia, one month after Lee surrendered to end the American Civil War. He later said he had always been well treated by white Virginians. And he was careful not to complain about white racism when he returned to the United States after achieving such national fame that when he toured with Booker T. Washington, he received top billing. In 1910, a white woman in Waynesboro said, "He was such a good darky. When he returned from Africa he remembered his place and always came to the back door."[8]

As a young man who had just graduated from Stillman College (later renamed Institute), and the Southern Presbyterian Theological Seminary for Colored Men in Tuscaloosa, Alabama, Sheppard applied to the church to be sent to the Congo as a missionary. The church had never before sent a black missionary to Africa, but it granted Sheppard's request with the provision that he go there in the company of a white missionary who would be the head of the church's mission. Sheppard readily agreed, and after a considerable search his colleague and superior was found, another young man just out of seminary training, Samuel N. Lapsley, the son of Judge James W. Lapsley, a wealthy former slave-owner from Alabama. Before beginning his theological training, Lapsley had entered the University of Alabama at the age of fifteen, and the university's president later said that he had been the most outstanding student to attend that university since the end of the Civil War.[9]

Early in 1890, the two young men met, liked each other, and set sail for England. Sheppard was treated as a gentleman aboard the ship, and when the two missionaries arrived in London, with the financial help of a wealthy British Presbyterian layman they had met aboard ship, they purchased "tropical" clothing, including pith helmets, and food staples such as flour, sugar, butter, and lard, as well as valuable items for trade such as cowrie shells, salt, beads, and brass wire.[10] They also equipped themselves with the most modern Martini-Henry rifles and large amounts of ammunition. They soon crossed the channel to Brussels, where, with the help of an American confidant of King Leopold, the French-speaking Lapsley was received by the king, who encouraged him to set up a mission in the Congo Free State, recommending the largely neglected district of Kasai in the central Congo as the best place to do so.[11]

The missionaries then set off for the Congo, and after a three-week voyage they docked at Shark's Point at the mouth of the Congo River, then sailed to the now modernized and sanitized Boma, where they found a comfortable hotel, government buildings, a Catholic mission station, African soldiers in red coats, and as Lapsley put it, "a crowd of darkies . . . looking out for 'dash' "—meaning any money they could extort from a European.[12] The marshes around Boma had been cleared, there were far fewer mosquitoes than in earlier times, and the heat seemed more bearable. From there they sailed to Matadi, where they had to leave the Congo River and march through dense underbrush and cross smaller rivers on a 250-mile trek to Stanley Pool, where they arrived on June 27, 1890. There were only 950 Europeans in all of the Congo at that time.[13] Hungry tribesmen asked the young missionaries to provide meat for them by shooting hippopotamuses. Sheppard and Lapsley were delighted to oblige, shooting no less than thirty-six animals and enjoying the "sport," as they called it, immensely.[14]

From Stanley Pool, the two young Presbyterians took a thirty-day steamboat ride for a thousand miles to a place called Luebo in the Kasai district, a relatively healthy and cool location at an elevation of fourteen hundred feet, where they would attempt to establish a mission station. The two men worked well together, with Lapsley referring to Sheppard as a "treasure." Sheppard's small, black pet monkey, named Tippu Tip, was a great hit with the Africans.[15] Some of the tribespeople Lapsley met disappointed him: "These natives are lean and ill-favored, too grasping and treacherous to trade."[16] But others were described as having "good morals." The Bakuba traders whom the two missionaries met were called a "fine race, very proud," and the Basongye, or Zappo Zaps, as they were called after the sound of their guns, although warlike cannibals, particularly impressed Lapsley as "magnificent men and handsome women, and carry themselves quite as an aristocracy."[17] But Lapsley was concerned when he saw little girls imitating the lascivious dances of grown women: "Poor children, who have not known what a pure mind is."[18] Lapsley and Sheppard bought one of these young slave girls from the Zappo Zaps for the equivalent of seventy-five cents. By freeing her they hoped to cleanse her "impure" mind and introduce her to God, as Lapsley put it.[19] She was one of seventy slaves the two men ransomed before Lapsley's premature death.[20]

The two young missionaries worked hard and had yet to see anything of the terrible atrocities being committed by Leopold's Free State soldiers or his Zappo Zap allies. They had no idea that George Washington Williams, another young black American, born in Pennsylvania in 1849, who was also a minister, had reached the Congo a few months before them and would soon startle the world with his accusations of brutality by King Leopold's self-proclaimed "civilizing" men. Little is known about Williams's early years except that his father was an illiterate free Negro who married a woman described as "as a genuine Pennsylvania Dutch girl."[21] Like his father, Williams was almost completely uneducated, but we do know that at the age of fourteen he joined the Union army and was wounded in combat during the Civil War's last year of fighting in Virginia. After the war ended, he volunteered to fight for Mexico to overthrow Emperor Maximilian's government. Even though he was still a teenager, he received a commission as a lieutenant in a Mexican artillery battery. After that war ended in Mexico's victory, he served as a sergeant in the American West with the U.S. Tenth Cavalry, the "buffalo soldiers," receiving another wound, to his left lung, that would plague him the rest of his life. Because his wound was not received "in the line of duty," Williams received a discharge in 1869. He was only nineteen years old.

After leaving the military, Williams unexpectedly turned to theology, joining a Baptist church in St. Louis and quickly becoming licensed as a minister. Although still barely literate, he applied to newly opened Howard University and was accepted. For some reason, he soon left Howard and was admitted to the Newton Theological Institution near Boston, where despite his previous lack of education, he not only graduated in four years, but surpassed the achievements of most of his white classmates, all but three of whom had received college educations at places such as Amherst, Brown, Colby, Harvard, and the University of Vermont. His commencement address in 1874 was titled "Early Christianity in Africa."[22] As a twenty-four-year-old college graduate, Williams had amazingly transformed himself into a literate man with an elegant writing style.

Williams took up the post of pastor of Boston's Twelfth Baptist Church, but after only a year of service he resigned. He then traveled briefly in the Deep South, witnessing the "religion of revolver and rifle," as he put it, before returning to Washington, D.C., where he worked in the Federal Postal Department for a few months, then moved to Cincinnati, where he once again became a pastor, early in 1876. Obviously, he was a young man searching for his role in life and not finding it. As his quest went on, he was not above taking creative license with his past. When a reporter from the Cincinnati *Daily Enquirer* interviewed him, he was told that Williams had been a Union army officer, was a graduate of Harvard University, and had been political editor of the prestigious *National Republican,* a post he had never held.[23]

If anyone noticed these embellishments, it did not prevent him from being elected to the Ohio state legislature in 1879, the first black ever to serve in that body. Williams took office at the age of thirty. He had not yet passed the Ohio bar but gave his occupation as "attorney-at-law." He also married, fathered a son, and was extremely active in state politics, but became increasingly dissatisfied with his life, neglecting his wife and son, then abruptly deciding not to pursue his political career. Instead, he threw himself full-time into being a historian. Three years later, he produced the first book ever written on the history of the African American people. This two-volume work was scholarly, accurate, and a major achievement that was well-received by the *New York Times*.[24]

Restless as always, Williams next moved to Massachusetts, where he practiced law and became a frequent public speaker about the history of blacks in Africa and the United States, including current issues in African-American life. He also wrote a novel about a romance between a black man and a white woman that was published by installments in the black press. Given later events in his own life, this novel might be seen as prophetic. In 1885, President Chester A. Arthur nominated him to be minister resident and consul general of the United States to Haiti. Although the U.S. Senate approved Williams's appointment, there was political opposition and he never took up the post. The following year, Williams sued his wife for divorce on the grounds of desertion, but the suit was eventually dropped when it became clear that it was he who had deserted her.

Seemingly undaunted, Williams continued to deliver high-profile, well-received lectures on African-American history, receiving an honorary doctor of laws degree from the State University at Louisville, Kentucky, after a presentation there. In 1888, he went to London to attend the Centenary Conference of Protestant Missions, where his interest in King Leopold's Congo was sparked. The following year, his pulmonary health, which had bothered him since he was wounded in the chest while serving with the Tenth Cavalry, worsened, and his physician recommended that he go to a warm climate. Instead, he published an article decrying the slave trade in Africa, and in September 1889 he sailed to Brussels, where he hoped to interview King Leopold II as a special correspondent for the Associated Literary Press, a prominent American publication of that time. Thanks to the intervention of the Belgian minister to the United States, Alfred Le Ghait, whom Williams had met earlier, he was granted an interview.

Speaking English, a language he knew well, Leopold told Williams about his Christian commitment to the Congo, dissembling grandly, "What I do there is done as a Christian duty to the poor Africans; and I do not wish to have one franc back of all the money I have expended."[25] Williams was dazzled by the tall, regal Leopold, concluding his article by referring to him as "one of the noblest sovereigns in the world."[26] Allowing himself to be thought of and referred to as "Colonel" Williams—perhaps because he held the honorary title of colonel in the Grand Army of the Republic, a veterans' organization—he impressed observers in Brussels and attempted to arrange a meeting with Henry S. Sanford, a confidant of Leopold's and former U.S. minister to Belgium, whom he had met in the White House when President Arthur had introduced the two men. Fittingly, Sanford, who had never served in the Civil War at any rank, but had used some of his family fortune to buy artillery for the First Minnesota Regiment, chose to be addressed as "General." Sanford knew that Williams had been befriended by Collis P. Huntington, the American railroad millionaire who hoped to finance Leopold's planned railroad into the Congo, and also to bring the slave trade to an end. Williams had told Huntington of his own interest in ending the slave trade and sending young African-Americans there to help the Congolese people in a variety of ways.

Sanford favored the return of black Americans to Africa, too, although hardly for altruistic motives, but he warned Leopold against Williams, saying that he was supported and financed by Huntington, who hoped to take control of trade in the Congo for his own profit. During a whirlwind three weeks back in the United States when he attempted to recruit blacks willing to go to Africa, Williams spoke to President Benjamin Harrison about his planned trip to the Congo, something that interested Harrison because he had not yet ratified the Berlin Act of 1885 that had created the Congo Free State. With Huntington's financial support assured, Williams bought equipment and supplies in London to outfit a large expedition to the Congo. His ship from Liverpool to Boma docked so often in West Africa that the journey took fifty-three days, but Williams invested his time well, making visits to missions and schools, learning all he could about Europeans' treatment of Africans.

When he finally reached the Congo in late February 1890, his first impressions were anything but positive. He wrote to Huntington that "this seems to be the Siberia of the African Continent, a penal settlement," referring to the large numbers of Africans he saw being held as captive laborers by officers of Leopold's Congo Free State.[27] Everything he saw around Boma appalled him. He vividly compared the poverty of Africans to the lavish lifestyle of the governor-general in his elegant Victorian mansion surrounded by uniformed servants and sentries. Before long, he became convinced that Leopold's Congo Free State was brutally corrupt. Despite his shortage of funds, his ill health, and his lack of experience in African travel, Williams recruited a party of eighty-five men, armed many of them, and set out to explore the Free State on May 15, 1890, six weeks before Lapsley and Sheppard arrived at Stanley Pool. He traveled through plains as "treeless as our prairies," as well as "dense, dark, damp" forests. Wherever possible, he stopped at missions, talking at length to the Reverend George Grenfell of the Baptist Missionary Society of London, who was married to a black West Indian. Grenfell listened to Williams's accusation that some Free State officials were brutalizing the people of the Congo, but stopped well short of agreeing that Leopold was responsible for such actions. The Africans whom Williams met looked upon the light-skinned American as a white man, but they willingly spoke to him nonetheless.

After two months of travel, Williams reached Stanley Falls, noting as he marched through varied landscapes the remarkable variation in the physical appearance and cultures of the people. He also noted that the Congo was depopulated. Instead of the 49–50 million people Stanley had estimated to live there, he judged the population at no more than 15 million, a figure that was, if anything, too high. While at Stanley Falls, Williams composed an "Open Letter to His Serene Majesty Leopold II." After taking a steamship back to Stanley Pool, Williams visited Luanda, on the coast of Angola, then sailed to Zanzibar, Aden, and Cairo, where he suffered a severe bout of lung congestion and had to be hospitalized in critical condition.

Williams's "Open Letter" had been sent directly to Leopold, but a copy had also been received by the *New York Herald*, assuring widespread knowledge of its charges. It began by accusing Leopold of spending not "one franc" for African education in the Free State but instead stealing the Africans' land, burning their villages, and enslaving their women and children, along with other terrible crimes. Williams then set out twelve specific charges against Leopold's Free State government: (1) it lacked the necessary moral, military, and financial strength to govern so vast an area; (2) government soldiers regularly stole from local people to secure provisions; (3) the government regularly broke its contracts with foreign soldiers, mechanics, and workmen; (4) its courts were unjust; (5) its cruelty to prisoners, who were chained and brutally whipped, was barbaric; (6) women were used for immoral purposes by the state; (7) the Free State's trade practices were unfair to other countries; (8) the Free State regularly stole from natives, (9) raided villages to take slaves, and (10) regularly sold slaves. Two other charges alleged the creation of Arab military posts and the misrepresentation of the construction of the railway.

Williams also asked the native peoples he met, as he followed the same route along the Congo upstream that Stanley had followed downstream, what they remembered about him. He reported that Stanley's name "produces a shudder among this simple folk when mentioned; they remember his broken promises, his copious profanity, his hot temper, his heavy blows, his severe and rigorous methods, by which they were mulcted of their lands."[28] According to Williams, by the use of "dirty tricks" Stanley and his men—representing Leopold—had duped the tribal chiefs and persuaded them to cede their lands to the king's men. Stanley used many well-rehearsed sleight-of-hand tricks including the "lens act," in which the white man lit his cigar with a glass through which the equatorial sun shone. The white man then explained his intimate relation to the sun and declared that, if he requested the sun to burn up his black brother's village, it would do so. By this and other means, Williams wrote, "too silly and disgusting to mention, and a few boxes of gin, whole villages have been signed away to your Majesty."[29]

Williams concluded his "Open Letter" by asserting that the natives of the Congo had shown "unexampled patience, long-suffering and forgiving spirit" against the "deceit, fraud, robberies, arson, murder, slave-raiding, and general policy of cruelty" of Leopold's government. He then told Leopold that these crimes had been committed in "your name, and *you* must answer at the bar of Public Sentiment for the misgovernment of a people whose lives and fortunes were entrusted to you by the August Conference of Berlin, 1884–1885."[30]

On his ship back to England from Cairo after he had recovered somewhat from his serious bout with lung congestion, Williams met Alice Fryer, a young Englishwoman returning from India, where she had been a governess with an English family. They quickly struck up a friendship, and by the time their ship arrived in London, they were engaged to be married. After a few weeks of recuperation on the oceanfront at Blackpool, where Alice and her mother lovingly cared for him, Williams seemed better, but suddenly suffered a violent chill, and on August 2, 1891, at the age of forty-one, he died. Alice Fryer was not only disconsolate at his loss, but crushed to learn after his funeral that her fiancé had not told her that he had a wife and a son.

As might be expected, reaction to Williams's "Open Letter" varied from loud applause in some quarters to cold condemnation in others. Not until later denunciations of King Leopold's Congo Free State confirmed Williams's charges would the world unite in condemning Leopold, finally removing his Congo fiefdom from him in 1908. But of all the European and American men and women who traveled in the Congo, hating the vicious brutality they saw, only Williams spoke out immediately. Grenfell certainly avoided doing so, and so did Joseph Conrad and Roger Casement when they first visited the Congo. One who did speak out relatively early was the Reverend J. B. Murphy of the American Baptist Mission Union. In late 1895, he gave an interview to Reuters in which he accused Free State officials of brutality in the collection of rubber and ivory. His charges did not seem to hit home in America, but they were favorably publicized in Britain because an English trader named Charles Stokes who was accused of selling guns to the Arabs had just been hanged by Leopold's notorious Force Publique without a trial and without recognizing his right to appeal to the Free State government in Boma.[31] Even William Sheppard waited for years before writing about the horrors he had seen. Yet, eventually he did so, and what he wrote had a powerful effect.

But that would not happen for several years. While Williams was examining conditions in the Congo Free State, Lapsley and Sheppard were clearing land for their mission station in Luebo, hunting and fishing, teaching school, learning the local languages, receiving visitors, and whenever possible preaching the gospel, although with little visible effect. Lapsley came more and more to rely on Sheppard, writing in a letter home to his mother that "his temper is bright and even—really a man of unusual graces and strong points of character. So I am thankful to God for Sheppard."[32] Both Lapsley and Sheppard suffered acutely from high fevers. Despite his regular use of quinine, Sheppard had twenty-two bouts of malaria during his first two years in the Congo, but he was a large, powerful, robust man who thrived despite his illnesses. He was always dressed in white—a white suit, white tie, white pith helmet, and white shoes. But he did wear black puttees. While Lapsley, a relatively frail man who was weakened by frequent febrile diseases, remained in Luebo, Sheppard explored the Kasai to the south on a sixty-eight-day expedition during which he discovered a previously unknown lake, an accomplishment that later led to his election as a fellow of the British Royal Geographical Society. While Sheppard was away, Lapsley grew increasingly worn, tired, and ill, but on Sheppard's return, he was revitalized by Sheppard's plan to learn the language of the Bakuba, whose nearby kingdom was completely closed to outsiders. The idea of bringing Christianity to these people excited both men, and they began to study the language from Bakuba traders who passed through Luebo.

Before much progress had been made, Lapsley had to return to Matadi on a steamer to conduct some business with the government of the Free State. When the steamer returned, Sheppard was handed a brief message saying that Lapsley had died on March 26, 1892, of hematuric fever, an affliction that had produced a cascade of blood in his urine and a temperature that reached 110 degrees.[33] Although distraught and lonely, the only Westerner for hundreds of miles, Sheppard carried out the plan that he and Lapsley had made to move farther east and establish a second mission station at Ibanche, close to the capital of the Bakuba. He accomplished this goal and with the help of passing traders soon learned the language well enough to carry on everyday conversation.

Shown the way to the Bakuba capital by Bakuba traders, who repeatedly warned him that any stranger who entered Bakuba territory without the king's permission would be killed, Sheppard brazenly marched ahead. When he was confronted by armed men on the cleanly swept streets of this ten-thousand-person town, he shocked everyone by speaking their language. Taken to the king, Sheppard must have made a good impression, for he was declared to be the reincarnation of a revered royal ancestor and warmly welcomed.[34] Sheppard protested that he was not of royal birth, but the elders insisted that he had returned from the land of the dead.

> He was escorted to an impressive residence furnished with woven mats, carved wooden bedstands, ivory encrusted chairs, beautiful quilted coverings, and clothes racks. Four days later, the monarch's sons, Toen-zaide and M'funtu, led him to the heart of the capital where he witnessed the arrival of the king in his royal hammock. To the accompaniment of music, his bearers gently lowered him within a half-ring lined with leopard skins and blankets extending for about 100 yards in an open square. As Sheppard described him, Kot aMbweeky, who appeared to be between seventy and seventy-five years old, wore a blue savalese cloth trimmed with beads and cowries, a blue and white beaded crown with a white tassel in it, and small brass rings, the sign of royalty, around his neck and legs. In many ways, the monarch, who Sheppard believed had 700 wives, was a God on earth to his subjects, who prostrated themselves before him, sneezing when he sneezed, coughing when he coughed and clapping in unison after his every sentence.[35]

Given free access to activities throughout the kingdom, Sheppard was harshly critical of some Bakuba practices—witchcraft, killing slaves to accompany their dead master to the afterlife, and poison ordeals—but he soon came to respect the rest of Bakuba culture, praising the people for their dignity, courage, honesty, industriousness, moral family life, and hospitality. He was also impressed by their legal system of police and courts, which effectively controlled theft, gambling, and drunkenness.[36] He enjoyed watching happy children playing, although he noted that they had few toys, and he was pleased to discover that, except for royalty, Bakuba men took only one wife. Most of all, he was dazzled by their artwork, describing their arts of weaving, embroidery, woodcarving, and smelting as the "highest in equatorial Africa."[37]

Although Sheppard had found a way to penetrate the closed Bakuba Kingdom, something even Leopold's Free State government had been unable to accomplish, after four months he had been unable to convert a single person to Christianity. At that point, he had to leave the Bakuba because he was recalled to the United States by the Southern Presbyterian Church to report on the activities of his mission. On the way home, he stopped in London to speak about the lake he had discovered to the Royal Geographical Society and was elected fellow, the first black American so honored. When Sheppard returned to the United States, he gave many speeches to schools and churches about the Congo. He also married a Southern Presbyterian schoolteacher named Lucy Gantt, to whom he had become engaged before he had originally left for the Congo. They had written regularly while he was away, and Lucy had been thrilled when she received a cable from London saying that he was on his way home.[38]

Lucy Gantt Sheppard was born in 1867. Her mother, Eliza, was a former slave who was deserted by the father of her child. Eliza had no schooling but taught herself to read and write while somehow acquiring sixty-seven books, all of which she read. While working as a housemaid, she taught Lucy to read, and even though there were no public schools for black children, Eliza used most of her earnings to place Lucy, her only child, in a small private school. As fortune had it, a Southern gentlewoman who roomed with Eliza's employer took an interest in Lucy, using her influence to gain admission for her to Talladega College, a missionary school for blacks in Alabama. At the age of eleven, she was the youngest student in the school. Eliza earned only $10 a month but sent $8 to Lucy each month. Lucy was an outstanding student as well as a soprano soloist who traveled through the Northern states singing Negro spirituals with a group called the Jubilee Singers. When Lucy graduated from Talladega in 1886, her mother, though ill, came from Florida to her graduation. Lucy became a teacher, and while she was teaching in Birmingham, Alabama, she met William Sheppard.[39]

Because the Southern Presbyterian Church couldn't find white ministers willing to go to the disease-ridden Congo, Sheppard was asked to recruit more black American ministers to accompany him back to the Congo. He successfully recruited two men: Joseph E. Phipps, who had been born and raised on St. Kitts and believed that his grandfather had lived in the Congo until he had been sold into slavery;[40] and Henry P. Hawkins. Sheppard also recruited two African-American women. The head of these new missionaries, as well as Sheppard, would be William M. Morrison, a white man from a politically prominent family in Virginia. He would take over the mission station at Luebo while Sheppard would move on to the new mission near Ibanche, on the fringe of the Bakuba Kingdom.

When the Sheppards returned from their honeymoon, which included raising money for their mission and attempting to recruit still more black American missionaries, they sailed to Britain, where they purchased a full year's supply of food and clothing. Lucy craved a cooking stove, but with her limited funds had to settle for a few enameled dishes. Three weeks later, the Sheppards arrived at Boma. Lucy would never forget the coffee-colored waters of the Congo River, which inspired her to compose this eloquent entry in her diary: the river was "a symbol of the people whose bodies reflected its deep, dark sheen; whose souls had been as unfathomable as its depths; whose struggles for centuries had been as varied and as consuming as its rush to the sea; and whose future still remained as unknown as the depths of the river's bed in its whirlpool regions."[41]

While still at Boma, Lucy became delirious with a high fever and had to be carried in a hammock 263 miles to Leopoldville, where she and Sheppard plus the new missionaries would take a steamer to Luebo, then walk another fifty miles on foot to Ibanche. Life at Ibanche was a struggle in every way, with diseases a daily threat. Lucy's first child, a daughter, lived for only a few weeks. With Sheppard's help, Lucy distracted herself by building a house to live in while battling the elements, biting ants, and even leopards that walked on the roof at night. She gave birth to a second daughter, but this child only lived for eight months.

Undaunted and much in love with Sheppard, Lucy set up a school where she taught children of all ages, as well as a clinic where she practiced her self-taught nursing skills every day except Sunday. She was often dangerously ill, especially once after suffering a scorpion bite. When she gave birth to her third daughter only seven months after her second daughter died, Sheppard convinced her to return to the United States with the prematurely born baby. There she remained for two years, nursing the baby and regaining her own health before returning to the Congo, where she had a son, William Lapsley Sheppard. After taking the boy to the United States to be cared for by relatives, Lucy returned to the Congo to teach school, direct her clinic, and care for her husband, who was often ill with febrile diseases and under great duress as he more and more actively opposed the atrocities of the Congo Free State.

The Reverend Mr. Sheppard worked hard to build a comfortable mission station, create a fertile garden, and hunt game.[42] The Sheppards' attempts to educate African children went well despite their lack of resources, and a few Bakuba, although not many, actually became interested in Christianity. From the start, Sheppard was Morrison's right-hand man. Always respectfully addressing him as "Dr." Sheppard, Morrison wrote that he had "unusual tact and wisdom in the management of the native . . . there is no man in all this country who has the influence over this people that Sheppard has."[43]

While the American Presbyterian missionaries and the British evangelists of the Baptist Missionary Society were hard at work in the late 1890s, the most forceful critic of the rubber-seeking terror tactics of the Congo Free State was a Swedish Baptist missionary, E. V. Sjöblom. In a public meeting in London in 1897, Sjöblom told the audience that he had personal knowledge of Force Publique soldiers being rewarded for the number of hands they collected from Africans who had not produced the amount of rubber demanded of them: "[An] agent told me that he had himself seen a state officer at one of the outposts pay a certain number of brass rods to the soldiers for the number of hands they had brought. One of the soldiers told me . . . 'The Commissioner has promised us if we have plenty of hands he will shorten our service. I have brought in plenty of hands already, and I expect my time of service will soon be finished.' "[44]

In many countries the public response to this accusation was outrage. The outside world did not yet know that ears, noses, penises, and even heads were also cut off by Free State orders, or that men who had not delivered enough rubber were made to eat the feces from European latrines and were sometimes shot.

At this time, the Force Publique was under civilian control to such an extent that district commissioners not only commanded Force officers, they regularly inspected the troops. They also ordered that rubber be collected, as this exchange between an irate Belgian district commissioner and a Norwegian officer of the Force whose men returned without any rubber illustrates: "Where is the rubber? Loafer! Thief! Show me the supplies! No rubber? Then what do you have, you bloody fools, you loafers!" The Norwegian's only response was *"Oui, Monsieur le Commandant!"* [45]

After witnessing the conditions in fifteen rubber factories, a German doctor, W. Doerpinghaus, described

a well organized system of compulsory labour, for the maintenance of which the agents employ, with the tacit toleration of the management, every means which brutality and coarseness have ever invented. . . . The history of modern civilized nations has scarcely ever had anything to equal such shameful deeds as the agents in the Belgian Congo have rendered themselves guilty of. That the Company is aware of the doings of its agents, tolerates them, and encourages them, I can produce flagrant proof. . . . I must add that the natives of the region in question are harmless and only rise to attack when driven to extremities. I frequently travelled for days without escort. There is therefore not the slightest excuse for the murders and atrocities. [46]

In September 1899, distraught refugees from a neighboring group of Bakuba pleaded with the Reverend Mr. Sheppard to stop the Zappo Zap atrocities against the Bakuba. They told him that fifty thousand Bakuba were hiding in the forest to prevent the Zappo Zaps from killing and eating them by the order of the Congo Free State government. Sheppard felt powerless to act and was also admittedly afraid for his own life. He said of the Zappo

Zaps, "You can trust them as far as you can see them—and the farther off you can see them the better you can trust them."[47] But a few days later he received a hand-carried letter from Morrison at Luebo "directing" him "immediately upon receipt of this letter to go over and stop the raid."[48] Sheppard somehow convinced eleven Kasai warriors to accompany him on what seemed a suicide mission against close to a thousand Zappo Zaps armed with modern rifles and a taste for human flesh.

He soon found himself face-to-face with sixteen Zappo Zaps, who cocked their guns and took aim. "I leaped forward, threw up my hands and cried out in a loud voice, 'Don't shoot; I am Sheppard!' "[49] The leader of the Zappo Zaps recognized Sheppard because they had frequently met, and the Sheppards had once treated him for a life-threatening wound. Grateful for this past medical attention, he welcomed Sheppard, talking freely about the raiding, burning, and killing he had done. He also sent for M'lumba, his commander, who soon arrived with a large number of armed men. Sheppard described the seven-foot-tall M'lumba as "a most repulsive looking man," because his teeth were filed to sharp points, his eyebrows were shaved, and his eyelashes plucked out. M'lumba led Sheppard to a stockade where some five hundred Zappo Zaps were living. They flew the "lone star" flag of the Congo Free State. Assuming that all Europeans were supporters of the Free State, M'lumba took Sheppard to the place where the slaughter had taken place, which was still reeking with the stench of corpses. Sheppard was brought water by a soldier whose "hands were even then dripping with the crimson blood of innocent men, women and children."[50]

M'lumba told Sheppard of inviting Bakuba men and women into an area his men had surrounded and then giving them the choice of paying their state-imposed taxes or being killed. The exorbitant government tax they had been sent to collect from tribal leaders had included sixty slaves and tens of thousands of balls of rubber, but only eight slaves and twenty-five hundred balls of rubber had been received. "I think we killed between eighty and ninety," M'lumba acknowledged.[51] Sheppard counted forty-one bodies and was told that the rest had been eaten. He noticed that the cannibals had carved steaks off the lower parts of three bodies. The forehead of one decapitated person had been used to make a bowl for rolling tobacco. Sheppard saw sixty women prisoners huddled together, awaiting their turn to satisfy the sexual appetites of the warriors.

Seeing the corpse of a young woman lying nearby without her right hand, Sheppard asked for an explanation. M'lumba stated that his men always cut off the right hand of each person they killed to give to Leopold's agent on their return as proof of the number of persons who had not paid taxes and had therefore been killed. Sheppard was then taken to a shed where the right hands of victims were being slowly dried out over a fire. He counted eighty-one hands and saw human flesh on bamboo sticks drying out to preserve the meat. M'lumba informed Sheppard that in addition to the people whom his men had just assaulted, the Free State had sent him to collect tribute from other areas of the Bakuba confederation. What is more, he said that the Bakete—in whose territory Luebo was located—as well as the capital of the Bakuba were soon to be invaded. He also told Sheppard details about the rifles and ammunition he had received from the Free State.

Sheppard's investigating party remained for two days in the sickening company of the armed Zappo Zap raiders, then rushed home. Sheppard quickly submitted a report to an official of the Congo Free State, and to the surprise of the missionaries and the Zappo Zaps, the women hostages were ordered to be released and M'lumba was arrested. The understandably puzzled M'lumba said to his superior Free State officer, "You have sent me to do this and yet you have put me in chains!"[52]

To document the atrocities he had seen, Sheppard took snap-shots with a Kodak camera, which had only recently been introduced. He was among the first to use a camera for social reform. In an album at the Presbyterian Historical Foundation, a photograph provides visual proof of three young men without their right hands. Another photo is of a young woman with a locked chain about her neck. Morrison realized that Sheppard's report was too shocking and inconceivable to be widely accepted without the testimony of another witness, so he sent Lachlan Vass, a fellow white missionary, to examine the alleged barbarity and carnage. Vass also reported seeing many corpses with their right hands removed, adding, "The whole country is pillaged and not a village left standing."[53] Vass counted forty-seven corpses, some of them partially eaten.[54]

In addition to these horrible deaths, untold thousands of men had died who had been pressed into service as porters by Free State officers, still known as Bula Matari or BM. In 1898, a Swedish missionary wrote, "Sometimes it feels as if we wander through an enormous cemetery, when we see heaps of skeletons. These are the skeletons of porters, who during the extensive transport on behalf of the State, have fallen ill and been left to die in the wilderness."[55] Another missionary added, "Now there is not one village to be found on the route to Diadia. All have fled in terror of BM. One can surely say that such a government eats up its people. Information has also been received that many of the porters who were forced to go to Mpumba to carry, are now dead and buried."[56] A third Swedish missionary concluded, "The porterage system gnaws like cancer and breaks multitudes of the country's strong young men and brings them prematurely to the grave."[57]

Desperate to prevent more state-sponsored Zappo Zap slaughter, Morrison sent Sheppard's report to Congo Free State officials at Luluabourg, asking that the Belgian *chef de zone* where the attacks took place, a man named DuFour, be held accountable. As the Protestant missionaries applied increasing pressure, the Free State administration agreed to carry out an investigation. It issued a rebuttal by a loyal Belgian priest, who concluded that Sheppard's report was an "absurd fabrication." The priest wrote that the state had no influence over M'lumba or the Zappo Zaps and, what is more, that the "victims" Sheppard and Vass alleged to have seen had initiated the trouble by attacking M'lumba's men. The report found DuFour and other Free State officers blameless, and M'lumba was immediately set free. In an attempt to avoid any international implications, the U.S. government was informed that agents of the Free State had never been responsible for *any* acts of cruelty.[58] Morrison exploded, calling the Belgians "a nasty piggish lot of fellows who would make a decent man sick without a storm."[59]

Morrison and Vass did all they could to end the slaughter by agents of the Free State and the Force Publique, appealing to foreign governments and the British Aborigines Protection Society, led by its sympathetic secretary, H. R. Fox Bourne, while Sheppard wrote numerous articles in missionary magazines that were reprinted and widely quoted in the United States and Europe. There were also eyewitness reports by travelers such as the British explorer Edward S. Grogan who had walked the length of Africa and was stunned when he discovered a three-thousand-square-mile tract in the northeast Congo that was "depopulated and devastated." "Every village has been burnt to the ground, and as I fled from the country I saw skeletons everywhere; and such postures—what tales of horrors they told!"[60] Strangely silent were the British missionaries, who were still unwilling to criticize the Free State government. Their leader, the Reverend George Grenfell, was made aware of atrocities as early as 1896 but believed that Leopold knew nothing of their occurrence and, moreover, that it was impolitic to criticize the Free State, to whom he was beholden for the right to carry out his missionary work.[61] When another influential British Baptist, W. H. Bentley, published a two-volume book about missionaries in the Congo in 1900, he made no mention of Congo Free State misconduct, but did describe at length the cordial relations that existed between the missionaries and the government.[62] Fox Bourne reproached him in the British House of Commons and in his own publication, *Aborigines Friend*.[63] Only after the soon-to-appear Casement Report did Grenfell accept Leopold's responsibility for the crimes, and by 1905, he openly criticized Free State policy to its governor-general.[64]

Not until Morrison left the Congo on leave in 1903 was the impact of his charges felt in full. First visiting Europe, then returning to the United States, the articulate Virginia gentleman described the Congo atrocities with great power. Fox Bourne of the Aborigines Protection Society said, "The gallant Virginian William Morrison turned up unexpectedly from the Congo . . . with a tale of continued infamy, with particulars of brutal and odious deeds; with a heart aflame with passion. There was nothing of the fanatic about him; no rhetoric; no invocations to the Deity; no prayerful entreaties. He was merely a capable, honest, strong, fearless man and he told his story with a moral force which thrilled all who heard it."[65]

Leopold immediately attempted to discredit Morrison by turning to Sir Hugh Gilzean-Reid, an influential British publisher and lay Baptist with hidden economic ties to Leopold, who had successfully challenged the evidence given by Sjöblom a few years earlier. Gilzean-Reid obligingly wrote a letter to the London *Daily News* refuting each of Morrison's accusations, assuring readers that members of the British Baptist Missionary Society had provided him with a picture of altogether positive conditions in the Free State. He also used his influence with leaders of the British Baptist Missionary Society to silence all criticism of Leopold.[66]

A senior Baptist Missionary Society officer actually praised Leopold for lowering taxes on the missionaries and for his "enlightened rule."[67]

By then, Morrison was in the United States, where he wrote widely read articles describing the devastation that forced "helpless men and women of the villages near to our mission station at Luebo [to flee] into his house . . . seeking protection."[68] Morrison was then introduced to a radical British reformer, twenty-seven-year-old Edmund D. Morel. The tall, handsome Morel, son of a French father and an English Quaker mother, had originally become suspicious about the Congo Free State when he worked in the Congo Department of the major British shipping line Elder Dempster. He discovered that the line took valuable ivory and rubber out of the Congo but returned virtually nothing to it except rifles and ammunition for the Force Publique. Moreover, the Free State refused to make public what was exported.[69] He left the shipping line to pursue his investigations of the Free State, joining with the British consul for the Congo, Roger Casement, a Protestant Irishman from Ulster, to create the Congo Reform Association on March 24, 1904. This was years before Casement would fight to free Ireland from British rule and be executed by the British as a result. Morrison even managed to meet with President Theodore Roosevelt, who listened, expressed concern, then requested that the American minister in Belgium, Lawrence Townsend, look into conditions in the Congo. Townsend chose to do nothing that might upset Leopold.

Although thwarted by Townsend, Morrison attempted to reach members of Congress, while he and Morel addressed several international congresses, often expressing open criticism of the British missionaries. That same year, Roger Casement published the "Report of a Parliamentary Paper"—based on his eleven-week tour of the Congo, always in the company of his pet bulldog, John—that described in sickening detail the atrocities of the Force Publique and other authorities in Leopold's Congo Free State. Casement interviewed many victims who had survived atrocities, and the experiences they related were chilling. Morel met with Casement and heard his reports of the horrors he had seen and heard about: "The daily agony of an entire people unrolled itself in all the repulsive terrifying details. I verily believe I *saw* those hunted women clutching their children and flying panic-stricken into the bush; the blood flowing from those quivering black bodies as the hippopotamus-hide whip struck and struck again; the savage soldiery rushing hither and thither amid burning villages; the ghastly tally of severed hands."[70] Casement described not only instances of torture and murder, but the wholesale destruction of villages and entire tribes with such agonizing power that the British public responded with outrage. Politicians, lords, and archbishops joined ordinary people in writing letters to British newspapers expressing not only their horror but the need to remove Leopold's control from the Free State.

Soon after, Morel cited some of Casement's descriptions of Congo Free State atrocities, along with those provided by many other observers, in his book, *Red Rubber,* first published in 1906. For example, he quoted an American Baptist missionary who had seen Congo Free State soldiers cut off a man's hand, while his "poor heart beat strongly enough to shoot the blood from the cut arteries at a distance of fully four feet."[71] This review in the *Daily Mail* was typical of the British press reaction: "The most appalling indictment of personal rapacity, cruelty, expropriation of life and labour, maladministration and tyrannical atrocity ever recorded on irrefutable proof against any one man in any country or any age. Contention as to facts has disappeared. The truth in all its international dangers—the horror of it all—stands out naked."[72]

In response to the growing criticism, Leopold spent lavish

sums to discredit all those who criticized the Congo Free State, actually setting up a large and well-paid lobby in Washington. As controversy swirled back and forth over the next several years, the tide of world opinion, led by Britain and the United States, turned against Leopold with even leading Belgian Catholic priests attacking his Free State system.[73] Leopold made many concessions to the now irate missionaries, but by 1908, he had no alternative but to allow his Congo fiefdom to become a dependency of Belgium, a seemingly triumphant outcome for the Presbyterian critics and their allies. It soon became obvious, however, that their victory was less than they had hoped for. Belgium preserved all existing legislation in the Congo Free State and upheld the legality of the trade monopoly concessions already in place there. What was even worse, virtually all of the Free State officials were retained, enabling them, if they chose, to administer the same laws and policies that had outraged the world.[74] For four long years, these same officials continued their brutal policy of food taxation and the enforced collection of rubber.[75]

The only portion of the Congo Free State, now renamed the Belgian Congo, that was not controlled by ivory and rubber monopolies was the Kasai, where the American Presbyterian missions, among Leopold's most vocal critics, were located. Because the Kasai Company, which controlled trading in the region, allowed traders to compete in Kasai, wages were higher there and brutality less commonplace. The Bakuba were an exception. Because these people, whom Sheppard and other missionaries had come to like and respect, refused to collect rubber, they were fined, taxed, flogged, and imprisoned. When Sheppard could tolerate their suffering no longer, he wrote an article in the *Kasai Herald* of January 1, 1908. Reminding readers that, only three years earlier, the Bakuba had been "happy, healthy, and strong," now their farms are growing up in weeds and jungle, their king is practically a slave, their houses now are mostly only half-built single rooms, and are much neglected. The streets of their towns are not clean and well swept as they once were. Even their children cry for bread.

Why this change? You have it in a few words. There are armed sentries of chartered trading companies who force the men and women to spend most of their days and nights in the forests making rubber, and the price they receive is so meager that they cannot live upon it.[76]

The Kasai Company, Sheppard's obvious target, was furious and immediately discussed a lawsuit against him for libel. For reasons that are still not clear, almost a year passed before charges were filed—a $10,000 claim against Morrison and a $6,000 claim against Sheppard. Thanks to an error by a clerk of the Belgian Congo court that would hear the case, the claim against Morrison was dropped and only Sheppard would stand trial. Before the trial took place, the British vice-consul, Wilfred Thesiger, visited the Kasai and, with Sheppard as his guide and translator, spent three months in the interior of the Congo. He submitted a report to the British Foreign Office confirming the missionaries' accusations in graphic detail. The report shook the Belgian government, but they attempted to portray Thesiger as an open advocate of the Presbyterians.

When the case finally came to trial in 1909, an honest Belgian lawyer, Emile Vandervelde, a socialist leader, defended Sheppard without fee. He did so in court for two hours with such clarity, force, logic, and eloquence that the judge promptly found Sheppard not guilty and ordered the Kasai Company to pay court costs.

Morrison, who did not know that charges against him had been dropped, had to travel with Sheppard one thousand miles from Luebo to Leopoldville for the trial. The journey took two months, five days of which Sheppard graciously spent nursing a sick white agent of the Kasai Company back to health. This long march and the trial itself left Sheppard so exhausted that he decided to leave Africa in 1910 to be with his wife and their two children, who were being raised by relatives in the United States. They would have an emotional, heartwarming reunion, and Sheppard was applauded by the press. Under the headline, "First to Inform World of Congo Abuses," the *Boston Herald* wrote: "Dr. Sheppard has not only stood before kings, but he has also stood against them. . . . This son of a slave . . . has dared to withstand all the power of Leopold."[77]

Even though Sheppard was widely welcomed as a returning hero, he would soon find himself the center of unwanted controversy. The American Presbyterian missionaries in Africa hid their indiscretions well, but like other groups of missionaries, they were not all Christ-like in their conduct. In addition to internal bickering, there were instances of racial and gender bias, self-enrichment, and sexual misconduct. For example, Samuel Phillips Verner, a white Southern Presbyterian missionary in the Congo, was sent home in disgrace after he attempted to obtain rights to land where he could develop his own private diamond mine. Several missionaries had sexual relationships with African women. Others attempted to enrich themselves through ivory, Kuba cloth, and various kinds of artwork.[78] Sheppard had collected over four hundred of pieces of art, giving many of them away but selling others to the Hampton Institute for $5,000. While this sum hardly enriched him, the sale did raise some eyebrows.[79]

Verner's case was extraordinary. The son of a wealthy, politically powerful, and racist family in South Carolina, he had graduated first in his class at the University of South Carolina in 1892, but soon after suffered what contemporaries described as a "mental breakdown."[80] After recovering, he suddenly became interested in evangelism and turned to his influential relatives, who somehow arranged for him to be ordained in a single day—the usual path to ordination was three years of study in a recognized seminary. A Southern Presbyterian, he was sent to the Congo in 1896, where he met and quickly came to respect William Sheppard. Although he had a long history of ardently expressing his racist belief that whites, especially white ministers, were superior to blacks, he was so impressed by Sheppard that he stopped doing so. However, he led an unusual ministerial life. He had more than one sexual relationship with African women, fathering a daughter by one. Also, his interest in the Batwa Pygmies, who lived near his mission station, led him to study them intensively for two years instead of preaching the gospel.

Sent home after his aborted quest for diamond-rich land, in 1903 Verner became involved with the anthropological organizer of the St. Louis World's Fair. He accepted a commission to return to Africa to recruit eighteen Pygmies willing to come to America for the fair. He could only recruit three Batwa, but he found a fourth man, Ota Benga, from another Pygmy tribe. He had been enslaved by the Force Publique after they had killed his wife and most of the other people in his home village while he was away hunting elephant. Ota Benga returned from his hunt just as the slaughter ended. After unsuccessfully assaulting the Belgian commander, he was overcome and sold into slavery. Verner freed him, and the two men began a relationship that would take them to the World's Fair, various parts of America, and back to the Congo, where Ota Benga would remarry, only to have his second wife killed by a snake bite. Ota Benga then accompanied Verner back to the United States, where after an unpleasant time spent living in the Museum of Natural History, he became an immensely popular exhibit at the New York Bronx Zoo, where he shared a cage with an ape, creating much income for the zoo and much controversy about the propriety of such an exhibition. This phase of his life was brief, followed by some ten years of aimless and unrewarding life in America, most of it with Verner's relatives in the South. Increasingly despondent, Ota Benga shot himself to death in 1916. Verner, then quite demented or perhaps simply deranged by malarial infections, lived on until 1943. He was seventy when he died. The story of his life with Ota Benga has been poignantly told by his grandson Phillips Verner Bradford, with the help of a professional writer.[81]

Ota Benga's life was a profound human tragedy; Verner's was also tragic. Some who knew him thought him a fine Christian man, but others held him in contempt. In 1904, the Reverend Mr. Morrison wrote to Morel saying that "some doubt the man's sanity." Later that year, the Belgian ambassador promised Verner financial support and favorable treatment for his diamond-mining schemes in the Congo if he would deliver a series of speeches defending Leopold's Free State. Even though Verner had seen atrocities by the Force Publique and railed against them while he was in the Congo, he accepted the offer, not only making a series of speeches but also writing articles supporting Leopold.[82] Despite these deceitful efforts, he never received the promised financial support or the land he had been promised.

Morrison was so outraged by Verner's support of Leopold that in 1907 he wrote an "open letter" explaining that the Presbyterian mission had written the Southern Presbyterian Executive Committee in 1899 asking that Verner, who was then at home on leave, not be allowed to return to the mission,

> a request . . . never made before or since in the history of this mission. . . . In view of the gross exaggerations, misrepresentations, and what we know to be positive falsehoods which he acted out in life and which are found in more or less all his published writings, we do not hesitate to say that no confi-

dence whatever can be put in anything he may say or write. He is shrewd, deceitful, conscienceless, clever, revengeful, plausible, and wields a ready pen, but to those of us who know the facts his stories are for the most part the merest Munchaussen [sic] romances.

He is selfish to the last degree, and, worst of all, he will resort to any means, no matter how low, to carry out his purposes. . . . Leopold has evidently found Mr. Verner a willing tool, and one willing to sell the truth for a few royal favors.[83]

Even Sheppard came under fire. He was accused of having sexual relations with African women, one of whom bore him a son. Fellow black American missionaries Phipps and Hawkins were also accused of sexual affairs by other missionaries, and both men resigned. When Sheppard was accused of sexual misconduct he broke down in tears, then made a public confession of wrongdoing when he addressed his presbytery in North Carolina soon after returning to the United States: "Sometime in the years 1898 to 1899, while my wife was at home and I was left alone in my work, I fell, under the temptation to which I was subjected in my relations with one of the native women at Ibanj [Ibanche] Station [Kasai] and was guilty of the sin of adultery. My wife was away from me for about two years, and during this time the action was repeated twice with the same person."[84]

Some months later, Sheppard added this: "During the last four years I spent in Africa I fell into sin with three different women. These sins occurred only once and at different periods. I do now, brethren, make a clean breast of the whole matter."[85] Sheppard was suspended for almost a year, until April 1912, when he was reinstated as a minister, becoming a pastor in Louisville. He remained together with his wife and their two children until his death in 1927. More than a thousand people came to his funeral. Lucy Gantt Sheppard lived until 1955, when she died at the age of eighty-eight.

Lucy was not the only black American woman to have an impact on the Congo. When she enrolled in Talladega College, her personal supervisor was a forty-year-old woman named Maria Fearing. Weighing only one hundred pounds, and standing only five feet tall, Fearing was not pretty and at forty was without male suitors. A slave until the age of twenty-seven, Maria had received no education until she entered Talladega at the age of thirty-three. The target of student teasing because of her age, Maria nevertheless proved to be such a fine student that she stayed on at Talladega as a supervising matron until 1894, when she was fifty-six years old.[86] Despite her age, this tiny woman decided that she had to go to the Congo to help with the missionary movement of the Southern Presbyterians.

In 1894, she offered her services to the American Presbyterian Congo Mission (APCM). She was quickly rejected because of her age, which, it was said, would make her too vulnerable to African diseases. Undaunted, Fearing put her house up for sale, took her life savings and $100 in gifts from churchwomen who supported her missionary zeal, and went to the home of the late Samuel N. Lapsley's wealthy and influential father, where she expressed her devotion to the cause that his son had died for, and her willingness to pay all of her own expenses. Greatly touched, Judge Lapsley generously purchased her house and wrote a fervent endorsement of her missionary zeal to the Presbyterians' Executive Committee on Foreign Service. She was promptly accepted and traveled to the Congo in 1894 as one of the Reverend Mr. Sheppard's recruits.

Maria Fearing taught and preached not only at the Luebo mission station, but in scores of nearby villages, where she sang and played with children lovingly. She also literally became the mother of some one hundred kidnapped or orphaned girls, whom she raised in her newly created Pantops House for Girls. She was so loved that she became widely known as "the foreign mother."[87] Her good works became known to the leaders of the APCM, who soon paid for her food and, after two years, paid her a full missionary's salary. After twelve years of service, Fearing was so ill, her teeth falling out and her vision blurred, that she had to return to the United States in 1906. When she left, she wept and so did her girls. After responding well to medical and dental treatment, Maria returned to Luebo in less than a year and renewed her role as loving mother to the one hundred girls, who were overjoyed to have her back.[88] By 1915, almost all of her girls had become Christians, grown to maturity, and married. At the age of seventy-seven, Maria Fearing left the Congo for good, her mission carried out. She lived to be ninety-nine, often speaking lovingly of the Congo and the girls she had mothered there.

Yet another devoted black American missionary was Lillian May Thomas, like Lucy Sheppard a student at Talladega while Maria Fearing was a matron there. When William Sheppard visited the college during Lillian's senior year in 1894 searching for more missionaries, she happily agreed to join him. Although Thomas was thirty-four years younger than Fearing, the two women immediately became friends, living in the same house together in Luebo for fourteen years. Only after June 1908, when Lillian married American missionary Lucius A. DeYampert, did she and Maria Fearing live separately.

Like Fearing, she worked in the Pantops House for Girls, where she taught domestic skills such as washing, ironing, cooking, and sewing, and she also taught children how to set type for the mission's printing press. With Lucy Sheppard, Lillian Thomas took a leading role in creating the Luebo day school, which proved to be a great attraction for Congolese children. The school began in 1894 with no tools for teaching and only a few children. By 1900 there were thirty-seven students; by 1901, eighty; and by 1903, there were almost two hundred and fifty.[89] In 1915, the DeYamperts joined Fearing in taking a leave in the United States. A medical exam showed that she had such dangerously high blood pressure she could not safely return to the Congo. She and the Reverend Mr. DeYamperts lived in Selma, Alabama, until her death from a heart attack in 1930.

Yet another notable black American woman missionary was Althea Maria Brown. Her former-slave parents had taught themselves to read and to excel at arithmetic. After Althea was born in 1874, they taught her at home until 1892, when she turned eighteen and was admitted to Fisk University, where she was voted the prettiest girl in the school.[90] She graduated in 1901 and was the only woman who spoke at commencement. She sailed to the Congo in 1902 with four other missionaries. Like other missionaries before her, she shopped in London, where she dressed in black and wore black, horn-rimmed glasses, perhaps to mute her beauty. She finally arrived in Ibanche after being carried the fifty miles from Luebo in a hammock and saw the mission station for the first time: "The men gave a loud yell which was answered by the firing of guns, and soon all the people of the station, men, women, and children, ran at full speed to meet us."[91]

Althea Brown described Ibanche:

As we came nearer we saw the station in its beauty. From the top of a tall flag pole floated the banner of the Congo Free State, a single gold star in a background of blue. In front of Mr. Sheppard's home, the French and the Belgian flags, the Union Jack, and the Stars and Stripes were also flying. The station is surrounded by broad avenues bordered with fruit trees. On the north is Pennsylvania Avenue, on the south Rankin Avenue, on the east Palm Avenue, and on the west,

Chester Avenue. Running east and west through the Mission is Grand Boulevard, gracefully adorned with delightful shade trees, two magnificent clusters of bamboo, and beautiful flowers. At the east end of the boulevard, in the center of a grass-covered mound, is a tree, seventy feet tall and five feet in diameter, with great outspreading branches. Beneath the shade of this giant is the Market Place. North of the market is Lincoln Park. All the station buildings face the boulevard, the most beautiful of which is the new Lapsley Memorial Church with its tower pointing heavenward.[92]

The Reverend Mr. Sheppard was away on a trip, but Althea was greeted happily by Lucy Sheppard, her small son, and Mr. Phipps. Her mission was about to begin.

Althea became the matron of the Maria Carey Home for Girls, the counterpart of Pantops at Luebo. Along with more than one hundred children, most of whom had been ransomed from slavery—one in return for a pair of scissors—were numerous pet dogs, cats, parrots, monkeys, and even some eagles and a hawk. But in 1904, the Bakuba people whom Sheppard had tried so hard to convert unexpectedly attacked Ibanche. The missionaries and their students barely escaped with their lives to Luebo, but the mission was burned to the ground. Just before the attack, a new black American missionary had arrived at Ibanche, Alonzo Edmiston, a reverend who had also studied medicine. He helped everyone escape the attack of the Bakuba. Later, he built a successful industrial school that taught printing and carpentry and soon after married Althea.

In 1907, she returned to Alabama with her sickly infant, and her husband joined her a year later. They returned to the rebuilt station of Ibanche in 1915. Their little son was now well and enjoying mission life while his parents were busy all day. The morning and afternoon schools both enrolled 350 children, and more than 1,000 people came to Sunday school.[93] When the Edmistons left the Congo in April 1920, Luebo had a population of twenty thousand. Ibanche was also large, and there were several new mission stations in even more remote areas. The Edmistons returned to the Congo for the last time in 1930, taking up posts at the new station of Mutoto. Their fellow missionaries gave them a silver wedding anniversary, featuring a beautiful cake with silver frosting and a chest of silverware.

But Althea would soon suffer severe attacks of malaria and sleeping sickness, which recurred with increasing intensity until June 25, 1937, when, despite the care provided by two doctors and two nurses, she passed away with her husband at her side. As her husband wept in anguish, she was buried in the Congo next to one of her dearest friends, a nurse who had died there in 1931.

While African-American missionaries like these men and women were devoting their lives to the Congolese people, King Leopold II was forced to yield control of the country to Belgium, and the new Belgian Congo came into existence. Christianity flourished in the Congo, but by the time of independence in 1960, 80 percent of these Christians were Roman Catholic, products of six thousand Catholic missionaries at 669 mission posts and thousands of Catholic primary schools. The Protestants had continued their missionary labors, but they remained outsiders to the government.[94] Most Congolese could not grasp the often-preached concept of the "unity of man in Christ" while watching the Catholics and the Protestants quarrel over virtually everything.[95] Although Catholic missions would always outnumber Protestant ones, by the time of independence, there were nonetheless forty-six different Protestant missionary groups in the Congo.

 5

THE BELGIAN CONGO

As the missionary-led international pressure against Leopold's Free State mounted, the king intensified his propaganda efforts, denying any wrongdoing yet promising wide-ranging reforms. Increasingly worried, he also agreed, albeit reluctantly, to the creation of an international Commission of Enquiry composed of three distinguished lawyers—one from Italy, another from Switzerland, and a third from Belgium—to investigate the charges made in the Casement Report. Leopold's hopes that the Commission would repudiate the Casement Report were crushed when the lawyers returned from a five-month tour of inspection of the Congo Free State that had closely followed Casement's itinerary through the rubber-rich areas of the Congo. To Leopold's dismay, they confirmed every one of Casement's findings. Incredibly, while the Commission was at work documenting the brutality of the Free State's collection of rubber and ivory, Leopold actually extended his personal control over the Free State, altering his monopoly trusts to increase his personal profits, issuing even more millions of dollars' worth of bonds, and ceaselessly building still more monuments to himself in Belgium—

triumphal arches, museums, palaces, seaside resort promenades, parks, royal châteaus, and even golf courses.

With some of his immense profits from the rubber trade, Leopold had earlier purchased an expensive estate on the French Riviera, where he used the luxurious, fifteen-hundred-ton, steam yacht *Alberta* as his residence and office. With him aboard the *Alberta* were dozens of servants and his private secretary. In a lavish villa on his nearby estate, he installed his French mistress, the beautiful, buxom, young Caroline. They had met in 1900 when he was sixty-five and she was sixteen, then the mistress of a former French army officer named Durrieux, who found it profitable to rent her to other men when he was in need of money, which was often, given his predilection for betting on horse races. Leopold II lavished her with every luxury, including castles. In return, she gave him two sons, and four days before his death Leopold married her, naming her Baroness DeVaughan and willing her his fortune. Long after his death, she wrote lovingly of their life together in a book entitled *A Commoner Married a King*. She did not mention her remarriage to her longtime French lover, Durrieux, which took place within a year of Leopold's death.[1]

His life aboard his yacht on the Riviera was the ultimate in self-indulgence, but Leopold also used the time to create three corporations, each with a monopoly to exploit the vast mineral wealth of Katanga. One of these companies would be responsible for building a railroad from Katanga to the mouth of the Congo and another to Rhodesia; the other two would mine and smelt copper and other minerals. Needless to say, a large percentage of the companies' profits would go to the Free State, that is, to Leopold himself. Although Leopold was never blind to his own profit, he may also have been concerned with the long-term economic development of the Congo, but he had no concern for the welfare of the men who labored in its mines and smelters.

While Leopold frolicked with his mistress and grew ever more wealthy, many thousands of Congolese died.[2]

By 1908, when international opinion, led by Britain and the United States, called for Leopold's personal ownership of the Congo to end, Belgium was anything but eager to take control of the Congo. But after intense national debate, much of it acrimonious, in August 1908 the Belgian parliament voted to annex Leopold's Congo Free State by the hardly overwhelming count of eighty-eight in favor, fifty-four opposed, and nine abstaining. After the vote, the majority applauded timidly and some of the opponents hissed.[3] On November 15, 1908, the Congo Free State ended and the Belgian Congo came into existence. No sooner had parliament voted for annexation than smoke began to billow out of Brussels' Congo Free State offices next door to Leopold II's royal palace. When the furnaces stopped burning eight days later, Leopold had destroyed virtually all evidence of his actions in the Congo Free State.[4] Similar fires blazed in the Congo itself as Free State administrators followed his orders to cover their tracks.

On November 15, 1908, the day that annexation formally took place, there was little public rejoicing in Belgium. Every November 15 was St. Leopold's day in Belgium, an occasion for King Leopold's grateful subjects to send him messages of thanks and congratulations. In 1908, few of these messages congratulated the king for his "abdication" from his personal empire. Instead, many were frankly critical. Leopold was upset by the letters and deeply resentful about annexation, which he saw as a "base and unjust" act.[5] However, his feelings did not prevent him from making a deal with the Belgian government, which, in return for his capitulation, called for Belgium to assume his debts of over 110 million francs, give him another 45.5 million francs to complete his building projects, and yet another 50 million francs in "gratitude for his great sacrifices made for the Congo."[6]

King Leopold II died the following year at age seventy-four. He had never set foot in the Congo. He had, however, imported masses of Congolese artifacts, especially artworks, to Brussels' museums, and in 1897 when the World's Fair came to Brussels, he arranged for 287 Congolese, including two Pygmies, to display themselves in newly built villages, where they sang and danced. Others paddled a canoe in a pond. Many male visitors expressed disappointment because the Congolese women covered their breasts.[7]

In 1908, Belgium was wholly unprepared to govern the Congo. As noted in the previous chapter, four years would pass before any administrative reforms would even begin to have an impact. One reason for this was that Belgium had no previous experience as a colonial power. Also, the vastness of the Congo, a place more than eighty times larger than Belgium, posed an intimidating administrative problem for Belgian officials. For example, Kasai Province was a low-lying savanna rich in cotton, maize, rubber trees, and diamonds, but it was the size of New Mexico. Many of the Congo's people had never seen a Free State administrator, and virtually every Congolese man owned a musket. The Congo's tribal diversity was also daunting, as was the disorganization of tribal political institutions. The Congo's emptiness was also a problem. The depopulation caused by Leopold's slaughter, the Arab slave raids, starvation, exposure, an epidemic of sleeping sickness, and a dramatic drop in the birthrate left the Congo seemingly empty. In part, this was also a result of Leopold's practice of conceding property rights to European corporations over any land that appeared to be empty, making it impossible for its tribal owners to reclaim it when it was needed. By 1908, 67 million acres had been appropriated in this way.[8] The Congo's population had fallen from something over 20 million people in 1880 to little more than 6 million in 1908.[9] There were simply not enough people alive in the Congo to develop its mineral or agricultural resources as Belgium had hoped.[10]

Tiny Belgium actually held more people than the Congo, 7.5 million. It was the most densely populated country in the world. It had huge industries as well. Surprisingly, despite the population density and the presence of such wealthy industries, the Belgian government was almost entirely free of corruption.[11] Unfortunately, the Congo would not follow in this tradition. Into its vastness would come Europeans from many parts of the world, and with them would come corruption of many kinds. In 1914, seventeen Belgian Congo officials were prosecuted for embezzlement, fraud, and illegal trading activities.[12] Others could have been. As we shall see, Belgium's administrative woes in the Congo were also a product of the inadequacy of its administrative personnel, as well as their mistrust of one another, especially Walloons versus Flemings. This mistrust was so common and deep among Belgians in general that it was widely recognized as a national characteristic.[13]

Neither Belgium's new king, Albert I, nor its parliament had any vision for the Congo's future or for the best policies to inform that future. The only clearly stated principle was the need for the colony's budget to be balanced.[14] All agreed that the Belgian Congo would have to pay for itself. To achieve this goal, Belgium continued Leopold's policy of granting land and mineral concessions to large Belgian corporations with the state taking a portion of the profits. This practice led to the profitable exploitation of Katanga's mineral riches, the development of an extensive railway system, and even the creation of some valuable agricultural exports such as cotton. Allowing Belgian corporations not only vast concessions but considerable control over the government itself led to dramatic economic growth. The largest concession was to Société Général, a holding company with more assets than the House of Morgan, Anaconda Copper, the Mutual Life Insurance Company of New York, and the Pennsylvania Railroad combined. It owned 20 percent of Union Minière and had interests in virtually everything from cotton to beer, railroads, insurance, diamonds, and automobiles.[15]

The Union Minière du Haut Katanga (UMHK) dominated this province's wealth in cobalt, tin, gold, manganese, iron, copper, and uranium. The Belgian Congo would soon become the fourth-largest copper producer in the world behind only the United States, the British Empire, and all of South America.[16] As early as 1920, the Belgian Congo exported over £12 million of minerals and agricultural products, six times the value of exports in 1913.[17] The exploitation of minerals also led to a rapid influx of Europeans. In 1908, only three thousand Europeans were in the entire Congo, and when copper was discovered in Katanga in 1911, only a handful of Europeans lived in a shantytown where the city of Elisabethville would be built. Ten months later, one thousand Europeans lived there within a newly built city complete with hotels and a major men's club called the Cercle Albert which welcomed European women as well as men. It was the largest collection of Europeans in any place in the Congo at that time.[18]

Today, Elisabethville—renamed Lubumbashi in 1967—is a city of over 350,000 people. Its history and that of Katanga mirror the achievements and the problems of the Belgian Congo. The city was built on a stretch of infertile grassland at an elevation of four thousand feet in the extreme southeast of Katanga Province, near the border with northern Rhodesia (now Zambia) along what became known as the Copperbelt. The small Lubumbashi stream that ran nearby later gave its name to the city. The city grew rapidly because of the success of the copper mining industry. In 1920, the old town of Elisabethville was flattened and a new one was constructed modeled on the rectilinear grid pattern of the Rhodesian city of Bulawayo.[19] Elisabethville had an affluent, relatively modern, Europeans-only city center, surrounded by thousands of huts built of sticks, mud, and savanna grass for Africans who had walked there from distant parts of the countryside. It also had a Force Publique military camp and several company towns belonging to large railroad or copper mining firms. But it was best known for a huge chimney to carry away fumes, and a giant slag heap, both belonging to the Union Minière.

One key to the city's growth was the large salaries in the railroad and mining businesses that attracted so many Europeans. But African laborers, at much lower salaries, were needed as well. They were attracted to wage earning by the Belgian imposition of a "head tax" in 1914 that forced every able-bodied man in the Congo to pay an annual tax in currency. The only way for African men to obtain the money for this tax was to work for Europeans. In 1914, 7,044 Congolese from Katanga were in Elisabethville, along with another 3,000 Africans from northern Rhodesia and Malawi.

The exodus of young men from the Katangan countryside to Elisabethville left food production solely in the hands of old men, women, and young children, with the result that food became so scarce that malnutrition set in, followed by disease. To escape this growing peril, many women also went to Elisabethville to work as maids or laundrywomen for Europeans, bringing their children into the ever more crowded and unsanitary African quarter of the city. Some women even worked long, hard days as road builders, singing all the while. Because women did not pay a head tax, they were paid in much cherished salt, not currency.[20] The lives of Africans in this city were anything but healthy. In the years before the outbreak of World War I, the annual death rate for Africans in the city was an appalling 24 percent.[21] The Spanish flu epidemic of 1918 would kill many thousands more throughout the Congo, especially in its new cities.

Ever the economic opportunist, in 1900 Leopold had given ten years of exclusive rights to prospect for minerals in Katanga to a Scottish engineer, Robert (later, Sir Robert) Williams, a close friend of Cecil Rhodes. To no one's surprise, Williams hired primarily British prospectors, with eighteen Britons in his employ in 1906, and forty by 1909. Five Britons, including Lord Arthur Butler, were also on the board of directors of the Union Minière.[22] Belgian administrators of Katanga Province soon came to fear that the British, with their soldiers only a few miles away in Rhodesia, planned to seize Katanga, which is exactly what Cecil Rhodes hoped to do. They also feared that the opening of the railroad from Rhodesia to Elisabethville would bring into Katanga all manner of British troublemakers, and it did bring many Britons, some of whom did prove to be troublesome. To prevent the British from taking over the Copperbelt, as the area was known, the Force Publique sent a thousand well-armed troops to Elisabethville, while administrative stations, guarded by soldiers, were set up all along the border with Rhodesia. The intent was to stake an unmistakable Belgian claim to the riches of Katanga. Belgian police and magistrates also dealt harshly with Britons who were already in Katanga.

While the semi-independent administration of Katanga attempted to deal with its influx of Europeans as well as Africans from other countries, the first Belgian minister of the colonies, Jules Renkin, studied the colonial history of other European nations. During his rule from 1908 to 1918, he virtually eliminated government-led atrocities, reduced compulsory labor, lifted many trade restrictions, and gave African chiefs wider powers. He divided the Congo into chiefdoms (*chefferies*) and sub-chiefdoms (*sous-chefferies*) in which the Congolese "chiefs" were paid by the state to carry out administrative and police duties. They even had limited powers of criminal jurisdiction. However, many of these appointed "chiefs" were not tribally recognized leaders at all, but men loyal to the state who lacked respect or cooperation from their own people. Because these chiefs had no idea how to collect taxes in a way acceptable to the people, entire villages often fled, many people died, and few taxes were collected. Another problem was the incredible proliferation of these chiefdoms. In 1917, there were 6,095 such administrative units for a population of just under 6 million people.[23] In the sparsely populated Équateur Province, by 1921 there were 2,710 chiefdoms, and no attempt was made to reduce the number of these administrative units until 1933.[24]

In addition to these thousands of chiefdoms, Renkin set up hundreds of administrative districts ruled by district commissioners, territorial administrators, agricultural officers, and other officials, all but the most senior of whom were required to wear uniforms that included khaki safari jackets and short pants, with knee-length khaki socks, and sun helmets bearing the same badge of authority formerly used in the Congo Free State.[25] But even in the most isolated stations they also had to possess and sometimes wear five dress uniforms, three of them white, two blue, as well as a civilian suit. As was the case under Leopold, the Congolese called these men Bula Matari—"rock smashers." It was not meant as a compliment. When Belgium annexed the Congo Free State, it had 756 such state officials, most of them known as a *chef de poste*. Of these, 486 were Belgian, but 92 were Swiss, 69 were Swedish, and 57 were Italian. Almost all of these men were carryovers from the Congo Free State. By 1913, the number of officials had risen to 1,611. Some of these men, especially the Italians, were hopelessly incompetent, as Viscount Mountmorres noted: "Almost every unsatisfactory State official whom I have met was Italian, and they are far from satisfactory even in the capacity of military officer."[26] But others, including Henri Rolin, a Belgian judge and university professor, criticized all officials: "All the witnesses whom we heard were unanimous in confirming what we ourselves observed: our *chefs de poste* are too young and incompetent; they are sent out, without knowing the native language, without serious training, without a probationary period, to a distant place where they are usually alone. Isolated, powerless, able only with difficulty to leave their headquarters, they do not travel enough in their district, they do not get to know the villages."[27]

Even officials who were conscientious and able were forced to work under difficult conditions, including spending twenty days of every month in the field with uncooperative native peoples. When they were in their offices, the workday began with a bugle call at 5:45 A.M. and lasted well into the evening. Despite the many vaccinations officials received, they still had to endure the ravages of tropical diseases. In 1890, for example, 15 percent of these officials died, and although health conditions and medical care would improve dramatically, during 1905, 5.42 percent of the officials died. By 1920, the death rate for these officials had fallen to 1.34 percent per year.[28] Disease slowly came under control, but government officials were still irked by the requirement to don formal attire for dinner, even in remote tribal areas. In Belgium, the question asked about anyone who took up service in the Congo was "Why? What has he done?"[29]

Renkin proposed a series of reforms, including an end to the monopoly system of commercial exploitation and the development of medical and social services, but years would pass before there were any noticeable changes. One reason for this was that the great majority of the new Belgian Congo administrators could not cope with their duties. For one thing, many lacked the language skills necessary for them to communicate with their subjects. In addition to this crucial deficiency, these men were asked to be all things at once—tax collectors, census takers, policemen, judges, agronomists, road builders, sanitationists, and wise counselors—all while they were poorly paid and often ill. To make matters worse, Flemings and Walloons not only spoke different languages, most openly disliked one another. One able Belgian administrator took this dim view of his colleagues:

> In numerous regions, the actions and faults of former *chefs de poste;* their frequent almost total incomprehension of native institutions; their inability to take a general and detached view, taking into account all aspects of the problem; their frequent tendency to follow a policy aimed at personal prestige, to the detriment of the authority of the traditional rulers, to this day weigh heavily on the shoulders of these entrusted with the political and economic development of native societies.[30]

Speaking to his Presbyterian missionary colleagues, who, like governmental officials, had great power, William M. Morrison urged them to "remember first and last that the natives should be treated as kindly and courteously as white people . . . we are their servants not their masters. Under their black skins they have feelings and sensibilities similar to ours, which ought to be respected. If we laugh at their customs, appearances, or fetishes, we destroy their confidence in us and repel them."[31] As we have seen, some missionaries listened to Morrison, but others did not.

Most of the Belgian officials recruited after 1908 were young men with little formal education who hoped somehow to make money and leave the Congo before they fell dangerously ill.[32] Like Leopold's officials, these men still ordered all kinds of forced labor and collected taxes at gunpoint, both enforced by the Force Publique, whose officers complained bitterly that their men had no time for military training because civilian administrators so frequently ordered their use as messengers, orderlies, escorts, and honor guards.[33] These civilian officials were still permitted to order the flogging of Congolese, although the number of strokes permitted by law declined over the years. Many ordered flogging as a matter of principle, insisting that without it they would have no respect. Some actually enjoyed giving such orders and watching the suffering as the *cicotte* tore into men's backs and buttocks.[34] Flogging was not forbidden entirely until 1955. The Belgian Congo eventually had more European civil servants and officers in administration, the magistrature, and the army than any other country in Africa. There were ten thousand such men by the time of independence in 1960.[35]

As these men struggled to administer Belgium's new colony, its commercial and industrial developments grew, especially in Katanga. Almost all of the Congo's badly depleted population still lived in traditional village settings. Except for Elisabethville, they did not move to cities or industrial centers in large numbers until World War II made jobs for Africans plentiful in urban areas. Village life still saw men and women engaged in traditional economic tasks, and women were usually bare-breasted. Traditional dances, rituals, and healing ceremonies took place as before, with elderly healers promising to cure virtually any physical or mental malady with magical incantations and medicines made up from snakeskins, the mummified organs of birds and animals, dried flesh, and all manner of dried leaves and herbs. Most women still carried heavy loads on their head and a baby on their back. Some people, such as the artistically talented Bakuba, not only rejected Christianity, they maintained their traditional culture well into the 1930s, and in some of the more distant parts of the Congo such as the far northeast, European influence was virtually nonexistent. Conversely, by 1950, one hundred thousand Baluba, with a far less traditional and tightly integrated culture than the Bakuba, had migrated to cities across the Congo. Because of their urban living and success in business, they referred to themselves, as others did, as the "Jews of the Congo."[36]

As a British visitor in 1883 noted, a Congolese market was a busy and vibrant place:

> An African market with so many commodities to sell and so many eager sellers and loungers, is a most animated scene. The din of voices may be heard afar off, and when you enter the great open square, where, under the shade of great trees, perhaps a thousand people are disposed in little chaffering groups round their heaps of wares, it is worse than the parrot-house at the Zoological Gardens. The women are the keenest traders, they haggle and scream and expostulate, and chuckle aside over their bargains, whilst the hulking men lounge about in good-humoured listlessness, or squat in rows stolidly smoking. Although the strife of tongues is great, few real quarrels occur. There is in most cases a chief of the market, perhaps an old Fetish man, who regulates all disputes, and who so heavily fines both litigants that all are chary of provoking his arbitration.[37]

In most parts of the Congo after Belgian rule took hold, a visit to a native market would quickly reveal the spread of European influence. Women in a market setting usually wore cloth sarongs or calico dresses that covered their breasts, and they smoked cigarettes, while many men who passed by wore tattered European clothing as well. Some men and women even wore shoes. Although women still dominated market transactions, and traditional vegetables, eggs, dried fish and meat, pots, woven goods, and native jewelry were still on prominent display, there were also a host of European-made trinkets, not to mention scissors, safety pins, padlocks, metal combs, and mirrors in all shapes and sizes. And transportation improved rapidly. Most markets would be close to a navigable river where many new steamships plied their trade. There were many miles of new railroad tracks as well, some three thousand miles in place by World War II. And new roads stretched out in seemingly every direction, one hundred thousand miles of them by 1950. Few were paved, and initially there were few motor vehicles, but more and more cars and trucks arrived every year, and these roads bore heavy foot traffic, mostly women carrying heavy burdens and trailed by their small children. But there were oxcarts, too, and men on bicycles.

And of greatest concern to the Belgian administrators and European settlers were the so-called *évolués*—mission-educated, Westernized men who tried to dress like Europeans, spoke French, largely rejected their traditional cultures, and yearned to become assimilated as Europeans. One of these was Patrice Lumumba. These men would grow in numbers as mission schools were opened to more and more Congolese. There would eventually be almost thirty thousand public schools and two universities. But not until 1955 were even a few Congolese children admitted to white schools, and as late as 1958 a large number of Congolese students were removed from white primary schools in Elisabethville on the grounds of their poor hygiene and health. However, they were told that their condition did not warrant medical attention at state expense.[38] The Catholic Lovanium University opened in 1956, as did a state university in Elisabethville. Both soon became interracial, but by 1960 there were only 344 African students in Lovanium University and 77 in Elisabethville University.[39]

While the Belgian Congo's administrative officials struggled to come to grips with the new colony, in 1909 young King Albert I, Leopold's nephew and heir, took a three-thousand-mile tour of the Congo by train, steamship, canoe, bicycle, and even on foot. When he returned to Belgium, he praised Leopold for making the Congo such a "splendid" country, but he also urged parliament and Renkin to expedite the development of railroads. In that same year, the first copper foundry in Katanga went into production, managed primarily by Britons and Americans under the direction of Sir Robert Williams. Copper production grew rapidly, and in September 1910, when the first train ever seen in Katanga arrived from Rhodesia, a flood of immigrants seeking a new Eldorado arrived from Britain, South Africa, Australia, and several European countries.[40] One such was a self-proclaimed Balkan count who arrived in Kivu wearing a thick tweed shooting coat, green velveteen britches, pigskin gaiters, and a pith helmet with a bright blue feather on the side. He kept a large knife in one gaiter and carried a huge, heavy walking stick.[41]

Each incoming train brought building supplies, mining equipment, and new settlers—artisans, merchants, fortune seekers, and prostitutes. Some of these early settlers built mud and grass huts, while others lived in tents. Two men actually dug a shelter inside a ten-foot-tall anthill.[42] By Christmas of 1911, of the more than 1,000 Europeans in Elisabethville, only 140 were women, and 25 of them were prostitutes.[43] Serving these 1,000 Europeans, were no fewer than forty-seven bars, all of them heavily frequented. As one might expect from the history of the Free State, almost half of the Europeans were Belgian, but 127 were British, and 100 were Italian. Another 86 were South Africans of British ancestry, 81 were Greek, 57 were Russian, 41 were German, 33 were Turkish, and 74 came from other parts of the world, including the United States. At least 150 of these immigrants were Jewish, most of them from Russia and Turkey.[44] Despite their diverse origins these Europeans quickly came to refer to Elisabethville as E-ville, while Leopoldville was Léo, and Stanleyville was Stan.[45] In that same year of 1911, 43 of these Europeans died of disease.

As these all-too-hopeful but largely destitute and often non-French-speaking Europeans tried to settle in, they were soon followed by thousands of low-income Belgians recruited by the government. With no state-funded housing available, most of these new immigrants lived miserably, and many rapidly fell ill. Few found jobs, yet prices soared. Most were soon forced to return to their home countries, with the Belgians being repatriated at considerable expense to the Belgian Congo government. Despite these economic woes, mining continued, with the first copper exports being sold in Antwerp in late 1911, and by 1913, 7,400 tons of copper were sold at a profit of £160,000. In that same year, both cobalt and uranium were discovered, but their future importance could not yet be known. Both of the atomic bombs dropped on Japan at the end of World War II were made with uranium from Katanga. Gold had been discovered at Kilo, just west of Lake Albert in the far northeast corner of the Congo. By 1923, some sixty Europeans employed six thousand Congolese in their gold mines near Kilo, compelling them to work seven days a week under appalling conditions.[46]

With the eruption of World War I, most of Belgium was quickly overrun by Germans troops. Belgians were conscripted to work for Germans, and much of the country's wealth was confiscated.[47] The Congo was necessarily left to its own devices. The Force Publique sent its poorly trained men and their women to fight the Germans in Cameroon, Ruanda-Burundi (then a single country), and Tanganyika. Others fought against the Italians in Ethiopia. On the whole, these Congolese soldiers led by white officers performed well. But the greatest impact of the war on the Belgian Congo was economic. The Allies needed raw materials, sending copper production soaring from the 7,400 tons sold in 1913 to 27,500 tons in 1917. There was also a growing market for rubber and agricultural products, although agricultural productivity was low until 1917, when a new law was passed requiring each tribal community to grow and market cash crops. This change not only produced commodities such as cotton and coffee for outside markets, it raised so much food that famine would seldom be a problem again. But because these compulsory crops had to be sold at a price fixed by the state, not free market prices, there was much annoyance and resistance.[48] In partial compensation, the state did away with the tolls, tributes, and labor services that chiefs had formerly imposed on their people.

Because so many Belgians left the Congo to join the Belgian army still fighting to reclaim Belgian soil, some Congolese were temporarily appointed to positions previously reserved for whites only. By the end of the war, two thousand new businesses had been established. Yet 70 percent of all business in the Congo would be controlled by only five companies, all of which were partly owned by the state. These businesses, along with the Catholic Church, were driving forces in the governance of the Belgian Congo.[49] "Parastatals" like these had a history in Belgium itself, and in the Congo they took on governmental roles involving public housing, utilities, transportation, and even maintenance of a central bank.[50]

After World War I, the government of the Belgian Congo initiated large public works programs. Ports, roads, and electrical supplies were greatly improved, and as early as 1920 there was air service from Belgium to the Congo. Development was particularly extensive in Katanga, previously the most barren and impoverished region of the Congo. Smelting works, refineries, factories, electrical power stations, laboratories, and repair shops were joined by hospitals, clinics, schools, and all sorts of housing from single-family homes to large apartments. Most of the houses and apartments were made of brick, and each block had its own water supply and sanitary facilities. There were even beauty salons and luxury hotels, such as the one in Matadi that had five stories, elevators, and a cinema.[51]

The Union Minière provided increasingly modern housing, child care, and education for its workers and their families. Gécomines, the Belgian Congo's second-largest parastatal, provided an even more extensive array of services. Located three hundred miles north of Elisabethville, Gécomines paid its employees very little in cash, fearing that they would immediately squander it on alcohol and gambling, but the company gave each employee a comfortable house for his family and scientifically balanced rations for their meals, including milk, porridge, and vitamins for their children. Each employee's wife was given a small cash allowance as well as free clothing for her children from the company store. All family members received free medical care, and the children received free schooling. When the worker retired, he received a pension as well as a free house in the most attractive part of the city. A huge, ultraluxurious "workers' club" contained a cinema, a library, and a fine restaurant with an all-electric kitchen. Everything in the club was provided without charge except for the restaurant's lavish meals, complete with a bottle of European beer, that were served for five francs although each meal cost the company twenty francs. Soccer was played in a football stadium on weekends, and a workers' brass band played between matches.[52]

Gécomines and the Union Minière no longer recruited single men to work in the mines on limited-time contracts, but rather men with families who would settle into the area with a contract for a minimum of three years. By 1940, over 75 percent of these men renewed their contracts.[53] By 1929, Africans in Elisabethville had the best food and housing in all of Central Africa.[54] And by the time of independence in 1960, the Union Minière employed 41 doctors with access to 1,417 modern hospital beds to care for its 22,000 employees and their families.[55]

Similar developments, although less rapid, took place elsewhere in the Congo. There were diamond mines in the Kasai, tin, diamond and gold mines in Kivu, and large agricultural plantations in several regions. From 1920 to 1930, diamond output increased more than eightfold. Many Congolese greatly improved their standard of living, and much improved health care led to far greater chances of survival for their children and longer, happier lives for adults. Yet progress was decidedly uneven. By the time of independence, the Congo had more hospital beds than any other country in Africa. Yet the Congo's hospitals were racially segregated, and in some parts of the country health care was slow to develop. In Kasai Province in 1923, for example, 1.3 million Congolese and one hundred Europeans were served by a single doctor.[56] A similar shortage of medical care was found in other parts of the Congo.

In 1929, the Wall Street collapse devastated the Congo as it did most of the world. Prices fell drastically, businesses closed, and copper production fell by 60 percent from 1930 to 1932.[57] In the European residential area of Elisabethville, Katanga's largest city, one in every three houses was vacant, and most businesses were for sale. By 1935, the economy rebounded. Copper production rose and new found deposits of lead, zinc, and manganese along with newly valuable cobalt let to the development of new industries including hydroelectric power stations. The Belgian Congo administration also limited immigration to the country to persons with substantial means. The idea was not simply to avoid a repetition of the calamitous flood of low-income immigrants during the prewar years, but to prevent Europeans of low income and education from competing with Africans for low-income jobs as had happened in South Africa and the Rhodesias. As a result, although the average per capita income in the Belgian Congo was low by Western standards, it was higher than in many African countries, including Kenya, Nigeria, and Uganda. Almost all of those Congolese with wage employment lived in towns or cities, where they were able to afford some of the best housing anywhere in Africa, Western clothing, and adequate food, not to mention tobacco, Western-built furniture, radio sets, and bicycles. By 1954, the Congo had 1,146,000 Africans in wage labor, more than twice as many as in the country with the second-largest number of wage workers, Kenya.[58]

But this prosperity was not without tension. In 1941, a strike at Union Minière provoked soldiers to kill 95 civilians and wound 150 more.[59] Other labor disturbances followed. In 1948, the state extended forced recruitment in the Force Publique to the urban and educated segments of the Congo. The decision pleased no one because neither state officials nor managers of corporations wanted to see their skilled mechanics, carpenters, radio operators, or truck drivers drafted into the army. What is more, the Force did not want highly educated, and therefore potentially insubordinate, recruits either. Such people were drafted anyway, but they served shorter terms than uneducated recruits. Women were still recruited, even drafted, but were given no education or training even though one-half of all men in the Force served with their "wives" as late as 1945.[60]

With the outbreak of World War II, the Belgian Congo's economy received another powerful boost. Its mines not only worked overtime, so did newly built refineries. Some sense of the magnitude of this expansion can be had by looking at copper production. During the entirety of World War I, Katanga produced 85,000 tons; from 1940 to 1944, it produced 800,000 tons. There were similar increases in the production of tin, zinc, and especially cobalt.[61]

The postwar years saw unprecedented prosperity in the Congo. Urbanization took place at a rapid pace. For example, the population of Leopoldville in 1923 was 17,000. By 1938, it had risen to 40,000, and by 1950, more than 190,000 people lived there. By 1955, the city held 325,000 people. Today, it is a city of over 4 million people. Other cities experienced a similar percentage of population increase. A growing number of these urban residents were Africans who owned their own shops,

restaurants, or other businesses, while others worked as crafts-
men, bus drivers, plumbers, roofers, and in the building industry.
The mining areas shared in this growing prosperity, where more
and more African families hired by mining companies such as
Union Minière, lived in modern, European-style housing in centers with municipal halls, schools, churches, recreation grounds,
hospitals, and maternity wards. These centers had running water,
electricity, and sewage facilities. But they also had marked tension
among members of different ethnic groups who found themselves living among strangers with different customs and attitudes. Loneliness and distrust were commonplace. As a British
scholar observed, "The rural African [new to urban life] quickly
discovers that he is no longer a member of a family, even of a
tribe; that his neighbor is not bound by the same beliefs that
bind him, and so cannot be relied on to behave as a reasonable
man. The only sensible and safe thing to do is to mistrust one's
neighbor, to think for oneself alone, to have no consideration
for others."[62]

In attempting to cope with the problems of urban life, or
depressed by life in largely abandoned villages, many Congolese
turned to strange mixtures of Christianity and traditional African
religions. These messianic and nativistic movements began in
1921 when Simon Kimbangu, a devout Bakongo member of the
British Baptist Missionary Society, but also the son of a native
doctor, began to heal the sick through spirit possession while
quoting from the Bible and shouting "Be healed in the name of
Jesus Christ."[63] Eyewitnesses reported that Kimbangu "tossed his
head, rolled his eyes, and jumped into the air, while his body
twitched all over."[64] He could not cure blindness, deafness, sleeping sickness, or many other serious conditions, but he did have
enough apparent success with other ailments that he quickly attracted a large following in the Lower Congo region among people who believed that missionaries ignored faith healing, gave

people too little emotional uplift, and ignored ancestor worship.[65] People came together to hear Kimbangu recite biblical passages, then followed his injunction to confess their sins and abandon alcohol, marijuana, polygyny, and adultery. Soon they joined him in ecstatic shaking as the ancestral spirits entered their bodies, then they fell to the ground or leaped into the air as God's spirits gave them ecstasy. At the same time, evil spirits were driven away and health was restored.[66]

Congolese radicals began to use Kimbangu's movement for their political ends, preaching hatred of Europeans and encouraging opposition to government programs of all sorts. Within a matter of months, soldiers from the Force Publique were ordered to arrest Kimbangu, but thanks to the intervention of his followers, he escaped. Fearing that harm would come to his believers, he turned himself in a few days later, consciously emulating Christ and still quoting the Bible that he always carried. After a rigged trial by the government, encouraged by the Catholic Church, which felt threatened, he was condemned to death, but later in 1921 the sentence was commuted by King Albert to life in prison. He served the remaining twenty-nine years of his life in a prison in Elisabethville, where he died in 1950.[67]

Despite Kimbangu's imprisonment, his movement flourished as huge congregations of true believers, many of them sick, came together to enter hypnotic trances to the accompaniment of ear-splitting blasts from bamboo pipes, drums, rattles, and bells. New prophets arose to continue Kimbangu's mission, becoming possessed, speaking in tongues, and finding their health restored. Some of these movements abandoned Christianity, but in the 1930s new Christian sects emerged, led by the Salvation Army, promising true followers immunity to witchcraft as well as holiness and eternal bliss. And as late as 1951, Watch Tower or Seventh-Day Adventists became active. Kitawala, as Watch Tower was known, preached both pacifism and antinationalism, provoking violence in many parts of the Congo, yet as late as 1936 it had many followers among the workers at Union Minière. They were followed by Jehovah's Witnesses, who spread confusion by denying the divinity of Christ.[68] As recently as October 14, 1959, police broke up a Kimbanguist prophetic cult meeting, beating many followers so severely that twenty-eight had to be hospitalized.[69]

Much of the Belgian Congo's budgetary surplus after World War II went to the improvement of medical care. By this time, deadly malaria and sleeping sickness had been largely controlled. Each one of the Congo's 135 smallest administrative units *(territoire)* had a population of about one hundred thousand. Each administrative unit had a hospital, maternity and infant care centers, as well as numerous small clinics and dispensaries. In addition to these state services, missions, industries, and agricultural corporations provided up-to-date medical care. So many mobile medical teams toured the Congo in the 1950s that one-half of the population was seen each year.

Primary school education was also well funded. By 1958–59, 97 percent of all primary-school-age children were attending racially segregated classes, almost all of which were provided by state-supported Catholic mission schools.[70] By design, the education provided was agricultural and vocational. The government did not want to educate and thus create an elite that would demand independence. As a result, few students went to secondary school, something even rural Congolese bitterly resented. As recently as 1958–59, less than 2 percent of primary school students went on to secondary school. Instruction was in native languages, or in lingua francas such as Swahili or Lingala. French was taught only as a foreign language.[71] This policy of leaving education in the hands of the clergy led one critic to describe the Congo as the last surviving theocratic state.

University education, a prerequisite for leaders of a soon-to-be independent nation, was even less available than secondary school. In 1957, for example, six hundred African students were attending universities in the United States. Only two of them were from the Congo.[72] So few Africans went on to university education in the Belgian Congo that, by 1960, only seventeen had earned a university degree.[73] However, by 1959 over six hundred had become priests and over five hundred had been ordained as Protestant pastors.[74] Those who most longed for advanced education were the *évolués*, whose discontent would fuel the Congo's passion for independence. In 1950, a newly arrived Belgian administrator encountered such a young man riding his bicycle wearing a black tuxedo jacket with two gleaming fountain pens in his breast pocket and a wine-red fedora on his head. The Belgian waved in greeting; the *évolué* spat on the ground.[75]

By 1955, the European settler organization Fedacol stated its goals frankly: "We must organize a class of *évolué* natives, who will declare their acceptance of the ideals and the principles of our Western civilization, and who will be . . . the allies it is indispensable for us to find in the native communities. This middle class will be the black bourgeoisie which is beginning to develop everywhere, which we must help to enrich itself and organize itself and which, like all the bourgeois of the world, will be opposed to any disruption, internal or external."[76]

While the Europeans in the Congo attempted to create a non-confrontational black bourgeoisie, life in cities like Leopoldville continued its strict racial separation. Unlike Brazzaville, across Stanley Pond, where Africans and Europeans ate in the same restaurants and whites sometimes stood in line behind blacks in stores, in the Belgian Congo, Africans and Europeans rarely met on social occasions.[77] Hotels, restaurants, bars, theaters, and sporting events were all segregated, as were many shops and stores, and although black Congolese served or waited on whites in all these places, they were not welcome as patrons or guests. And Europeans rarely visited the so-called African or "macaque" (monkey) quarters, where life bore little resemblance to that as lived by white people. Some of the irony of this black and white separation could be experienced any night. Every building in Leopoldville and every other city was guarded throughout the night by a black watchman, who built a fire just outside the building's doorway where he wrapped himself in a blanket and slept all night.[78]

Not all Congolese were affected by "Europeanization." Many people in the northeast were largely unchanged, as were some peoples in the east of Kivu. But no people were as untouched as the Bambuti Pygmies of the Ituri Forest. By the late 1950s, they still subsisted by hunting with their poison arrows in the dense forest, then trading game in nearby Bantu villages for fruits and vegetables, especially bananas. They had no European education, and just as the Europeans referred to the Bantu as "monkeys," the Bantu looked upon the Pygmies as "monkeys." Disturbed by the Belgian Congo administration's failure to do anything to improve the Pygmies' quality of life, a junior Belgian administrative officer named Jean-Pierre Hallet convinced an agricultural agency to give him a small financial grant that he hoped to use to bring the Bambuti into at least part of the Congo's growing prosperity.

Although Hallet stood six feet five inches tall and had previously blown off his right hand while dynamiting fish to feed some Bantu farmers who had been brought to the brink of starvation by drought, he flourished in the forest and somehow convinced many Bambuti to accept his gifts of axes, machetes, and hoes to take up farming to supplement their hunting. Some one thousand Pygmies soon did so, planting and harvesting corn, beans, peanuts, manioc, and sweet potatoes. They also built sturdy houses and, even more remarkably, went to class where they

quickly learned to read, write, and do arithmetic. The program
was such a success that it attracted publicity in the Belgian Congo
press, angering Hallet's superiors, who appeared to be jealous of
his achievements. Rather than accept his resulting transfer to a
far-distant post, Hallet resigned in disgust and the Pygmies soon
reverted to their traditional way of life.[79]

Over time, the Europeanization of the Belgian Congo took
many forms. An American visitor to the Congo in 1923 was struck
by the national diversity of the Europeans he encountered. In
Kabalo, he met several Greeks from America who read the New
York *National Herald*, keeping up-to-date on baseball scores and
the plays on Broadway. One of these men, however, readily
adopted Congolese culture, marrying three African women before buying a beautiful twelve-year-old from her father to become
his fourth wife.[80] In the more bustling city of Tshikapa, in addition to Belgians the same American visitor met Americans as well
as Europeans from Ireland, Britain, Russia, Norway, and even
Brazil and Peru.[81] In one small town, he met four Europeans—
a Swiss, a Belgian, an Italian, and a Russian—said to be related
to the tsar—who directed the building of a railroad.[82]

Whatever their country of origin, Europeans in the Congo
tended to maintain cordial relations, often strengthened by sharing similar jobs as well as by their memberships in private clubs
that allowed them and their European wives to enjoy a gin and
tonic or two, a fine meal, and the opportunity for their women
to wear the latest Paris fashions. But Europeans did not mingle
with black Congolese. Instead, the Belgian Congo maintained
rigid racial segregation both by law and social practice. Whites
lived apart from Africans in residential areas that were separated
from African quarters by parks, golf courses, zoos, and commercial areas. Whites and blacks also attended separate schools and
did not mix socially. In 1947, a liberal Belgian lawyer in Elisabethville said, "The most ferocious Anglo-Saxon color bar had

never produced so many discriminatory laws, had never enacted so many measures of so rigid a segregation as our Belgian tutelage."[83] The Belgian administration denied being racist, but racial segregation was its official policy and so was racial discrimination.[84] And racist, too, was its control of the press and radio, neither of which was free to print or broadcast anything objectionable to the state.

Alan P. Merriam, an American anthropologist who lived in the Congo in 1951–52 and again in 1959–60, wrote, "Belgians in my experience seldom had true African friends, seldom invited Africans to their homes, seldom felt that Africans were their intellectual equals. On the contrary, the sentiments most often expressed were that the Congolese were, in truth, savages, and I cannot count the number of times that their differing cultural behavior was explained to me in terms of the 'fact' that 'they were up in trees just fifty years ago.' "[85]

Belgium joined with Europeans in the Congo in the hope of educating a conservative middle class or "black bourgeoisie" that would maintain the Congo's status quo by opposing all potentially disruptive changes, whether internal or external. But they both opposed an "elite" of highly educated and potentially troublesome Congolese. Catholic mission-educated men were known as *évolués*, "the evolved," meaning someone who had evolved "toward" being civilized, although it was not thought that they would ever completely achieve a "civilized" status. However, the Belgian Congo government went so far as to create an identity card in 1950 called the *carte du mérite civique* or "civilized person" card for *évolués*, but when priests were told that they were eligible to apply first for the card, they indignantly refused, saying that it added nothing to their stature. Possessors of such cards were permitted to eat in some white restaurants and hotels, and even to live in white neighborhoods, but over the next decade, only 217 *évolués* accepted these cards.[86] In 1955, while Europeans were trying to create their quiescent black bourgeoisie, Belgian university professor A. J. J. van Bilsen dropped a bombshell when he called on the Belgian parliament to adopt a thirty-year plan for the Congo's independence. He stressed the need to educate many more Congolese to enable them to lead their newly independent country, pointing out that the Congo had not yet educated a single black doctor, engineer or even veterinarian.[87] He also criticized the overemphasis on industry and the lack of any colonial policy. The *évolués* were ecstatic.

In that same year, Belgium's new king, Baudouin, returned from a trip to the Congo to tell his nation, "I want to insist on the fact that the basic problem which now confronts the Congo is that of human relationships between black and white. It is not enough to equip the country materially, to endow it with wise social legislation, and to improve the standard of living of its inhabitants; it is imperative that the whites and the natives should show the widest mutual understanding in their daily contacts. . . . Before we realize this high ideal, gentlemen, much remains to be done."[88]

Baudouin was referring to attitudes like the one that led a Belgian lady on board a steamship to assault two *évolués* who had the temerity to stand on the customarily "whites-only" upper deck.[89] The idea that force was necessary to control the behavior of Congolese was widespread. The British wife of a Belgian in Kivu spoke for many when she insisted that Congolese had "a complete lack of personal responsibility," instead displaying "deceit, laziness, and pretension." She insisted that the only means of dealing with such ones consisted of "a solid kick in the seat of the trousers."[90] Many others recommended even sterner means to control the inherent deficiencies of the *évolués*.

Many whites were not reluctant to express their contempt for Africans quite openly. For example, it was common to refer to them as *macaques* (monkeys) and insist that they had only recently come down from the trees. The term *sale macaque* (filthy monkey) was also used in public as a wounding insult. In 1944, when some Belgian men overheard an American telling some *évolués* with an interest in boxing that the world's heavyweight champion was a black American, Joe Louis, they were furious, telling the American that the Congolese must not be encouraged to have such aspirations.[91] When a Belgian writer took an African journalist to a bar on Leopoldville's posh Boulevard Albert in 1959, European patrons openly made snide remarks until the visitors left to loud applause.[92] Even *évolués* with "civilized person" cards were not served in many European bars and restaurants, and European movie theaters were closed to them as well. It was even illegal to sell alcohol to Africans until 1955. Perhaps most pervasive as a form of racism was that whites routinely addressed Congolese not as *vous* but as *tu*, the familiar form that when used with strangers was a patronizing expression of vague contempt.[93]

Belgium did nothing to encourage racial equality in the Congo, any more than it chose to provide university education for the Congo's best African students. And the political leaders of the newly independent Congo would not be among those few Congolese who had earned university degrees. Neither Joseph-Désiré Mobutu nor Patrice Lumumba, who would become the Congo's first prime minister, had even finished secondary school, and Joseph Kasavubu (also spelled Kasa-Vubu), its first president, was the grandson of a Chinese laborer who had helped Stanley to build the railroad, and a Bakongo grandmother. He had studied for the priesthood but had no university education. Before entering politics he had been a Catholic-school teacher. His lack of education, his priestly manner, and his poor public-speaking ability did not prevent the short, stout Kasavubu from being intensely ambitious.[94] The fifty-year-old Kasavubu was a passionate Bakongo patriot who struck strangers as quiet, even suspicious. He was conservative, slow to act, but tough and determined.

Lumumba's background would hardly seem to have prepared him for his country's highest political office. A secondary-school dropout, he was working as a postal clerk in Stanleyville in 1956 when he was convicted of embezzling $2,520 and sent to prison for two years. While in prison, he was held in European quarters, fed European food, and left alone to write a book, *Congo My Country*, which was published posthumously in 1961. He pleaded for clemency because he had returned 20 percent of the amount he had embezzled and planned to return the remainder. When his *évolué* friends repaid the remainder, he was released twelve months early.[95] He then moved to Leopoldville, took a job as a sales manager in a brewery, and became actively involved in politics. Despite his apparent psychological instability that led him to change his mind for no apparent reason, the tall, thin, handsome, thirty-five-year-old Lumumba was a brilliant orator with a fiery charm that dazzled many.[96] Quick to reach decisions and to take action, he could nonetheless talk for hours without stopping. He could also be ruthless. Although his parents were devout Catholics, unlike Kasavubu he was indifferent to religion.[97]

In August 1958, French president Charles de Gaulle gave a speech in Brazzaville offering the people a choice between joining the French Community of Overseas Territories or receiving "immediate" independence. The *évolués* in the Congo applauded loudly, giving voice to their own demands for immediate independence. Soon after, Lumumba attended the first All-Africa's People's Conference in Accra, Ghana, where he began what would become a close friendship with Ghana's prime minister, Kwame Nkrumah. When Lumumba returned to Leopoldville, he gave a public speech on December 28, 1958, loudly demanding immediate and complete independence for the Congo, saying that independence was not a "gift" but a "fundamental right of the Congolese."[98]

On January 4, 1959, Kasavubu organized a large political rally

in Leopoldville, but fearing violence, the Belgian Congo government canceled the event, triggering exactly what they had hoped
to prevent—widespread rioting. For several days, crowds sacked
missions, schools, and social centers. Shops were looted and set
on fire. Everything on the streets was destroyed—cars, street-
lights, signs, stoplights, bus stops, even trees and shrubs. European men were beaten, and many white women, including nuns,
were raped. When police and troops were finally called, they
quickly opened fire, killing 49 people and wounding another 258
according to the government. Observers placed the number
killed and wounded in the thousands.[99] A prominent historian
concluded, "It was at once the most decisive single event in the
surge to independence and singularly prophetic of the revolution without revolutionaries which followed in 1960."[100] Because
of the incendiary speech he had given a week earlier, Lumumba
was arrested and, despite the lack of any evidence, convicted of
inciting to riot and sent back to prison. Kasavubu, who was by
then revered by many of his fellow Bakongo as nothing less than
the reincarnation of Simon Kimbangu, was also imprisoned.[101]

In January 1960, Lumumba and Kasavubu were released from
prison to join 200 black Congolese who attended a monthlong
roundtable negotiation with Belgian officials in Brussels about
the Congo's future. Because Belgian Congo officials had seldom
allowed Africans to study in Belgium—only fifteen were there in
1959—and few had even been able to visit because a passport
cost $1,000, the presence of two hundred black faces in Brussels
prompted Belgians to stare at them in open amazement.[102] By
February 20, the Belgians agreed to virtually everything the Congolese had demanded, including independence. It was the most
radical decolonization plan ever adopted in Africa, and it is difficult to imagine a population less ready to carry out democratic
self-rule. Not only were no Congolese educated to lead such a
government, but also, despite pleas for unity, there were 120 po-

litical parties, many of them openly hostile to others. The country's ethnic groups were at odds, and rural Congolese had no knowledge of the world outside their villages. For them, independence was an incomprehensible concept. Nevertheless, elections were held and Lumumba was elected prime minister. Although Kasavubu contested the election and refused to speak to Lumumba after the results were announced, in an act of political expediency, if not wisdom, Lumumba asked Kasavubu to serve as president and form a government.

Lumumba had asked Mobutu to remain in Brussels until mid-June, keeping him out of the May elections, but Mobutu returned to Leopoldville in time to witness the independence ceremony on June 30, 1960. After King Baudouin delivered a speech officially declaring the Congo's independence in which he praised Leopold II, President Kasavubu made a positive and polite response, but Prime Minister Lumumba was furious, and when he spoke, the king was stunned. Accusing Baudouin of presiding over "a regime of injustice, suppression, and exploitation," he added: "We have known that the law was never the same for a white man as it was for a black: for the former it made allowances, for the latter it was cruel and inhuman."[103] He then said, "We have known ironies, insults, and blows, which we had to undergo morning, noon, and night because we were 'Negroes.' " Finally, he ad-libbed with a snarl, "We are no longer your 'monkeys,' " referring to the widely spoken Belgian nickname for the Congolese, "macaques."[104] The king flushed visibly as the Congolese in the audience stood and cheered. Lumumba had not forgotten the pain and the humiliation he had felt a few years earlier when he inadvertently bumped into a European woman in Leopoldville and she snarled *sale macaque* at him.

6

INDEPENDENCE—THE DREAM AND THE NIGHTMARE

For the first four days after independence, the cities and countryside alike were calm. Heavily armed, stern-faced, steel-helmeted troops led by white officers were watchful, well-disciplined, and in public view, but there was no sign of trouble. However, on the next day, the Force Publique mutinied against its all-white officer corps, and a few days later, the men of the Gendarmerie did the same. Men of both forces inflicted shocking abuses on many of their white officers and humiliated hundreds of European civilians, especially priests and nuns. Some Europeans were tortured, and others were murdered. Scores of European women were raped. A few days later, the Congo's richest province, Katanga, declared its secession, taking up arms to defend its own "independence." In response to this rapidly escalating chaos, much of the Congo's European population fled, most of them taking ferryboats to Brazzaville across Stanley Pool from Léopoldville, but others packed the country's two international airports, and some drove their cars to neighboring countries. While this panicked exodus was taking place, planeloads of Belgian paratroopers were landing to secure Leopoldville's airport and to protect the Congo's Europeans by whatever means they found necessary. There were few left to protect. Of the twenty-nine thousand Europeans in the Congo's three largest cities on July 1, 1960, only three thousand remained by July 10.

The trouble began on the evening of July 5 when some soldiers of the Force Publique met to air their grievances about their white officers. They were furious because Lieutenant General Émile Janssens, commander of the Force, had called a meeting of the Léopoldville garrison at Camp Hardy to tell them that there would be no changes in the Force, writing on a blackboard this confrontational message: "After independence equals before independence." Even more troubling to them was the announcement by the country's new prime minister, Patrice Lumumba, that he would retain the army's white officers and appoint Belgians to key national defense posts. Lumumba hurried to Camp Hardy in an attempt to calm the troops, but because he took Lieutenant General Janssens with him, the soldiers were not only suspicious, their rancor seemingly grew even more intense. When white officers of the Force attempted to break up this increasingly vociferous and unruly debate, the soldiers disarmed them and locked them up. The following day, armed soldiers from the Force Publique tried but failed to force their way into parliament, then later that day sent a large armed delegation to Lumumba to explain their grievances to him. Instead of explaining anything, they shouted, jostled, and threatened to shoot. They were outraged when Lumumba refused to yield to such intimidation, repeating his intention of retaining white officers and appointing Belgians to important defense posts.

The following day, July 7, more armed soldiers stoned the car of a cabinet minister, threatened again to march on parliament, and besieged Lumumba's residence. Lumumba suddenly did a complete about-face, joining with his cabinet in attempting to defuse the explosive tension in Léopoldville by agreeing to remove the commander of the Force, Lieutenant General Janssens, along with all his white officers. They also declared that all of the Force's African noncommissioned officers would be promoted one rank, with many becoming officers as a result. Only a handful of Belgians would be retained as advisers. Overnight, the entire European officer corps of more than a thousand men ceased to exist. Aging Victor Lundula was named general and made the Force's new commander in chief. However, Lundula, a member of Lumumba's tribal group, took little interest in the Force or its hundreds of new Congolese officers. The army was actually controlled by Mobutu, who had been named colonel and chief of staff, but despite Mobutu's efforts, the new Congolese officers had little or no control over their still unruly troops.

Lumumba's attempts at appeasement failed to bring peace. On July 8, heavily armed soldiers from the Force Publique resorted to mob violence in Leopoldville, while members of the Gendarmerie rioted in Matadi. The next day more armed violence occurred in Kasai and Katanga, and by the time Belgian paratroopers landed in Leopoldville on July 11, they were needed at trouble spots all over the Congo. Their presence quelled the violence in some places but fueled it in others. Belgian navy warships created even more havoc when they ill-advisedly attempted to end the rioting in Matadi by indiscriminately bombarding the city. Of Matadi's usual eighteen hundred European residents, only ten remained in the city at the time of the shelling, but the Force Publique radio network reported that hundreds of African Congolese had been killed by the naval bombardment. In response to this inflammatory news, whether accurate or not, troops of the Force took vengeance across the Congo.

On that same day, popular Moise Tshombe—the son of a wealthy and politically powerful trading and transport family—proclaimed the independence of Katanga. The following day, Lumumba implored the United Nations to intervene. Neither

Lumumba, Kasavubu, nor their advisers had foreseen any of these uprisings or the secession of Katanga. Lieutenant General Janssens was equally taken by surprise. The day before the mutiny erupted, he was asked about the security situation in the newly independent Congo. Janssens replied with the utmost confidence, "The Force Publique? It is my creation. It is absolutely loyal."[1]

The Force Publique in 1960 had 23,000 men led by 1,006 European officers. A year earlier, it had served loyally to put down bloody nationalist demonstrations in Leopoldville and Stanleyville, but it suffered from several inherent weaknesses. The bulk of the men were both illiterate and recruited from the most backward parts of the country. At the same time, the small cadre of somewhat educated men in the Force, such as Joseph-Désiré Mobutu, were not permitted to become officers. The Gendarmerie of some seven thousand men was also composed of illiterate Congolese and led exclusively by white officers. These men shared the widespread belief among Congolese that independence would not only bring the immediate departure of all Europeans from the Congo, but that all of their possessions would be left behind for the Africans to claim. Even so, the rebellion of these previously well-disciplined men surprised everyone.

How many of the eighty thousand Europeans who were in the Congo when the violence began were harmed during the mutiny has never been determined. Most fled out of harm's way before the violence could overtake them, but some escaping cars were fired on, and many abandoned homes were looted and burned. After the Force Publique's officers had been disarmed, all but a few were detained under guard. Some of these officers were civilly treated, fed, and exposed to few indignities, but others were stripped of their uniforms, beaten, spat upon, and forced to drink the urine that Congolese soldiers had deposited in tin cups. A few were shot and killed. Some European civilians suffered the same kinds of ill-treatment, Flemings being singled out as victims because they were thought to have been especially contemptuous of Congolese.[2] Priests and nuns were particularly targeted for abuse, often being stripped of their clothing and made to parade in public in the nude. Scores of European women including nuns were raped, several of them at least twenty times. Most of them were assaulted in front of their young children. A few of those who were raped were prepubescent girls themselves.[3]

A Belgian government investigation took evidence from many victims of these assaults and rapes. For example, it reported that one man

was imprisoned for two days without food, with his wife and three children aged less than 12, under the menace of an automatic weapon. After he was freed, he was arrested again on the 11th of July, around 3 o'clock in the afternoon. He was stripped, like the others, and hit with fists, feet and rifle butts. Two of his companions were mortally wounded. For two more days, they were deprived of food and drink. Soldiers tried to drown him in a barrel filled with water, but a sergeant prevented them.

On the same day (11th of July), his wife was assaulted in her bedroom. She was hit with fists and rifle butts by six soldiers, who got hold of her and made deep cuts in her arms, of which the Commission has found traces. They stripped her of her underwear and raped her. Six soldiers held her tight and motionless, while an undetermined number of soldiers raped her. They stood in line while waiting for their turn. Her three children were present at the scene, crying loudly.

Other soldiers got hold of her daughter aged less than 12 and raped her several times.

Shortly afterwards, three soldiers again entered her room

and raped Mrs. Z＿＿ in turn. While one of them raped her, the two others held her motionless. The children were again present.

Shortly after they left, other soldiers came to the house and raped Mrs. Z in the same manner.

These scenes continued from dusk till dawn.[4]

Despite atrocities like these, only some two dozen Europeans were killed. The intent of the mutineers, almost all of whom were soldiers and police, not civilians, was to humiliate Europeans, not kill them.[5] However, one who was killed was the kind, devoted, and effective government officer André Ryckmans, son of the stern, but fair, former governor-general of the Belgian Congo, Pierre Ryckmans. Even though the town of Thysville, near Léopoldville, where Ryckmans was assigned, had been evacuated by its Belgian inhabitants, he insisted on returning there to serve the Congolese. As his car approached the city, he and his companion were shot to death.[6]

When Belgian paratroopers arrived in the Congo, some of them parachuting in, they often shot first and asked questions later, if at all. Their actions not only inflamed many of the rebels in the Force Publique, they convinced many in the country's new government that Belgium intended to take back the Congo by force. This perception was strengthened after the Katangan secession when it became clear that important people in Belgium actively supported Katangan independence, as did most Europeans who lived in that province. With as much as 80 percent of the Congo's export wealth located in Katanga, Belgian corporate interests such as the Union Minière predictably wanted to retain power there. To emphasize this interest, a Belgian colonel was named to command the Katangan military forces. Lieutenant General Janssens seriously considered flying to Katanga himself to organize Katangan resistance, but finally decided against it.[7]

Urged on by Kwame Nkrumah in Ghana, on July 12, Lumumba and Kasavubu cabled the United Nations secretary general, Dag Hammarskjöld, appealing to him for urgent UN military assistance. In light of the more recent history of UN inaction in Africa, response was surprisingly prompt. In 1960, the world took Congo independence seriously. Its turmoil was front-page news. Only three days later, on July 15, several thousand UN troops from Ghana, Guinea, Mali, Morocco, and Tunisia were in Léopoldville. They would soon be joined by others from Liberia, Ireland, and Sweden. On that same day, Lumumba rashly declared that the Congo was at war with Belgium, and the next day he met with Ralph Bunche, then serving as chief of UN operations in the Congo, excitedly demanding that the UN troops then arriving be placed under Congolese command. Bunche refused, later saying that he thought "Lumumba was crazy and that he reacted like a child," an opinion shared by Bunche's chief assistant, Brian Urquhart.[8] On July 19, the U.S. ambassador to the Congo concluded that Lumumba's government had to go. Two days later, CIA director Allen Dulles called Lumumba "a Castro or worse" and concluded that he had been "bought by the Communists."[9]

Later in July, with UN troops then replacing the Belgians, and Congolese troops under better control, Lumumba surprised everyone by flying to the United States in an attempt to obtain U.S. support to end Katanga's secession. He also wanted financial and technical aid as well as the world's recognition that he was the distinguished head of a foreign state. He first went to the United Nations in New York to meet with Dag Hammarskjöld, who promised him support but did not agree that UN troops would invade Katanga. Disappointed, Lumumba flew to Washington, where he was honored by a nineteen-gun salute, then lodged in Blair House, where to the horror of Belgian public opinion, he slept in the same bed recently occupied by King

Baudouin.[10] However, neither President Eisenhower nor Vice President Nixon were in Washington at the time, and if they had been, they probably would not have received him. In fact, Eisenhower had already decided that Lumumba had to be removed from power by any means necessary. Lumumba had to settle for a meeting with Secretary of State Christian Herter, who refused to approve his request for U.S. aid, a loan, or a USAF aircraft complete with a U.S. crew. Lumumba also asked his American hosts to provide him with *"une blanche blonde."* The CIA actually hired a blond, white prostitute and tried to bring her to him, but the hostess at Blair House refused to let her in.[11]

Just before leaving Washington, Lumumba gave an interview to the Soviet Tass news agency in which he did nothing to mend fences with the United States, saying, "The Soviet Union has been the only great power which supported the Congolese people in their struggle from the beginning. I express the deepest gratitude of all our people to the Soviet Union and personally to Nikita Khrushchev for the moral support given by your country when we most needed it against the imperialists and the colonialists."[12] After meeting with Lumumba during his visit to Washington, Douglas Dillon, then undersecretary of state, declared, "He was just not a rational being," adding: "The impression that was left was very bad, that this was an individual whom it was impossible to deal with."[13] After leaving Washington, Lumumba went on to Ottawa, where he was also rebuffed by the Canadians, again leaving empty-handed.

On July 29, under growing UN pressure, Belgium agreed to withdraw its troops from the Congo. Then, during the first week of August 1960, Hammarskjöld announced that UN troops from Ireland, Tunisia, Ethiopia, and India would enter Katanga to take control from the Belgians. Tshombe refused permission for their entry. When some UN troops crossed into Katanga nevertheless, Tshombe declared a state of emergency. Another state of emergency was declared by Albert Kalonji, who was attempting to make southern Kasai, a district rich in diamonds, into another independent state. Led by Mobutu, Congolese military forces, by then named the Armée Nationale Congolaise (ANC), easily subdued Kalonji's rebellion, killing at least a thousand of his Baluba tribespeople. Many were innocent women and children. Lumumba was so horrified by the carnage that he stripped Mobutu of command. Mobutu would not forgive what he saw as an unfair rebuke.

At the same time, fifteen huge Soviet transport planes carrying trucks and complete with crews and interpreters arrived in Léopoldville and Stanleyville after Lumumba had courted Soviet economic aid in reaction to what he saw as Western despotism. The U.S. government was appalled, and the CIA immediately made plans to dispose of Lumumba, giving him the code name Stinky.[14] A CIA agent actually delivered lethal poison to CIA agent Larry Devlin in Leopoldville, but as a devout Roman Catholic, Devlin refused to use it to, as he put it, "commit murder."[15] On September 5, 1960, President Kasavubu took Mobutu's side and attempted to dismiss Lumumba as prime minister. He did so during a radio address but, apparently nervous, did not mention Lumumba by name, and by saying *premier bougmestre* instead of *premier ministre,* he inadvertently fired the mayor of Léopoldville.

Nevertheless, Lumumba understood perfectly well that he was Kasavubu's target, and after forcing his way into the national radio station, he responded with his own radio address in which he declared that he had removed Kasavubu from office, then went on to accuse him of treason.[16] The UN stood behind Kasavubu, but the Congo legislature voted to reinstate Lumumba. During this comedy of errors, Eisenhower expressed grave concern about Soviet intentions in Africa and warned them to withdraw their aircraft. On his orders, the aircraft carrier USS *Wasp,* supported by four other U.S. navy warships, took up a position just outside the mouth of the Congo River.[17] While Lumumba and Kasavubu were at a standoff, Kasavubu demanded that the UN seize Katanga. Hammarskjöld finally agreed and after eleven thousand UN troops entered Katanga in what was infelicitously named Operation Rum Punch, Tshombe agreed to UN demands and a cease-fire was declared.

Still in early September, as the UN announced its cease-fire, Lumumba attempted to seize a government radio station in Leopoldville. He failed and was soon after arrested on a warrant issued by President Kasavubu. Mysteriously, he was released, and protected by bodyguards from his own Batetela people, he drove through Leopoldville shouting, "Victory, victory!" to cheering crowds. He then took refuge in the prime minister's residence, where he was guarded by UN troops under Hammarskjöld's orders. As Lumumba struggled for power and was always near arrest, Colonel Mobutu was so buoyed by U.S. promises of support that he seized power on September 14, 1960. He was not yet thirty years old.

Although Mobutu actually controlled only Leopoldville, with Stanleyville under Lumumba, Kalonji in control of Kasai, and Tshombe still in power in Katanga, Mobutu nevertheless acted as if he were the leader of the entire Congo, immediately giving the Soviets, including all the staff in their embassy, forty-eight hours' notice to leave the Congo. While the Soviets were leaving as ordered, the UN forces continued to gain strength. By September 17, sixteen thousand UN troops drawn from twenty-eight nations were in the Congo.[18] Immediately after taking power, Mobutu attempted to avoid being seen as a dictator by announcing that he was handing all governmental power to a small group of college graduates he called the "general commissioners." Initially, Mobutu listened to their advice, but in reality, they exercised no executive power, and before long Mobutu stopped listening altogether.[19]

On September 14, 1960, fighting again broke out in northern Katanga when hostile Baluba tribesmen attacked a Katangan army patrol. Although UN troops were stationed nearby, they did little to intervene, and the Balubas apparently took revenge for their earlier slaughter by ANC soldiers. At this same time, Albert Kalonji again seized the diamond-mining area of southern Kasai with a large force made up of Balubas, about seven hundred of whom were well armed, and a few European mercenaries. Some of these Balubas took revenge against people in the north of Katanga who had opposed them earlier, taking as hostages several Europeans. In November, thirteen Italian airmen flew a C-119 transport plane into Kindu, in nearby Orientale Province, to deliver two armored cars to Malaysian UN troops who were attempting to maintain peace there. ANC troops beat, then shot them, throwing their dismembered bodies to a cheering crowd that had gathered.[20]

While the eastern Congo was in turmoil, drunken ANC troops, some inexplicably wearing bright pink lipstick, ran riot in Leopoldville, and UN soldiers did nothing to stop them. World opinion turned against the UN, and Hammarskjöld had increasing difficulty raising money to support his troops. Tensions grew everywhere with armed conflict breaking out in many parts of the Congo. Along with two associates, Lumumba was captured, escaped, and recaptured after being beaten so savagely aboard the plane that returned him that its Belgian crew had to close the cockpit door so that they would not be sickened. He was beaten again on live television by Mobutu's ANC soldiers after the plane landed. Flown to Katanga, he and his two associates were executed by firing squad in Elisabethville on January 17, 1961, apparently by the agreement of Mobutu, Kasavubu, Tshombe, and their Belgian advisers. A Belgian officer gave the firing squad, led by Belgian captain Julien Gat and Police Commissioner Frans Verscheure, the order to fire.[21] Lumumba was thirty-eight years old.

CIA operatives, still actively opposed to Lumumba and in support of the U.S.-leaning Mobutu, may have been involved in his death. A CIA officer, who had by then become a dissident, later wrote that another CIA agent had told him that he had driven around Elisabethville for some time with Lumumba's corpse in the trunk of his car trying to decide what to do with it.[22] This version of the event may be in doubt, however, as an authoritative source reports that, based on Belgian documents, two Belgians cut up Lumumba's body into small parts, then threw them into a barrel of sulfuric acid. His skull was ground up, with his bones and teeth scattered in the wilderness.[23] No trace of his body has ever been found.

Tshombe, who later admitted that he could have ordered the savagely beaten Lumumba taken to a hospital but did not do so, concealed his death for three weeks, then announced that Lumumba had escaped his custody only to be captured and killed by local people in an unnamed village. When Lumumba's death became known, Belgian embassies in several African countries were sacked, race riots exploded in the United States, and the Soviet Union accused Hammarskjöld of being the "organizer" of the murder. When Lumumba's wife soon after came to Léopoldville to claim her husband's body in traditional mourning dress with bared breasts, a shaved head, and holding the hand of her two-year-old son, ANC soldiers beat her and the boy and drove them away. The UN gave her refuge, infuriating Kasavubu.[24]

With Lumumba's murder, constitutional government in the Congo came to an end. Katanga, where over fifteen thousand Europeans remained, was the only portion of the country where any semblance of order prevailed. Fighting erupted across much of the eastern Congo in 1961 and 1962. By December 1962, the situation in Katanga became even more explosive as the Europeans there joined with Tshombe in believing that the time had come to use force to drive the UN troops away from Katanga's borders and insure its independence. At that time the UN had about twelve thousand men. Of these, the French-speaking, friendly Tunisians were popular with the Congolese people, but the Irish were not, and the Ethiopians were widely feared. The Indians and Gurkhas were respected but not liked.[25] Athough poorly trained and lacking discipline, Tshombe's forces outnumbered the UN troops, and they were led by several hundred white mercenaries, including some twenty pilots who flew military aircraft.

On December 26, 1962, Tshombe's men opened fire, killing an Ethiopian soldier and wounding several others. The next day, Tshombe cut off Elisabethville's water and power, while his troops fired mortars on UN positions. Two days later, UN air strikes led by Swedish pilots destroyed Tshombe's air force except for one plane, which made an ineffectual attack before being destroyed. UN ground forces led by tough Indian troops easily defeated the poorly led and hopelessly disorganized men of Tshombe's so-called National Congolese Army, driving deep into Katanga. The UN forces took losses, but the Katangan forces crumbled, and on January 14, 1963, Tshombe gave in, ending the secession and fleeing for his life to Spain.

The little more than two weeks of combat caused many Katangan casualties. Bombs and shells often fell indiscriminately, and fire from automatic weapons killed innocent civilians. An eyewitness described some of the UN troops, including the Indians and the Gurkhas, as "needlessly brutal."[26] Ethiopian troops sometimes executed prisoners, including white mercenaries, and killed three Red Cross workers.[27] UN casualties were not heavy. The Indian Brigade took the brunt of the combat, but had only four officers killed with two others wounded, while thirty-one in other ranks were killed and forty-two wounded.[28] But thousands of Katangan soldiers and civilians, many of them Europeans, died.

Even before the open combat of late December 1962 and early January 1963, the sporadic fighting that had flared up in various parts of Katanga had taken such a heavy toll that, by the end of 1962, forty-six Belgian doctors in Elisabethville joined together to express their anger over what they called "UN atrocities" in Katanga. They listed the names of European civilians who had been killed, raped, or taken hostage. They also described many thefts from Europeans' houses and wrote that some hospital orderlies from the Red Cross had been arrested and murdered. Others had been killed when their ambulances were fired on. Three hospitals were bombed, perhaps unintentionally but with deadly results. And close to forty thousand Balubas were held in UN detention camps under such appalling conditions that perhaps three thousand died. To reinforce their vivid accusations, the doctors included scores of photographs of mutilated bodies—black and white—and devastated hospital buildings.[29]

Mobutu's control over the Congo was tenuous at this time and would remain so until late in the 1960s, but he secured his rule in 1965 by placing Kasavubu under house arrest. He gradually increased his power, becoming the country's unchallengeable leader by 1970 and remaining in control of the country until 1997. Named after a famous warrior uncle of the small Ngbandi tribal group near the Congo's northwest border, Joseph-Désiré Mobutu was born October 14, 1930, to Marie Madeleine Yemo, who, only two months earlier, had married Albéric Gbemani, a cook who worked for a Belgian judge. Mama Yemo, as she would become known, had previously given birth to four other sons, the first two out of wedlock, the second a pair of twins fathered by a village chief whom she did marry. These twins died in infancy. Mobutu's father died when Mobutu was eight, and his mother had to rely on relatives to support him and her other boys.[30] Fortunately, the wife of the Belgian judge for whom his father cooked had taken the boy under her wing, teaching him to read, write, and speak fluent French while taking him every-where with her, tenderly holding his hand. Following the death of his father, Mobutu was taken away from her to live with an uncle in Colquilhatville. It was a painful separation for the boy, who for some time felt lost without his surrogate Belgian mother.

Life in Colquilhatville was hard, with food and clothing always scarce, but Mobutu attended Catholic mission schools taught by Flemish-speaking white priests. A tall, athletic boy, known to his friends as Jeff, Mobutu excelled at sports and was also a top stu-dent, but a troublesome one who was continually unruly. He not only made trouble for other students with endless pranks, but when one of the Flemish-speaking Belgian priests would make a mistake in their rudimentary, accented French, Mobutu would leap to his feet to point it out, sending the class into a fit of laughter. This practice did not endear him to the priests. At eigh-teen, Mobutu left school without permission to go to Léopold-ville, where he had a sexual escapade with a young woman for several weeks. Soon after he returned, he was accused of stealing books from the school's library to sell them. He was not only expelled, but as was common at that time, in lieu of a prison sentence he was ordered to serve a seven-year term in the Force Publique.[31]

In the Force, Mobutu came to appreciate discipline, and in the stern but compassionate figure of Sergeant Joseph Bobozo he found the surrogate father he had longed for. Thanks to his fluent French, he was soon given a desk job that allowed him the time and opportunity to read ravenously. European newspapers were available, subscribed to by Belgian officers, and all manner of books as well. Later in life, Mobutu remembered poring over the works of three men who he said influenced him most: Win-ston Churchill, Charles de Gaulle, and Niccolò Machiavelli.[32] He also advanced rapidly in rank, becoming a sergeant major, the highest rank an African Congolese could then hold.

He took a course in accountancy, and although he passed it, his incredibly profligate spending in later life betrayed no indication that he remembered anything about accounting or economics. He also studied journalism, and despite his poverty, he married Marie Antoinette, who was all of fourteen years old. Although she would remain loyal to him, she was never meek or subservient. She spoke her mind, often loudly. However, she did not object when Mobutu expressed his hostility to the Catholic Church by refusing to marry her in a Catholic ceremony.[33] When his term of duty in the military ended, he continued to study journalism both in the Congo, and in 1958, in Brussels. While there, he met some young Congolese *évolués* who were speaking out and demonstrating for their rights and for the independence of the Congo. One of those who became a personal friend was Patrice Lumumba, whom he served as a trusted aide, scheduling his activities and sometimes even sitting in for him during political meetings. He also met and was befriended by Larry Devlin, the CIA agent who knew that Mobutu was pro-Western. Mobutu actually worked for Belgian intelligence as an informer, and one of the *évolués* he betrayed was Lumumba.[34] Belgian intelligence not only paid Mobutu, it passed his reports on to Devlin.[35] Apparently, they did not pay him much, as in 1959 he said that he had only $6 to his name. When a Belgian warned Lumumba about Mobutu's work as an informer, he shrugged it off saying that Mobutu was engaged in innocent activity motivated solely by his urgent need for income.[36]

As the years passed and Mobutu's power, fame, and wealth grew, no one doubted his keen intelligence and astonishing memory, but he also had great courage. The CIA's Léopoldville station chief, Larry Devlin, who was frequently by Mobutu's side, often saw him take deadly risks as, for example, when he first calmed, then personally disarmed, mutinous police in 1960, even though they shouted at him not to come any closer or they would shoot. Devlin once also personally disarmed an assassin just as he was about to shoot Mobutu. Mobutu faced four other assassination attempts in that same week, and although unruffled by his near-death experiences, he did send Marie Antoinette and their children to Belgium as a precaution. She dropped off their children in Brussels, but returned to Mobutu within twenty-four hours, saying, "If they kill him, they have to kill me."[37] Mobutu did not have a monopoly on bravery in his family.

The Congo was calm enough in mid-1963 for Mobutu to come to the United States for a brief stint of paratroop training, after which he received a U.S. DC-3 complete with an American crew for his personal use. Needless to say, the crew filed reports with the CIA on his activities. Except for this brief interlude, the Congo was engulfed in almost perpetual warfare from the mutinies of July 1960 until the end of 1967. Some conflicts were the result of secessions by various regions, others from mutinies of the armed forces, still others from the perceived threat of take-overs by foreign powers. The fighting engaged various government troops, UN soldiers, European mercenaries, Belgian paratroopers, U.S. transport planes, and even CIA agents.

Larry Devlin, as mentioned earlier, not only refused to poison Lumumba, he displayed his own courage on several occasions. So did many mercenaries. Had it not been for courageous mercenaries like South African Mike Hoare, who fought for Mobutu's imperiled government, its stability might never have been achieved. Mobutu was in combat himself against the rebel Simbas (Swahili for "lions"). He displayed great personal courage, sometimes finding himself compelled to take absurd risks to inspire his timid ANC troops to advance.[38] Some of the most feared Simbas were Pygmies armed with poisoned arrows.[39]

Many of these battles made worldwide headlines. In late 1964, mercenaries and Simbas representing Christophe Gibenye, Pierre Mulele, and Gaston Soumialot's newly proclaimed People's Republic of the Congo, centered in Stanleyville, took 250 European hostages, including women, children, and several American consular officials and CIA agents. The Simbas, including scores of lower-ranking, little-educated officers, were illiterate, impoverished, and rebellious men mostly from the warlike and apparently still cannibalistic Batetela people. Some Simbas boasted that they had eaten a Belgian officer sent to scout their advance. Fellow Batetela Patrice Lumumba was honored by them as a fallen god. They were led by a "general" named Nicolas Olenga, who was virtually illiterate and had been in prison for theft. Olenga ordered all beer parlors to remain open for twenty-four hours, then appointed a virtual madman, Alphonse Kinghis, as his provincial president for Stanleyville. Kinghis had earlier spent two years in prison for attempting to crucify an enemy. While in power in Stanleyville, he often beat European hostages and killed so many people who refused his extortionist demands for money that Olenga eventually jailed him.[40]

Like many other tribal peoples throughout the history of Africa's resistance to colonial power, the Simbas had been convinced by their religious leaders that Europeans' bullets would turn to water against them due to the chants of their sorcerer leaders and their own protective amulets—feathers, bits of leopard and monkey skin, and a small piece of fur worn on top of the head to ward off attacks from the air. They were led into battle by a half dozen or more bare-chested sorcerers waving palm branches back and forth and chanting, "Power, power." Soldiers and sorcerers alike all smoked marijuana heavily before going into battle.

The thousands of Simba soldiers were mostly dressed in captured ANC camouflage combat uniforms made in Belgium and armed with modern weapons, many of them of Chinese and Soviet manufacture. In addition to the automatic rifles, pistols, hand grenades, and bayonets that each Simba soldier carried, they had many machine guns, bazookas, rocket launchers, and even some antitank artillery, most of this weaponry supplied by Egypt and Sudan. Like the sorcerers who led them into combat, many fought bare-chested, although their officers wore various versions of Belgian army uniforms, and General Olenga wore a Belgian officer's uniform complete with a field marshal's dress sword in a scabbard.

In a few weeks, they had seized all of the northeast Congo, an area almost as large as France. This takeover was so rapid that many Europeans, about two thousand in Stanleyville alone, did not have time to flee their homes and businesses. Others who could have escaped chose not to because the Simbas did not seem to be anti-European, and for the Europeans to have left would have meant the loss of all they owned. And for some months, the Simba leaders kept businesses open, published newspapers, saw to it that utilities functioned, and even managed to govern fairly. Simba soldiers who stole or raped were tried and jailed or executed.[41] However, while Europeans were being treated reasonably well, the Simbas were systematically executing Congolese clerks, teachers, nurses, postmen, foremen, and any other *évolués,* all of whom they looked upon as dangerous enemies.[42]

As long as their only opposition was the dispirited and disorganized ANC, the Simbas had little difficulty holding the many towns, cities, and native villages they had taken, but with Belgian and U.S. support, Moise Tshombe, whom Mobutu had in desperation named the new prime minister, was able to recruit several hundred white mercenaries from South Africa, Rhodesia, and all over Europe, under the tough command of Mike Hoare, a longtime mercenary soldier and former British army officer. Well-equipped with armored cars and ammunition, and with a sense of urgency driven by a widespread lust for looting among these young soldiers for hire, several columns of mercenaries drove into Simba territory. Followed by murderous if not often valiant ANC troops, they defeated the Simbas in battle after battle, causing Simba leaders to take European hostages, whom they threatened to kill if the mercenary advance continued. Among those taken hostage in Stanleyville were the American and Belgian consuls and four CIA men. Alternately pampered in a posh, air-conditioned hotel and an airport guesthouse, then starved and beaten in prison, for several months these men were threatened with death almost daily. They were also made to chew on American flags, were verbally abused, told that they would be killed and eaten, then were beaten, sometimes badly.[43]

As air strikes increased in intensity, some of them by U.S. crews clandestinely flying B-26s, the Simbas searched everywhere for radios that might have been used to direct "American" planes against them. One European man was killed because he wore a hearing aid, another because he nervously tapped a gold tooth.[44] When more and more Europeans were taken hostage and the Simba leaders sent cables and radio messages threatening to kill them all because "thousands" of American troops had attacked the Simba forces and the Belgians had dropped an "atomic bomb" that was said to have killed one hundred thousand people in a town called Beni, Belgian and American authorities reluctantly agreed that military intervention had become unavoidable.

American crews flew C-130s to pick up 545 red-beret-wearing Belgian paracommandos and dropped them on Stanleyville's airport at 6 A.M. on November 24, 1964, in what was dubbed Operation Dragon Rouge. Simbas at the airport opened fire while others drove more than two hundred European hostages into the streets as human shields. When the paratroopers advanced in a skirmish line, the rebels opened fire on the hostages, killing twenty-seven of them, including two young girls and five older women, while wounding another forty before they fled in panic and the other hostages were freed unhurt. In all, two thousand Europeans were safely evacuated. One who was killed was the missionary doctor Paul Carlson, who was riddled with fifty bullets from a submachine gun fired at point-blank range. Another was Phyllis Rine, a nurse.[45]

The next day, the same scenario was played out in a town 225 miles to the north of Stanleyville. There, twenty-two of three hundred and seventy-five European hostages were killed. The first to be killed was an American missionary, Joseph Tucker, who was tortured by gleeful Simbas for forty-five minutes before a stake was driven through his head.[46] The other Europeans were saved by the same paracommandos that had fought earlier in Stanleyville.[47] As the Belgians drove to the north, they liberated town after town, freeing thousands of Indians and Europeans, but over three hundred Europeans, eight of them Americans, were executed by the fleeing Simbas. General Olenga was killed by Hoare's mercenaries, while the civilian leaders of the rebellion fled. Throughout the entire campaign, although the Simbas often fought hard, they fired wildly, killing only two of the Belgian paratroopers and wounding six others.[48]

Captured documents left behind in Stanleyville when the Simbas fled described plans for a Marxist-Leninist political state for all of the Congo. They were printed in Beijing, where one of the Simbas' leaders, Pierre Mulele, had been trained in guerrilla warfare. Cuba's Ernesto "Che" Guevara, who had trained some of the Simbas in the eastern Congo, spoke in the UN accusing the United States and Belgium of "bloodthirsty butchery" in the Congo, calling for "free men" to avenge their crimes. He did not mention the Simbas' murder of the white hostages or their slaughter of twenty-eight Catholic missionaries including nuns.[49] Guevara did back his words with action, however, returning to the Congo early in 1965 with two hundred Cuban veterans of Castro's successful revolution. The Cubans fought well but soon left in disgust because, according to Guevara, the Simbas lacked the will to fight.[50] Three Simba units led by white mercenaries who had originally fought for Tshombe in Katanga continued the rebellion in the eastern Congo after Guevara and his men left, but eventually they were forced to take asylum in Rwanda.

On November 25, 1965, with the personal encouragement of Larry Devlin and the support of the CIA and U.S. government, Mobutu again seized power, and Tshombe again fled to Spain, where he received political asylum. Mobutu had him tried in absentia and he was found guilty of treason and sentenced to death. Soon after, a European mercenary hijacked a Spanish airliner in which Tshombe was a passenger, landing it in Algeria. While Algerian officials pondered Mobutu's demands that Tshombe be returned to the Congo, he died of a heart attack. His body lay in state in his home in Belgium.

As he had said in 1960, Mobutu insisted in 1965 that his actions in taking all political power into his own hands were a necessary military solution to the country's political chaos. When a reporter addressed a question to him as "Mr. President," Mobutu smiled and said, "Please continue to address me as General Mobutu. I intend to remain in the army."[51] Devlin was the first U.S. official to meet with the new president, and the two men worked together to assure U.S. recognition of his government, after taking care that some African countries would do so before the U.S. took action. Devlin also made certain that the substantial funds the CIA had given Mobutu since the early 1960s would continue. The raspy-voiced Mobutu was not yet the dramatic speaker he would later become, but on December 17, 1965, he told a huge, cheering audience in Léopoldville's biggest soccer stadium—the same one so often used by Lumumba and Kasavubu—that because it had taken five years for the Congo's "politicians" to drive the country to ruin, he would need five years in office to lead it to prosperity. The crowd roared its approval.

Devlin had nothing but praise for Mobutu as a young man. Acknowledging that he later became an absolute tyrant unrestrained by law or constitution, Devlin said, "But he was so different at the start. I can remember him as a dynamic, idealistic young man who was determined to have an independent state in the Congo and really seemed to believe in all the things Africa's leaders then stood for."[52] Many others noted his truly incredible memory, his charisma, and his sardonic humor. But not everyone cheered Mobutu's presidency. Although wars of secession had been controlled by late in the 1960s, rebel leaders still plotted coups. Mobutu dealt with them brutally. When some men were accused of plotting a coup against him, he paraded them, in the same sports stadium he had used earlier, before a large crowd chosen from his staunch supporters. As the crowd roared its loud support, each one was hanged. And when the thirty-six-year-old Pierre Mulele, one of the Simba leaders who had challenged Mobutu's rule in the east, was lured out of exile in Brazzaville by a false promise of amnesty and brought back to Léopoldville on Mobutu's luxurious yacht, men of Mobutu's private guard gouged his eyes out of their sockets and tore his genitals off before killing him. Other rebels and political opponents met similarly violent deaths. Even Europeans could be targeted. In the late 1970s, when an official of Bretton Woods offended him, Mobutu sent an army unit to his home in a quiet residential area of Kinshasa, where they beat him, then raped his wife and daughters. Neighbors called the police, but there was no response.[53]

However, Mobutu usually preferred co-optation of his opponents rather than violence against them. Potentially dangerous members of his government were dismissed, then arrested, tried by a military court loyal to Mobutu, and found guilty. After a few unpleasant months in prison, Mobutu would then pardon the official and welcome him back into the government. More dangerous opponents were "rusticated"—exiled to their home village for five years or more. *Washington Post* journalist Blaine Harden noted that between 1965 and 1975, only 41 of 212 senior gov-

ernment officials held high office for five years or more.[54] He
also observed that except for members of Mobutu's family, only
eighty people in all of Zaire seemed to be important. "At any
one time, twenty of them are ministers, twenty of them are exiles,
twenty are in jail, and twenty are ambassadors. Every three
months, the music stops and Mobutu forces everyone to change
chairs."[55]

The most remarkable example of this pattern is Nguz a Karl-i-
Bond. He served as Zaire's foreign minister in the early 1970s
before leaving that post to lead the country's only legal political
party. However, in 1977, Mobutu accused him of high treason
and had him sentenced to death, threatening to shoot Nguz himself. Instead of execution, Nguz was jailed and tortured, including electrical shocks to his testicles. One year later he was freed
from prison, and only a year after that, Mobutu named him
prime minister. After two years in that office, he fled to Belgium,
where he wrote a book attacking state corruption under Mobutu's rule. He then went before a congressional subcommittee
in Washington to describe Mobutu's years of theft from public
funds. Amazingly, Mobutu invited him back to Zaire, where he
was not only well treated, but in 1986 was appointed as Zaire's
ambassador to the United States. Two years later, he returned to
Zaire as foreign minister, and in 1991, with the country in turmoil, Mobutu made him prime minister for a second time.[56]

In 1971, before any of this bizarre history took place, Mobutu
gave himself a new name: Mobutu Sese Seko Kuku Ngbendu Wa
Za Banga, "the all-powerful warrior who goes from conquest to
conquest, leaving fire in his wake." He also promoted himself to
field marshal and adopted either a marshal's uniform complete
with decorations for valor, or a dark, tight-fitting Mao-style tunic
known as an *abacost* (from *à bas le costume*)—meaning "down with
the business suit." Affluent Congolese men rushed to buy an *abacost*, many of them choosing dark blue wool tunics despite the

heat.[57] Mobutu's head was invariably topped by a leopard-skin toque made in Paris, and his throat was swathed in a silk scarf. He always wore heavy, black-framed glasses and carried an elegantly carved ebony walking stick. He also referred to himself— and expected the population to follow suit—as "the Founder," "Guide of the Revolution," "Helmsman," "Mulopwe" (emperor or demigod), and "the Messiah." He also liked to be known as "the leopard" and had the face of a snarling leopard printed on banknotes, ashtrays, and his official letterhead. Referring to the period of 1960 to 1965 as one of "chaos, disorder, negligence, and incompetence," he did not hesitate to use force to bring about social order. For the Congolese people, he would become yet another Bula Matari.

His dictatorial rule was maintained by an electoral victory in 1970 thanks to armed poll watchers who observed how people voted, assuring him over 99 percent of the vote. He would later run for reelection unopposed. In that same year, King Baudouin paid a return visit to the Congo, his first since his painful independence day speech. Accompanied by a host of foreign journalists, Baudouin saw nothing but euphoric crowds and met only happy people. The reporters wrote rapturously about Mobutu and his country.[58] He continued to enjoy the support of the U.S. government, including large financial grants. His fame grew in 1974 when he hosted the heavyweight boxing championship bout between George Foreman and Muhammad Ali in Kinshasa. Television coverage of the fight included many shots of Mobutu. The "rumble in the jungle" attracted a huge American television audience, most of whom learned something about Mobutu and Zaire for the first time.

He was not universally cherished, however, as several attempted coups were discovered just in time to save him. In June 1975, after Mobutu's visits to China and North Korea led him to adopt a new program of Mobutuism that re-created some aspects of Maoism, the CIA was said to have been involved in an attempt on his life.[59] This alleged coup came at a time when congressional criticism was mounting over the CIA's increasingly obvious and controversial role in flying military supplies through Zaire to aid Holden Roberto's troops—he had married Mobutu's sister-in-law—and his South African allies for the control of Angola. Some believe the coup was "staged" to deflect criticism away from Mobutu and onto the CIA.[60] In 1978, however, sixty-seven army officers, made a serious coup attempt, nineteen of whom were executed. No generals were involved thanks to Mobutu's close financial ties to officers of that rank. After another coup in 1983, Mobutu's private armies cracked down even harder to prevent the organization of future coups.

By the early 1970s, Mobutu had learned that money was even more effective than violence in controlling potential opponents or rivals. Mobutu maintained his large sunglass-wearing private army called the Division Spéciale Présidentielle (DSP), and his equally feared Service National d'Intelligence et de Protection (SNIP), led by a man known as the Terminator, and their search for dissidents or potential enemies was as ceaseless as it could be brutal. However, as vast sums of money came to Mobutu from the bribes given him by large foreign corporations, including many in the United States, and as the percentage he took from the profits of all economic ventures in the country rose rapidly, he soon became wealthy enough to use money as his weapon of choice. He would make corruption the keystone of his administration, and untold thousands eagerly joined in.

State employees supplemented their inadequate and irregular salaries by postal and judicial fraud, false billing, extortion, embezzlement, outright theft, padding payrolls with false names, forgeries, import, export, and excise tax fraud, illegal taxation, and taking second or third jobs. Bribery was universal. No one could arrive at or leave from an international airport without paying a host of bribes, and military barricades set up on roads around the country extorted money from every traveler able to pay. Admission to a secondary school or university was based on bribery, not outstanding grades. Even university students joined in the corruption saying, "If there's anarchy, profit from it."[61]

Mobutu's self-enrichment program relied on direct bribes from foreign governments and security agencies, payments by investors, diversion of Zairean government funds, embezzlement of export earnings, and the massive diversion of foreign loans and aid. Estimates of the amount of money Mobutu stole from the Congo vary widely. The lowest estimates are 4–5 billion U.S. dollars, with some as high as $15 billion. He built and lavishly furnished over a dozen grand palaces in the Congo, led in grandeur by the one at Gbadolite, deep in the tropical forest of the northeastern Congo near his birthplace. It boasted a fifteen-thousand-bottle wine cellar. One of his favorites was a replica of a Chinese pagoda. His luxury cruiser on the Congo River was furnished with oyster-shaped settees in pink silk. He also had many properties in Europe on the French Riviera, in Brussels, Switzerland, Paris, and Madrid, not to mention Cape Town, Marrakech, Dakar and Abidjan. In Portugal, he had a twelve-bedroom estate with a fourteen-thousand-bottle wine cellar.

When Mobutu became president, the village of Gbadolite was a rustic backwater of seventeen hundred people. He gave it the country's best supply of water and electricity, not to mention television stations, telephones, and medical services. As the population rose to thirty-seven thousand, he also built a one-hundred-room hotel, luxury guesthouses, and plantations for palm oil, coffee, coconuts, oranges, and grapefruit, along with ranches for cattle and the five thousand sheep he ordered flown in from Venezuela on thirty-two flights of his government-owned DC-8. There was also an airport with daily flights to Kinshasa that could also accommodate jets landing from Europe.[62]

The year 1971 not only saw Gbadolite rise from rural obscurity to kingly splendor, it marked the start of "Zaireanization" and "Mobutuism." Both the country and river were renamed Zaire, not Congo. Foreign-born merchants, most of them Portuguese, Greek, and Pakistani, whose home countries had little leverage with Mobutu, were forced to leave the country, their businesses worth over $1 billion given to Mobutu's close military and civilian followers. Mobutu personally took possession of fourteen plantations that employed twenty-five thousand people, making him the third-largest employer in the country.[63] Most of these new owners had no experience in business, and within a few months, massive layoffs were reported, shortages of basic commodities were widespread, and many of the new owners simply liquidated their assets, then locked their doors. The economy went into a sharp decline, and with it came social unrest. The Zairean Highway Authority became known as the Department of Holes, and Air Zaire was referred to as Air Peut-Être—"Air Perhaps."

At the same time, Mobutu insisted that television, radio, and newspapers in every way imaginable advocate pride in Zaire, its autonomy from all other countries, and the elimination of all foreign influences. People with Christian baptismal names had to replace them with Zairean ones, and colonial place names were changed. Leopoldville became Kinshasa, Stanleyville became Kisangani, and Elisabethville became Lubumbashi. Reminiscent of the French Revolution, the terms of address *madame* and *monsieur* were changed to *citoyenne* and *citoyen*. Roads and squares with Belgian names were renamed after key events in the struggle for independence. A new national flag and anthem were created, and statues of Stanley, Leopold II, and King Baudouin were toppled. Mobutu insisted that he be known by one of his honorific titles such as The Guide or Messiah, and his photograph appeared everywhere, including on stamps and on the new currency, the zaire, which replaced the franc. His picture was even found on cloth that was sold for making men's shirts and women's dresses. He also changed the name of scenic Lake Albert to Lake Mobutu. And at the start of every state-television newscast, Mobutu was shown descending from the clouds like a god.[64]

The Roman Catholic Church, long dominant in the country, also came under attack. Mobutu had resented the Church even before his expulsion from mission school, and in 1971 he nationalized the Catholic Lovanium University outside Kinshasa and attempted to implant his newly formed secular Youth of the Popular Revolutionary Movement (JMPR) in Catholic seminaries, an audacity the church resisted with all its will. The following year, after all Zaireans were ordered to replace their baptismal names with African ones, Cardinal Malula protested and told his bishops to ignore the order. In response, Mobutu forced Malula into exile for three months and seized his residence and converted it into JMPR headquarters. A year later, Mobutu announced that Christmas would no longer be a state holiday, banned all religious instruction in Zairean schools, and ordered all crucifixes and pictures of the pope removed from schools, hospitals, and public buildings. If these bans were not confrontational enough, Mobutu ordered that photographs of him would replace those of the pope and the banned crucifixes.[65]

As the state took over the nation's schools, courses on Mobutuism replaced religious instruction. Students in formerly Catholic schools were led by JMPR members in chanting, "Mobutu here, Mobutu there, Mobutu everywhere." The Church fought back with pastoral letters by every bishop in Zaire denouncing the state corruption that was increasingly out of control as falling copper prices created near economic collapse and state officials brazenly stole millions from public funds. Prior to 1974, the Zairean economy had grown 7 percent every year. In 1974, it fell and continued to fall every year thereafter.[66] To make matters even worse for Mobutu, state officials proved so inept at managing schools that the educational system collapsed as well. Teachers were paid so little that they were known as two-shirts because that was all the clothing they could afford. In reaction, teachers began to demand gifts from their boy students and sexual favors from the girls.[67] Less than half of Zaire's students went as far as the fourth grade. In 1976, the educational system was in such dire straits that Mobutu was forced to allow the Church to resume its control of formerly Catholic schools, and religion was once again taught.[68] Protestant churches, especially the Church of Christ, had long supported Mobutu, and although their schools and hospitals did not receive state subsidies as their Catholic counterparts did, they were not subject to the same government control and harassment that the Catholic institutions suffered.

The medical system was near collapse as well. Sanitation was poor everywhere, garbage went uncollected, and most children were badly undernourished. As a result, infectious and parasitic diseases accounted for 50 percent of all deaths. The comparable figure for the United States at that time was 1.5 percent. AIDS, or the "syndrome invented to discourage sex," as it was known in Zaire, was taking on epidemic proportions, and because health-care professionals were so poorly paid by the state, doctors and nurses demanded a personal fee be paid to them by a patient's family before they would provide any care.[69] Some African governments are receiving Western assistance in their fight against HIV/AIDS, but infected Congolese still receive no help and the death toll is appalling.

In early 1977, with Zaire's economy and health and educational systems in such a troubled state, two thousand men from Angola led by Nathanael Mbumba, a former Katangan police officer, invaded Katanga, which had been renamed Shaba by Mobutu, a man he was determined to overthrow. At that time, twenty-one thousand Cuban troops were in Angola, and some of them apparently marched with Mbumba, although he denied it. Mobutu, who by then had a pilot's license, startled visiting European journalists who had no idea that he was a pilot by flying them over the battle zone. Despite Mobutu's scrutiny, his ANC forces fell back, and more Congolese flocked to Mbumba's cause. As Mobutu's poorly led and motivated men faced defeat, France stepped in, sending warplanes and fifteen hundred elite Moroccan infantrymen, who quickly turned the tide. Mbumba withdrew to Angola, but early in 1978, he returned with twice as many men. This time, both France and Belgium sent troops, who were flown to the combat zone around the copper-mining center of Kolwezi, northeast of Elisabethville (now Lubumbashi). The European troops drove Mbumba's men out of the city. Belgian troops reported that they rescued 2,155 Europeans in Kolwezi, but the Red Cross reported that 96 European civilians had been killed with 49 more missing. Mobutu led European journalists through the battered city, showing them the bodies of 32 Europeans, including women and children he said had been shot by the rebels.[70]

At the same time that Mobutu was spending untold millions, probably billions, of dollars on himself and his family, he was lavishly paying off his friends, associates, and administrators, along with any prominent businessmen or politicians who might otherwise become threats to his rule. His motto was "Keep friends close but enemies closer still."[71] He surrounded himself with yes-men who constantly told him what a great man he was and routinely received cash bounties in return. He also paid six hundred thousand civil servants to do work that the World Bank estimated could easily have been done by fifty thousand. He also overpaid the many generals and colonels in his army while he badly underpaid the soldiers, who could not pose a threat to him without the leadership of senior officers. Many ANC soldiers were forced to steal from civilians at gunpoint in order to eat. All of Mobutu's payoffs were in cash. He never used a checkbook or a credit card. His assistants always kept huge supplies of dollars ready for his disbursement or personal use. Not surprisingly, a good many of these dollars found their way into his assistants' pockets.

His wife, Marie Antoinette, held off his most demanding kinsmen, but after her death in 1977, these people were a constant plague on his riches. Mobutu soon married his beautiful mistress, Bobi Landawa, then took her identical twin as his mistress. These two women helped him spend his riches in grand style, rapidly growing quite plump.[72] Mobutu not only had no sense of economics, he had no idea what anything actually cost. He could not even guess the price of ordinary commodities or the Mercedes-Benz and Peugeot cars he gave away by the thousands. He also paid little heed to sexual propriety, regularly having sexual relations with the wives of his many subordinates.[73] In addition to women, he loved expensive ceremonies. When his pretty daughter, Yaki, married Belgian Pierre Janssen—who described her as "fragile as a tropical flower"—the wedding ceremony was stupefyingly lavish. She appeared in a $70,000 wedding gown, and the jewels she wore that Mobutu had given her were worth an estimated $3 million. Guests drank over a thousand bottles of *grands cru* wines, there was a huge fireworks display, three orchestras played, and a huge Parisian wedding cake flown in that day at a cost of $65,000 was devoured before it could melt. The couple then honeymooned at a royal Thai beach resort, followed by a stay in a villa in Brussels. At the wedding, Mobutu handed Janssen an envelope containing $300,000.[74]

Janssen later wrote a book about becoming a member of the family in which he described Mobutu's total lack of concern for the cost of anything and the complete lack of accountability for the flow of money into or out of his hands.[75] He also graphically described Mobutu's lifestyle. The Messiah arose at six-thirty and by seven was in the hands of a team of Chinese masseurs. After reading international newspapers, he ate a lavish breakfast on the terrace, then by nine would be in his study sipping the first of his several daily bottles of Laurent-Perrier pink champagne. Lunch was usually fried mussels flown in from Belgium, washed down by a 1930 *grand cru* wine, chosen to commemorate the year of his birth. The afternoon might witness the arrival of a barber from New York, a hairdresser from Paris, a couturier or a florist, all flown in from overseas. Mobutu loved to listen to Gregorian chants, but he might also attend what Janssen called a "voodoo session" or a secret meeting with Freemasons. Painfully superstitious, he regularly consulted a marabout from Senegal.[76] Dinner was an elaborate social affair with family members and sycophantic guests, all of whom, Janssen said, were obviously there with their hands out. Mobutu responded with $100 bills that he routinely kept stuffed in his desk drawer. Janssen said, "I looked into his eyes and I felt sorry for him."[77]

As recently as 1987, with the Cold War still alive, the United States continued to provide military support to Mobutu. Under pressure from Congress, the State Department admitted that for several years the United States had carried out secret joint military exercises with Zairean troops in Shaba, at Kamina Air Base. The CIA also flew military equipment into Zaire to arm Angolan rebel FNLA forces under Holden Roberto, which were opposed to that country's Communist regime.[78] But by 1990, the Cold War had ended and so had U.S. support for Mobutu. By 1990, Zaire was bankrupt, unable to pay its huge foreign debts, and its people were destitute. Its roads were impassable most of the time, and its state-owned river transport system had collapsed, replaced by highly unreliable private entrepreneurs. Its national airline rarely operated. Major cities were in collapse, too. Kisangani seldom had electricity, and the city of Kikwit, once considered the most modern and elegant in all of Zaire, was without both electricity and running water. Banks were closed, Zaire's currency was worthless, and no taxes could be collected. Across most of Zaire, the cost of food was so great that most people ate only one meal a day, and children were even more seriously malnourished than in earlier times.[79] Overseas, several Zairean diplomatic missions had their telephone and electrical services cut off for nonpayment of bills, and in 1992 in Denmark, the Zairean ambassador was found sleeping under a railroad trestle. He had been evicted by his landlord for nonpayment of rent.[80]

Throughout all of this, Mobutu and his huge entourage continued not only to enrich themselves but to take lavish state visits abroad in his private jumbo jet. In June 1989, one year before the dissolution of the Soviet Union and the end of Cold War, his cronies accompanied him as he visited President George Bush, whom he had known earlier in his role as director of the CIA. Bush happily greeted Mobutu with these words: "Zaire is among America's oldest friends—and its president—President Mobutu— one of our most valued friends. . . . And so I was honored to invite President Mobutu to be the first African head of state to come to the United States during my presidency."[81] Bush also praised Mobutu for brokering an Angolan peace settlement at Gbadolite attended by eighteen African heads of state. Soon after Bush's accolades, the settlement collapsed.

By 1990, Mobutu was forced to acknowledge the calamitous social conditions in Zaire as well as the impact on his country that the end of the Cold War would clearly have. Various members of the U.S. Congress visited Zaire to urge Mobutu to make fundamental changes, pointing out that if he did not, U.S. support for his government could not possibly continue. The *New York Times* published an editorial on April 21, 1990, praising these men, explaining, "The end of the Cold War removes any possible justification for this taxpayer subsidy to a repellent dictator." Only

three days later, Mobutu responded, announcing that he was converting Zaire into a three-party state and would soon name a
transitional government, although he would retain control over
defense, foreign affairs, and "territorial security." Two weeks later,
Mobutu's troops fired on students at the University of Lubumbashi who had apparently taunted students from Mobutu's tribe,
the Ngbandi. Mobutu admitted that one death occurred, but human rights groups reported as many as forty.[82] Soon after this
attack took place, Mobutu vanished from public view, moving
from one of his palaces to another without warning and spending
so much time on his yacht that the people of Kinshasa nick-
named him Noah.[83]

In September 1991, Kinshasa experienced its worst violence
since 1960 when Zaire's seldom-paid army rioted, looting stores
in the city's center for two days before they began to strip private
homes in the suburbs. Over a hundred Congolese were killed
with fifteen hundred wounded. Mobutu ended the violence by
announcing that not only the troops but underpaid civil servants
would receive a 2,000 percent pay raise. Needless to say, few ever
saw any of this money. While foreign residents fled, most of them
to Brazzaville, France and Belgium flew in over a thousand troops
to protect them. The U.S. State Department reported that it had
evacuated 830 Americans and that several hundred more had
escaped on their own.[84] Senator Paul Simon, chairman of the
Senate Africa Subcommittee, urged Bush to persuade Mobutu to
leave Zaire. Bush did nothing of the kind, but a few days later
Mobutu appointed Nguz prime minister. Nguz soon after gave
an interview to the *New York Times* in which he bluntly said,
"Zaire's situation will probably not improve until President Mobutu is removed from office."[85]

When Laurent Kabila with his Tutsi troops from Uganda and
Rwanda invaded Zaire in late 1996, after learning of plans for
forty thousand Hutu militiamen from Zaire to attack the many

Tutsi who lived in Zaire, and then to invade Rwanda, the Zairean army could barely put up token resistance.[86] The Zairean army was then controlled by four utterly corrupt generals who were more thieves than military men. They clandestinely sold Mobutu's fleet of Mirage fighter jets for personal profit and even sold arms to Kabila's forces. When Mobutu ordered them to take their eighty-thousand-man army out of the suburbs of Kinshasa and fight the invading troops, they ignored him. In desperation, Mobutu hired white mercenaries, including Frenchmen, Russians, and Serbs, who were paid $2,500 per month but did little to battle Kabila's advancing army. In December 1996, Mobutu returned to Zaire from France, where he had been undergoing treatment for prostate cancer. He was greeted enthusiastically by a huge crowd that hoped he could save the country. Instead, he introduced a new currency that promptly created hyperinflation, then returned to France for more prostate therapy. His new currency was widely referred to as "prostate money . . . just like cancer, the new bills can kill."[87]

When Mobutu's troops were forced to engage the rapidly advancing Tutsi soldiers, they fired all of their ammunition wildly, then stripped off their uniforms and fled. Meanwhile, the United States and Nelson Mandela attempted to broker peace by bringing Mobutu and Kabila together, and after much delay, the two men actually met aboard a South African navy ship off the coast of Zaire. A ramp had been built enabling the terribly weak Mobutu, by then so seriously ill with prostate cancer that he could not walk, to drive onto the ship in his Mercedes. Nothing was achieved because Kabila had no interest in any outcome except Mobutu's departure from Zaire. When the DSP soon after mutinied, killing General Malele, who was pleading for peace, Mobutu's family put Zaire's desperately ill leader in a Mercedes, drove it into the belly of a huge Soviet cargo plane, and took off. His previously loyal DSP troops actually opened fire on the plane, which landed safely in Togo with Mobutu in tears over the betrayal of so many who were near to him, people he had supposed to be loyal.[88] Mobutu's son, Kongolo Mobutu, a short, stocky, bearded captain in the dreaded DSP, scoured Kinshasa for those he believed had betrayed his father, killing about a hundred people before, like almost everyone else in the DSP, he changed into civilian cloths and fled to Brazzaville, where he would soon after die of AIDS.[89]

Kinshasa fell to Kabila's ragged but well-disciplined troops, wearing their trademark Wellington boots, virtually without a shot on May 17, 1997. By this time, Mobutu was near death from cancer, and except for his real estate, worth perhaps only $40–$50 million by that time, his wealth had apparently been exhausted. He would die in Rabat, Morocco, on September 7, 1997. President Yoweri Museveni, whose Ugandan troops had played a central role in Mobutu's defeat, was exultant: "The big hole in the middle of Africa has been filled up, and now we can build roads from east to west. We want a common market from east to west and from South Africa to the west."[90] A few days earlier, South Africa's President Mandela had been even more optimistic: "I am convinced that our region and our continent have set out along the new road of lasting peace, democracy, and social and economic development. The time has come for Africa to take full responsibility for her woes and use the immense collective wisdom it possesses to make a reality of the ideal of the African renaissance, whose time has come."[91]

Kabila inherited a national debt of $9.6 billion and a host of doubters. Nevertheless, President Clinton's special envoy to Zaire spoke for many when he said, "The jury is still out on Kabila. But he has potential; we should give him a chance."[92]

7

THE CONGO AND KABILA—
FATHER AND SON

The flight of Mobutu did not herald the start of an African renaissance in the Democratic Republic of the Congo (DRC), as Kabila promptly renamed Zaire, also removing *Zaire* from all road signs and public buildings, and banning miniskirts, which were said to excite men's passions unduly. He also banned all political activity.[1] He ordered that all the "leopard" statues Mobutu had erected in his own honor be destroyed, and he also gave his DRC a new flag—inexplicably, it was a gold star on a blue background, just like the one used in the Congo Free State by King Leopold II.[2] As Kabila moved his gleeful entourage into the five-star Hotel International in Kinshasa, he faced the stark reality that the country was profoundly in debt, its currency worthless, and its government nonexistent. If Mobutu's once immense cache of overseas wealth still existed, it could not be found, and while it was searched for in Switzerland and elsewhere, the Congo's 42 million people faced desperate shortages of everything from gasoline to basic food supplies. When Kabila took the oath of office as the country's new president before twenty-two justices in red robes with leopard-skin trim, as tens of thousands of people looked on in Kinshasa's Kamayola Stadium, he declared, "We should start from the beginning."[3] That beginning had little or no effect on the Congo's shattered economy, but it did include ruthlessly stamping out all political dissent by the arrest, torture, and execution of so many "innocent citizens" that Amnesty International called for the international community to take action.[4]

No effective action by international agencies resulted, but Kabila did take steps to improve his image by reappointing to office Sakombi Inongo, the man who had shown Mobutu on state television descending from the clouds. Sakombi immediately marketed Kabila as "Mzee"—the respectful Swahili word for "elder." And under the headline "Here is the man we needed," he plastered billboards of the corpulent, grim-faced Mzee, with his huge bald head, all over Kinshasa.[5] Sakombi also created the slogan "*Debout Congolais*" (arise Congolese), which was shown regularly on television news. Thanks to Sakombi, Kabila was no longer the ludicrously dressed man whom one correspondent described during the military campaign to unseat Mobutu as a "stout man who wears alligator shoes, a Mirabella baseball cap, and well-pressed military attire."[6]

Kabila quickly alienated many Congolese by his refusal to invite Étienne Tshisekedi—a popular political opponent of Mobutu's who had called the Messiah a "human monster" and had been brutally beaten by Mobutu's security men for his political opposition—to serve in his transitional government.[7] After Tshisekedi organized protest marches against the newly installed Kabila regime, he and his entire family were arrested at midnight, then held for ten hours and treated harshly before they were released with a deadly warning of what would happen to them if Tshisekedi did not "stay out of politics." Despite brutal dictatorship like this, most Congolese were delighted that Mobutu was gone and looked to Kabila to restore their country. He immediately fumbled the chance.

When Kabila's regime took office, Western nations saw a new opportunity to share in the Congo's still rich mineral wealth. Hopeful that Mobutu's ouster meant a new political order and economic responsibility, the IMF and the World Bank offered financial aid, as did several individual countries, including the United States. International mining corporations also rushed forward with offers of loans in return for promised concessions. Kabila quickly squandered the aid he received, pocketing a good portion of it. He also seized and nationalized Sizarail, the national railway company owned by South African and Belgian interests. It was immediately transformed from a profitable enterprise to bankruptcy. Although he publicly declared his intention to model the Congo's future on the capitalism adopted by Museveni in Uganda, Kabila was still imbued with the Marxist ideology of his youth and was so hostile to Western governments and their economic institutions that he tried to play one off against another until he had alienated them all to such an extent that they withdrew their interests. Frustrated Western businessmen returned from visits to Kinshasa reeling from what one called Kabila's "Marxist mumbo jumbo."[8] It seemed to them that he had no economic policy.

Questions about the legitimacy of Kabila's presidency arose as well. On November 1, 1996, soon after the ADFL "Alliance" (Alliance of Democratic Forces for the Liberation of Congo-Zaire) rebels opened hostilities against Mobutu in the eastern Congo, Ugandan and Rwandan Tutsi rebel commanders agreed to appoint Kabila "spokesman" for the Alliance, apparently accepting his claim that he had long fought against Mobutu. His friendship with Museveni was no doubt also a factor. Kabila almost immediately began presenting himself to the international press as the Alliance's "president." This led Alliance general André Kisase Ngandu to remind Kabila in no uncertain terms that he was their "spokesman," not their "president." Kabila at first ignored the

general, but not long after accused Ngandu of plotting to over-throw him.[9] Shortly after "Kabila's" army took Kinshasa, General Ngandu was mysteriously murdered by Alliance soldiers.[10] Three days after General Ngandu's murder, Rwandan general Paul Kagame gave an interview to the *Washington Post* in which he admitted that the Rwandan government had "planned and directed" the ADFL rebellion that had driven Mobutu out of power, and that Rwandan officers and troops had led the rebel forces.[11] He made no mention of Kabila's role in the victory nor did he mention Ngandu's death.

As tensions rose between Kabila and the Tutsi soldiers from Rwanda and Uganda who had put him in power, the Mzee rapidly attempted to develop an army of his own that he hoped would be loyal only to him. It was trained by North Koreans. However, he did nothing to restore the economy, and living conditions throughout the country became even more indescribably grim with more and more families at best limited to a single meal a day of thin cassava porridge or simply bread. The beggars that were everywhere in Kinshasa were ignored by everyone with money, especially by the fashionable young women in high heels and Parisian dresses who still flaunted their beauty in the best hotels and restaurants. In 2000, inflation soared to an astonishing 520 percent, while the gross domestic product fell by 11.3 percent, on the heels of a 10.3 percent decrease in 1999.[12] Kabila's ban on foreign currency drastically limited imports, while the roadblocks set up by long-unpaid police and soldiers to extort money and food from every passing car and truck were devastating to the economy as well. Kabila's reputation as another Mobutu, growing rich while all but his generals and cronies starved, spread so rapidly that when he visited Brussels not long after taking power, the Belgians chose to provide no military honors for him at the airport, and King Albert pointedly did not shake his hand.[13]

Who was this man who had risen from obscurity to replace Mobutu after a seven-month war in which he personally never came close to combat? He was born in 1939 in Jadotville, Katanga, into the Baluba tribe, noted for their business acumen and their frequent migration to cities. Little is known about his early life, but he appears to have completed his secondary-school education in the Belgian Congo, then spent a brief time in Paris before the Congo gained its independence. He was also profoundly influenced by one wing of the Balubakat party, a radical political grouping that strongly supported Lumumba and was willing to take up arms to create a unified and socialist Congo. Communist ideology drove these so-called *le durs* (hard-liners).[14] After independence, Kabila became a leader of the Balubakat Youth, young men who became noted for their ferocity in battle as members of the Simba rebellion against Tshombe's forces, but also for their almost complete lack of discipline.[15]

Kabila spent most of 1961 studying at the University of Belgrade in Tito's Yugoslavia, an experience that apparently intensified his commitment to socialism. In 1962, he returned to the Congo, where at the age of twenty-three he ran for the North Katanga Legislature, winning election over sixteen other candidates.[16] When President Kasavubu shut down the national parliament in late 1963, Kabila joined other Lumumbist politicians in exile in Brazzaville, where he helped to found the CNL (Conseil National de Libération) as well as military training camps. In early 1964, the CNL sent Kabila along with Gaston Soumialot to Burundi, where they were to base themselves while promoting revolution in the eastern Congo, a movement that had some initial political success in attracting followers.[17]

In addition to his earlier studies of political philosophy in France, Kabila attended Dar es Salaam University in Tanzania, where he apparently met Yoweri Museveni. He also became a disciple of Pierre Mulele, a Chinese-inspired Marxist who was one of the leaders of the Simba rebellion for the independence of the eastern Congo in 1964–65. Kabila later met Ernesto "Che" Guevara, who had joined the Simba rebellion with a few hundred Cuban soldiers but found nothing to admire in the then twenty-five-year-old Kabila, saying that his promises meant nothing, that he was addicted to women and alcohol, and that he "seemed reluctant to visit the front and drove around Dar es Salaam in a Mercedes-Benz."[18] According to Guevara, Kabila sent letters promising everything but he delivered nothing. Instead of taking an active role in the Simba rebellion, Kabila devoted himself to making money by smuggling gold and ivory out of the eastern Congo. He also ran a brothel and a bar in Dar es Salaam, where he became known for his taste for fine wine and stylish clothing.[19] In 1965, while the Simba rebellion continued, he also made appearances in Nairobi, Cairo, and Paris.

After the defeat of the Simba rebellion, Kabila and some other rebels took shelter in the mountains of South Kivu, where they founded another political party designed to carry on the revolution and overthrow Mobutu. During the 1970s and 1980s, this party had no military success. Instead, they traded gold to the Zairean army in return for munitions and maintaining a peaceful status quo. Some of the party's activities were intended to develop a socialist society, but most of Kabila's energies went toward his gold mining and his networks of smuggling partners, who profitably took gold out of what was by then called Zaire. He also maintained homes and businesses in Dar es Salaam and Kampala, Uganda, where he renewed his acquaintance with Museveni. Kabila also outrageously made $40,000 by kidnapping three Stanford University students and a Dutch friend who were studying chimpanzees at Jane Goodall's Gombe Stream Research Center in Tanzania and holding them for two months before their ransom was paid.[20]

During the summer of 1998, a UN commission was actively

investigating reports that Kabila's Tutsi-led, rebel Alliance army had murdered thousands of Hutu militiamen and their supporters in Zaire. Mass graves had been reported, and many Alliance soldiers themselves asserted that their invasion of Zaire had originally been aimed at the Hutu militia who had slaughtered Tutsi in the appalling Rwandan genocide of 1994 before being freed to flee from Rwanda into eastern Zaire. The decision to march on to Kinshasa and remove Mobutu from power was apparently made in response to Mobutu's support of these Hutu and his persecution of the hundreds of thousands of Tutsi who had lived in northeastern Zaire for several generations. Once in power in the DRC, Kabila did all that he could to distance himself from his Tutsi advisers, and when he claimed to have become aware of an assassination plot against him, he not only dismissed the Tutsi in his entourage, he sent away the senior Rwandan and Ugandan officers who had provided the command structure of the Alliance army that had put him in power.

Rwanda and Uganda responded by seizing much of the eastern Congo. Kabila appealed to Angola, Zimbabwe, and Zambia for help, something those countries were willing to provide not only to prevent the feared seizure of the Congo by Rwanda and Uganda, but in return for promises of oil concessions and the right to mine and export diamonds and other minerals. Kabila immediately called on the people of Kinshasa, his main base of power, to kill Tutsi "infiltrators" in the region, something many of them did with obvious relish, unleashing a bloody pogrom. Soon after the killing of Tutsi civilians began, Rwandan troops drove all the way to the outskirts of Kinshasa, where they rescued some endangered Tutsi, but repeated bombing attacks by Angolan warplanes and Zimbabwean troops drove them back.

As infantry from Angola, Namibia, and Zimbabwe were joined by twelve thousand soldiers from Zambia, the fighting settled down to a largely static exchange of fire and an intense exploitation of the Congo's coltan, diamonds, gold, oil, and other valuable resources. Angola agreed to pay for most of the military expenses of Namibia and Zimbabwe, hoping to deprive the Angolan rebel leader Jonas Savimbi of access to the profitable diamond trade. The plan did not succeed. On the other side of the war, Ugandan and Rwandan forces became so competitive about mining gold, diamonds, coltan, and other precious minerals that, in June 2000, the two armies fought a six-day battle in which sixty-five hundred shells fell on the working-class areas of the city of Kisangani (previously Stanleyville), killing and wounding thousands of civilians.[21] Much of this conflict was driven by the rapid increase in the value of coltan, which, once it was refined as tantalum, became a key component in everything from cell phones and computer chips to Sony stereos, VCRs, and laptop computers. Rwanda alone is said to have made at least $250 million from the sale of coltan.[22] There were other battles as well, including some bloody ones against Kabila's allies, with the Zambians suffering substantial casualties.

Throughout this protracted period of widespread warfare in the eastern DRC, the Clinton administration maintained its diplomatic and economic ties with Kabila's government. In 1999, when Madeleine Albright visited Kinshasa, she said that "a commitment to open markets, honest government, and the rule of law" would enable the DRC to emerge as an "engine of regional growth. President Kabila has made a strong start toward these goals." As she spoke, Kabila stood beaming at her side.[23] Soon after Albright's visit, Kabila's "commitment to honest government" could be seen in the composition of the DRC's Constitutional and Legislative Assembly, the country's lawmaking body. All of its members had been appointed either by Kabila or his feared interior minister, Gaeton Kakudji.[24] Not a single member had been elected. Kabila also rejected the plan endorsed by the

so-called Lusaka Peace Accord of July 1999 to hold open constitutional talks with his opponents about the Congo's future.

Growing discontent within the army, particularly among the
kidogo ("little ones" in Swahili), the boy soldiers who had marched
with Kabila throughout his campaign of Alliance forces but had
received little pay and no attention since his victory, led to a
failed coup attempt against him in October 2000. A year later, a
military tribunal sentenced eight of the eighty men accused of
the plot to death, including Kabila's former friend and army
commander Anselme Masasu, who was executed in November
2000. Thirty-two others were sentenced to between five and
twenty-five years in prison. Forty men were found not guilty. The
UN denounced the trial as unfair because of the lack of legal
representation for the accused and also decried the "atrocious
torture" many of the accused were said to have suffered while in
prison.[25]

On January 16, 2001, another coup was attempted, and this
one succeeded. Laurent-Désiré Kabila was shot to death at the
age of sixty-one. For two days, the Kinshasa government issued a
farcical series of reports about his assassination followed by de-
nials that he had been killed before finally confirming that he
had been shot to death by a lone gunman, one of his bodyguards,
who was immediately shot dead by other security officers. As if
to confirm this report, the alleged assassin's family fled to Brazzaville immediately after Kabila's death. However, in March 2001
the French newspaper *Le Monde* reported that his killer was one
of the *kidogo* who had marched with him in the Alliance forces
four years earlier. According to *Le Monde,* once in power Kabila
was said to have increasingly neglected these young soldiers.
When he began to fear that these angry young men were plotting
to assassinate him, he ordered the execution of forty-five of them,
which he witnessed. Soon after this "outrage," as it was described

by one of the conspirators identified only as "A.L.," six teenage soldiers took part in the assassination plot. Two of them entered Kabila's office to kill him while four hid outside to give covering fire. One of these was killed, but the other five, including the actual assassin, were said to have escaped.[26] Over fifty people are still detained for their alleged role in the assassination, but no one has been formally charged. A human rights activist who was held in the same prison with these men was released without charge after seven months of confinement. He required medical attention for the wounds he suffered while tortured.[27]

After lying in state for several days, Laurent Kabila's flag-draped coffin was driven through Kinshasa as huge crowds looked on under heavy security. Friends and family filed past the open coffin, many of them weeping. But Joseph Olenghankoy, a political opponent who had taken refuge in the Belgian embassy, spoke for many others when he told the press, "The person who killed Kabila is Kabila himself. He did not have respect for human life. Even in his inner circle, he was humiliating them."[28]

Three days after his assassination, Laurent Kabila was succeeded as president of the Democratic Republic of the Congo by his oldest son, Joseph-Désiré Kabila, a young general aged either twenty-nine or thirty-one, depending on the source. At either age, he is the youngest president in the world and is as little known as any leader in all of Africa's history. One source has said that the thin, handsome, soft-spoken, teetotaling, non-smoking Joseph is the eldest son of one of Laurent Kabila's three wives, but others insist that his mother was one of Laurent's mistresses of Tutsi ancestry. Still others report that Joseph is the adopted son of a Rwandan man married to a Tutsi woman.

It is known that Joseph Kabila speaks fluent Kinyarwanda, the language of Rwanda, that he has had Tutsi girlfriends, and that he did everything he could to save Tutsi during the 1998 pogrom in Kinshasa that his father ordered. He does not speak Lingala, the lingua franca of the Congo. He is said to have received his primary and secondary school education at a French-language school in Tanzania, yet today his French is heavily accented while his English is fluent, as is his Swahili, the lingua franca of East Africa. He is said to have spent a year at Makerere University in Uganda, where English is the language of instruction, and he is said to have served at least one year in the Rwandan army. He is also reported to have spent three months in China undergoing military training. Just before his father was assassinated, Joseph was the commander of DRC land forces near the Katanga border, where he was defeated by Rwandan Congolese rebels.[29]

After his swearing-in ceremony, Joseph Kabila spoke to the nation on television in his labored French, saying, "Our country is going through one of the most painful crises in its history, but I believe that we, all of us together, will be able to overcome it." He promised free elections, a liberalized economy, and the deployment of UN troops to oversee implementation of the 1999 Lusaka peace agreement, which his father had rejected.[30]

Among many unknowns is who decided that Joseph Kabila should take power and who is maintaining him there. He insists, with great conviction, that even in his dreams he had no desire to become president.[31] According to Justice Minister Mwenze Kongolo, immediately after the assassination, the country's political and military leaders met to decide on a successor and chose Joseph Kabila as "somebody we could all trust."[32] Mwenze also denied that Kabila was Tutsi, saying that he was from an eastern Congo tribe known as the Bongo, a Nigritic-speaking people.[33] In late April 2001, Kabila surprised onlookers by removing Gaeton Kakudji from office along with three other senior ministers. Several senior army officers and civilians were placed under house arrest, strongly suggesting that by this time Kabila was sure of his position and his political backing.[34] Only four of the twenty-five members of the old government kept their positions.

Despite his youth, lack of experience in government, and virtual anonymity, the new president—known to the French and Belgians as *le Petit*—made a positive impression on international observers when he went on a tour to promote the Lusaka peace initiative in the Congo, the same one that his father had opposed. He first went to Washington on February 1, 2001, where he met with Rwandan leader Paul Kagame. Both men then met separately with Colin Powell. Kabila went on to Paris to meet with French president Jacques Chirac and to Brussels to confer with Belgian prime minister Guy Verhofstadt, who gave him impressive "red carpet" treatment. Frankfurt's liberal newspaper, *Frankfurter Rundschau* wrote on February 8, "Already he has managed to achieve . . . what his murdered father had bungled with equal speed: the support of important representatives of the international community."[35] In March, the European Union gave young Kabila $28 million to rehabilitate the justice system and set aside an additional $101 million conditional on progress toward peace. Belgium, in particular, has offered financial aid and help in ending the civil war. When Kabila was asked whether Belgium was welcome to play such an active role in the Congo, he answered, "Why not? The Belgians ought to get involved. It's not only a question of goodwill but a duty imposed by our historic links. Belgium cannot remain a spectator to what happens in the Congo."[36]

Significantly, Kabila reversed his father's position when he announced that he would invite former Botswanan president Ketumile Masire to Kinshasa to serve as a peace mediator, leading Dakar's Panafrican News Agency to comment, "The young Kabila is seemingly eager to distance himself from the unproductive position of his assassinated father."[37] He also refused to aggrandize himself, declining suggestions that he pose for billboard photographs, living modestly, and avoiding any form of excess. He even postponed his planned marriage to devote more time to the country's problems.

In mid-April, Kabila met with a reporter from *Time International* in Kinshasa's presidential palace, commenting:

> The expectations of the Congolese people are that their country should be reunified, that they should live in peace among themselves and with neighboring countries. The expectations are that they should have a democracy, because in the Congo since 1960 we've not had a democratic government that works for the people. The expectations are that there should be development, that there should be leaders who are responsible.
>
> We should not be fighting this war. I've always said it was a stupid war. Look at our people. They are being reduced to beggars. What the people of Congo need is not food, medicine, or some other assistance. What they need is peace. They can't cultivate their fields, they can't sell their produce. If everyone understands things from my perspective, then we should be seeing the end of the war quite soon.[38]

While young Kabila was making these widely acclaimed statements, it became obvious that not everyone shared his perspective. A UN committee denounced both Uganda and Rwanda for looting diamonds, gold, timber, ivory, and coltan, naming Museveni's brother, a major general, as one of the men closely involved in this. At the same time, it exempted Angola, Namibia, and Zambia from similar criticism because they had done so with the approval of the government of the DRC.[39] And thousands of blue-beret-wearing UN observers entered the country. The UN report was vehemently rejected by the governments of Uganda,

Rwanda, and Burundi, who pointed out that they had created the first Kabila regime and had at least as much right to determine the Congo's future as Angola did.[40]

Kabila promised many changes that would restore the Congo's economy, but by midyear 2001, some families were still surviving by eating rats, caterpillars, and cooked cow skin.[41] Food markets were largely empty and beggars roamed the streets, pleading for food. Malnutrition rates for children under the age of five reached 30 percent, the infant mortality rate was 41 percent, and according to a report by Oxfam, Save the Children, and Christian Aid, 16 million Congolese went hungry each day.[42] Due to fuel shortages, buses did not run and car owners hoping to obtain their quota of gasoline would line up at petrol stations the night before, sleeping on the hood of their car. Even with these precautions, the following day often saw no gasoline. Almost all roads were impassable, few medical clinics were open, and half of the country's children were not in school. The police and military grew more and more corrupt each day, extorting money from Congolese in every way possible.

Rural areas were beyond civil control as well. Even the northeastern Congo, where disciplined Ugandan troops were in control, was rocked in mid-July 2001 when 394 people were killed in a hunt for suspected witches. Eighty-nine people were under arrest for these murders.[43] Various international agencies, including the New York–based International Rescue Committee, have estimated that since 1997, the war has killed 3 million people, 350,000 of these at the hands of armed men, with the rest victims of hunger and disease.[44] At least one-third of the dead were children under five. The World Health Organization recently estimated that over 70,000 people die avoidable deaths every month in the Congo.[45]

Yet by midyear 2001, Kabila's regime liberalized fuel prices and the exchange rate and abolished the much criticized diamond-export monopoly of the Israeli firm International Diamond Industries. In August 2001, President Kabila also suspended 250 managers at fifty-seven state-run companies for corrupt mismanagement and embezzlement, barring them from leaving the country. Copper production at the state-run mining company, Gécomines, was used as an example. A decade ago, it produced 450,000 tons of copper per year. Last year the total fell to 30,000 tons. Over the same period, the annual state budget fell from $1 billion to $200 million. Most of the suspended managers had been appointed by Laurent Kabila.[46] After Joseph Kabila complained that a corrupt legal system had created judicial insecurity, the chief state prosecutor tried to explain, "You cannot think that widespread corruption is limited to the judiciary alone. It affects all sectors. . . . The destruction of the judiciary, the army, the police force, and the national economy took a long process that did not start today."[47]

Kabila also permitted the establishment of opposition political parties, a widely hailed extension of democracy in the Congo. However, these parties have not yet been allowed to hold public meetings or rallies. In mid-August 2001, when the four largest of these parties attempted to march down Kinshasa's main street, the Boulevard du Trente Juin, unfurling protest banners and singing, heavily armed police quickly dispersed the crowd and arrested forty protesters.[48] One party that Kabila has not recognized is led by Étienne Tshisekedi, the popular politician who had been jailed and beaten by Laurent Kabila. Tshisekedi recently challenged Joseph Kabila's right to determine which parties would be allowed to run for election, saying, "He knows very well that we never considered his father legitimate, and consequently he is not legitimate either."[49]

As noted earlier, the eastern Congo's rich supply of coltan, along with its many other valuable minerals, has fueled the warfare that continues there to this day. It has also created a paradox that is seemingly characteristic of this tormented country. Earlier in 2001, a kilogram of coltan was worth $80, and many hard-working Congolese rushed to become miners, many of them able to produce a kilogram with a day's work. In a country where most ordinary people lived on twenty cents a day, this was an irresistible lure for many farmers, who left their homes to mine in the streambeds of the Ituri Forest and elsewhere in the eastern Congo where coltan was concentrated. Some of the money they made was used to pay prostitutes, who rushed to the same area, while much of it found its way into other areas of the local economy, helping many families to improve the quality of their lives. Millions of dollars were stolen by warlords and profiteers, but many ordinary people also benefited.[50]

However, for various reasons, including a glut of coltan on the market thanks in large measure to the emergence of a large, new coltan mining company in Australia, by midyear 2001 the price of a kilogram of coltan fell to only $8. Worse still for the people of the Congo, when it was discovered that many profiteers, including Rwandans and Ugandans, as well as some ten thousand Congolese miners, were growing rich from coltan while slaughtering for food virtually all the gorillas that lived in a supposedly protected national park that was rich in coltan, the UN called for an embargo on coltan. Sabena, the Belgian airline that had previously carried coltan to Europe, declared that it would no longer do so, and several large American companies announced that they would no longer buy coltan from the Congo or bordering countries. The sad result was to reduce still further the income available to many long-suffering Congolese.[51]

Soon after President Kabila suspended the managers of state-run companies, he spoke at the 75th Agricultural and Commercial Show of Zambia, saying that his country was capable of feeding the entire continent, but due to the continuing warfare and the resulting political instability, it had to import food to keep its people alive. He urged the business community to take advantage of open-market policies to foster development in mining, textiles, agriculture, and tourism. He also asked them to invest in his country, saying that the Congo and Zambia should live as one people, sharing their resources and wealth. He concluded by saying that the political situation in the Congo was "calm in transition" and that the quest for peace and stability would continue.[52] Another positive note was struck on September 3, 2001, when Zimbabwe announced that it was removing its troops from the DRC, and Namibia announced that it would do the same.

And in late August, the former president of Botswana, Ketumile Masire, had unexpected success in forging a peace conference. At Kabila's behest, he brought together sixty delegates from the Kinshasa government of Joseph Kabila, as well as the various armed and unarmed opposition movements in the Congo and from "civil society." After six days of preparation, the delegates agreed to meet in Addis Ababa, where over 330 delegates from all parties and factions would come together for fifty days to agree upon a new political order in the Congo with a transitional government, a timetable for elections, and the creation of a new national army. However, on the first day of the peace conference, October 15, 2001, only 70 delegates were present, and these traded angry words, with few seeming to be willing to compromise. Neither President Kabila nor the key rebel leaders chose to attend the opening ceremony.[53]

Ketumile Masire blamed this impasse on the lack of funding to bring all of the delegates to Addis Ababa and maintain them there for a long conference. He had been unable to raise even half of the $5 million he said was necessary to support all the delegates for a fifty-day meeting. He tried to convene the conference with only 70 delegates, but this was seen as excluding so many legitimate participants that Kabila and other leaders boycotted the meeting. Masire then suggested that the conference

239

be postponed for thirty days before reconvening in South Africa, where the South African government had offered to pay for the expenses of the over 330 delegates originally invited. The proposed conference is the culmination of the Lusaka Peace Accord signed in Zambia in 1999 but pointedly ignored by Laurent Kabila. This accord did not call for the inclusion of the pro-Kabila government militia, the Mayi-Mayi, which Kabila demanded be included. His opponents saw this demand as an attempt by Kabila to strengthen his representation at the conference, and they refused to accept Mayi-Mayi delegates, citing the Lusaka agreement.[54] A week after the abortive Addis Ababa talks ended, the UN Security Council announced that Rwanda and Uganda had been reinforcing their troops in the eastern Congo, not withdrawing them as the Lusaka Accord required. Despite UN protests, these troops remained in the Congo, and heavy fighting was reported.

While waiting for Ketumile Masire to finalize a date and a location in South Africa for the aborted peace talks, and an agreement about the legitimacy of various participants, in early November, Kabila made a trip to the United States, France, and Belgium. In Paris, Kabila met with Jacques Chirac, who publicly called for the removal of all foreign troops from the DRC, the deployment of UN peacekeeping troops, and the release of promised aid from international financial institutions—$108 million from the European Union and $50 million from the World Bank. Kabila also spoke at length with the Belgian prime minister, Guy Verhofstadt. In the United States, he met with Colin Powell and George Bush Sr.

A week later, Kabila returned to the United States to meet briefly with President George W. Bush, to speak to the UN Security Council on the Congo crisis, and to attend the U.S.-Africa Business Summit in Philadelphia. This summit was hosted by the Corporate Council on Africa (CCA), which had a membership of 197 U.S. firms accounting for 85 percent of all U.S. investment in Africa.

When Kabila returned to the DRC, he expressed optimism that the South African peace talks could succeed, but then joined with the president of Malawi, Dr. Bakili Muluzi, to condemn Rwanda and Uganda for "looting" the wealth and natural resources of the Congo. As if in response, on November 17, 2001, the World Bank granted the DRC $50 million, the largest unconditional grant it had ever given to any country.[55]

And thanks to the good offices of President Obasanjo of Nigeria, the three major opponents in the struggle for peace in the Congo met in Nigeria's capital on December 10, 2001: Kabila and his two rebel opponents, the Rwanda-based Congolese Rally for Democracy, and the Uganda-led Congolese Liberation Movement. The long-planned peace conference was still expected to be held in South Africa in February 2002.

In mid-January, as President Kabila attempted to ready himself and his supporters for the impending peace conference, Amnesty International accused his police and security services of widespread human rights abuses against his political opponents, who were systematically arrested, jailed without charges, and brutally tortured. One week later, Dieudonne Wafula, a Congolese vulcanologist in the city of Goma on Lake Kivu, predicted that the 11,400-foot Mt. Nyiragongo, a volcano that had last erupted in 1977, was ready to do so again—and very soon. The 350,000 or so residents of Goma, tormented by the war that was still ravaging the eastern Congo, ignored his warning. On January 18, a river of fast-flowing molten lava sliced through Goma, cutting the city in half and driving almost everyone out of their home. Scores were killed. As many as half a million Congolese refugees walked across the nearby border of Rwanda—whose troops had occupied the eastern Congo for almost five years—hoping to find food and shelter.

Neither the Rwandan government nor the Rwandan people made any attempt to help. The Congolese slept in open fields and went hungry. "I spent the last two days in Rwanda, and no one offered me a drop of water, food—nothing," said a Congolese woman from Goma who had walked to Rwanda with her one-month-old daughter strapped to her back.[56] How many Congolese were killed by the lava is unknown, but hundreds are missing, and scores more were killed when lava ignited huge fireballs at one of Goma's gas stations. Not until six days after the eruption did the first UN food supplies reach the stricken city. One woman said that neither she nor her many children had eaten since the volcano had exploded.[57] As people struggled to find food, a vulcanologist hired by the UN warned that this recent eruption had created such deep fissures that the next eruption could bury Goma. People went about their business as usual. A week later, torrential rains caused such violent flooding that hundreds of people were swept away, and fifty are thought to have died.

The peace conference, dubbed the Inter-Congolese Dialogue, formally opened Monday, February 25, in Sun City, a luxury casino resort, 112 miles northwest of Johannesburg, South Africa. The talks were scheduled to last forty-five days. Holding these vital talks in a venue famous for gambling and drinking led several observers to comment that the Congo could never be taken seriously. President Joseph Kabila of the DRC attended, as did the host president, South Africa's Thabo Mbeki, President Levy Mwanawasa of Zambia, President Bakili Muluzi of Malawi, and the leaders of the two dissident organizations backed by Uganda and Rwanda. The chairmen of the Organization of African Unity and the Southern African Development Community were there as well. The conference was organized by Sir Ketumile Masire, the former president of Botswana. The opening ceremony was boycotted by one of the rebel leaders, Jean-Pierre Bemba, of the

Movement for the Liberation of Congo (MLC). There were 350 approved delegates, all of whom lived in a swank hotel at the expense of the South African government. Police turned away another hundred who tried to force their way in. The talks immediately became so heated that the conference had to be suspended the following day.

The talks resumed at the end of the week, but there was no agreement concerning the role of the two rebel armies in the Congo's future. Kabila's government insisted that these men be integrated into the DRC's army and accept orders from DRC commanders. The talks were so angry that no compromise could be foreseen. On March 14, the DRC representatives walked out of the conference, accusing the Rwandan-backed rebel troops of the Congolese Rally for Democracy (RCD) of deploying ten thousand troops against DRC forces at the town of Moliro, a strategic port on Lake Tanganyika in the southeastern Congo. France condemned the RCD troops for attacking and actually seizing Moliro. The rebel RCD leaders insisted that Kabila's forces had attacked them.

On March 15, Kabila's government announced that "it wishes to inform national and international opinion that it has just decided to suspend its participation in the national dialogue until Rwanda and the RCD order troops to cease hostilities at Moliro and pull back to their lines."[58] The next day, all parties agreed to meet on March 22 in Lusaka to search for a solution. Meanwhile, the Rwandan-backed RCD offered to put Moliro under the control of UN observers. Every day brought word of new fighting.

While all sides bickered about the ground rules for continuing the peace talks, a hand grenade was thrown into a crowd of Roman Catholics in the star-crossed city of Goma. Two people were killed with sixteen wounded. The reason for the attack remains unknown. After a week of round-the-clock arguments, the peace conference resumed, and it became clear that three issues dominated the delegates' attention: How should the rebel soldiers be integrated into the Congo's national army? When and how could elections be held to form a new government? And who should head a transitional government until the elections took place? The rebels and Kabila's government immediately clashed. The government insisted that President Kabila remain in office until the elections were held some twelve to eighteen months hence. The rebels firmly rejected this idea.

Meanwhile, despite the presence of UN observers, fighting continued around Moliro. While the talks dragged on with no sign of agreement, a variety of flamboyant characters made their presence known. François Lumumba, the son of Patrice Lumumba, returned from a thirty-two-year exile in Egypt and Europe to announce his readiness to serve his country in any way. The MLC president, Jean-Pierre Bemba, flew in and out of Sun City on his private jet. He was seen by many as a warlord not to be trusted. Raphael Katebe Katoto, a Belgian-based multimillionaire business-man arrived in two helicopters with a large entourage, glossy pamphlets, and even a CD recording his vision of the Congo's future. And Madame Nzuzi-wa-Mbombo, a plump, bespectacled woman who always dressed in black and gold, distributed another pamphlet describing her "crusade" for peace, unity, democracy, national accord, and prosperity, arguing that her "feminine touch" could succeed where men have only made matters worse.

The forty-five-day peace conference was scheduled to end on April 11, but the delegates could reach no agreement, and after an all-night session it was agreed to continue the talks for another week. But that same night, the delegates were evicted from their hotel by the British reggae-rock group UB40, which had long before booked themselves into the hotel, where they would stay while readying themselves for a concert. While this almost comic development was taking place, there were no signs that additional meetings would resolve the Congo's future. Kabila remained in office, the fighting that had killed well over 2 million people since 1998 in the eastern Congo continued, and there was no agreement about incorporating rebel soldiers into the national army. The 50 million Congolese people continued to live under the ravages of war, economic collapse, and political uncertainty, while 800 million Africans looked on, their own futures very much in doubt. On May 30, 2002, peace facilitator Sir Ketumile Masire told reporters in Lusaka that the peace talks were at a stalemate. He expressed no optimism.

When Joseph Conrad returned from his turn-of-the-century visit to the Congo to write *Heart of Darkness*, his most memorable words were Marlowe's despairing "The horror! The horror!" These words still ring true. The horror and the hopelessness go on. Even if an agreement about elections and army integration were, by some miracle, to take place, there is no reason to believe that peace would be restored, that fair elections would take place, or that a government dedicated to ending the suffering of the Congolese people would finally emerge from the ruins of the past.

As I have tried to show, Portuguese slavery began the horror in the west of the Congo, and it spread inland bringing with it warfare, famine, and cannibalism. Adventurous explorers, especially Stanley, brought the Congo to the world's attention but did nothing to end the suffering of its people. Arab slavers then created even more calamitous death and destruction in the eastern Congo before King Leopold's men brought about the inhuman slaughter and cannibalism that appalled Conrad. Leopold's overthrow and the resulting Belgian rule slowly ended the killing and most of the cannibalism, but it did nothing to prepare the Congolese people for self-rule, and it inflicted painful white racism on them. With independence, Patrice Lumumba became the

Congo's only freely elected leader, but his murder, civil wars, and brutal UN military intervention brought Mobutu to a position of supreme power that he held for thirty-two years, until Kabila's forces overthrew him. Soon after, Joseph Kabila replaced his father as president. For the Congolese people, independence has meant tyranny, corruption, police brutality, hunger, malnutrition, and an ever-shorter life expectancy. That a people should suffer so terribly for so long is truly tragic.

On July 30, 2002, South African President Thabo Mbeki brokered a peace accord between Rwanda and the Congo calling for United Nations and South African troops to monitor the planned withdrawal of Rwandan troops from the Congo within ninety days. Several observers have expressed doubt that this withdrawal will actually take place, but others are optimistic. Time alone will tell, but for once there is hope for the Congolese people.[59]

Notes

1. THE LAND BEYOND OBSCURITY AND DARKNESS

1. J. Vansina, *Introduction à l'Ethnographie du Congo* (Brussels: Éditions Universitaires du Congo, 1965).

2. H. Ward, *A Voice from the Congo: Comprising Stories, Anecdotes, and Descriptive Notes* (London: William Heinemann, 1910), 240.

3. H. H. Johnston, *The River Congo: From Its Mouth to Bolobo* (London: Sampson, Low, Marston & Company, 1895), 169.

4. R. W. Harms, *River of Wealth, River of Sorrow: The Central Zaire Basin in the Era of the Slave and Ivory Trade* (New Haven: Yale University Press, 1981).

5. J. Taylor, *Facing the Congo* (St. Paul, Minn.: Ruminator Books, 2000).

6. E. Torday, *On the Trail of the Bushongo* (London: Seeley, Service & Co., 1925).

7. J. Vansina, *Paths in the Rainforests: Toward a History of Political Tradition in Equatorial Africa* (Madison: University of Wisconsin Press, 1990).

8. Ibid., 61.

9. G. Balandier, *Daily Life in the Kingdom of the Kongo from the Sixteenth to the Eighteenth Century*, trans. Helen Weaver (New York: Pantheon Books, 1968), 94.

10. P. Forbath, *The River Congo: The Discovery, Exploration and Exploitation of the World's Most Dramatic River* (New York: Harper & Row, 1977).

11. D. Diène, ed., *From Chains to Bonds: The Slave Trade Revisited* (New York: Berghahn, 2001.)

12. C. Hibbert, *Africa Explored: Europeans in the Dark Continent, 1769–1889* (New York: W. W. Norton, 1982).

13. Ibid., 73.

14. F. Pigafetta, *A Report of the Kingdom of Congo and of the Surrounding Countries; Drawn out of the Writings and Discourses of the Portuguese, Duarte Lopez*, trans. M. Hutchison (1591, reprint, London: John Murray, 1881); and W. H. Bentley, *Pioneering on the Congo*, 2 vols. (Oxford: The Religious Tract Society, 1900), 20.

15. P. Hyland, *The Black Heart: A Voyage to Central Africa* (London: Victor Gollancz, 1988).

16. Johnston, op. cit., 60. Johnston met Henry Morton Stanley while in the Congo and

read his earlier books but inexplicably dedicated his book to Henry Moreland Stanley.

17. E. G. Ravenstein, ed., *The Strange Adventures of Andrew Battell of Leigh, in Angola and the Adjoining Regions* (London: The Hakluyt Society, 1901), 107; and C. R. V. Bell, *Portugal and the Quest for the Indies* (London: Constable, 1974).

18. Pigafetta, op. cit.; and Balandier, op. cit., 42.

19. J. Vansina, *Kingdoms of the Savanna* (Madison: University of Wisconsin Press, 1966).

20. Pigafetta, op. cit., 76.

21. G. P. Murdock, *Africa: Its Peoples and Their Culture History* (New York: McGraw-Hill, 1959), 297.

22. Ward, op. cit., 3.

23. J. H. Weeks, *Among the Primitive Bakongo* (London: Seeley, Service & Co., 1914).

24. Balandier, op. cit.; and W. MacGaffey, "Economic and Social Dimensions of Kongo Slavery," in S. Miers and I. Kopytoff, eds., *Slavery in Africa: Historical and Anthropological Perspectives* (Madison: University of Wisconsin Press, 1977).

25. S. Axelson, *Culture Confrontation in the Lower Congo: From the Old Congo Kingdom to the Congo Independent State with Special Reference to the Swedish Missionaries in the 1880's and 1890's* (Falköping, Sweden: Gummessons, 1970), 69.

26. Ibid., 74–75.

27. Ibid., 55–56.

28. Ibid., 76.

29. Ibid., 75.

30. Ibid., 134.

31. O. De Bouveignes, "Jérôme de Montesarchio et la découverte du Stanley-Pool," *Zaire* 2 (1948): 989–1013.

32. R. M. Slade, *King Leopold's Congo: Aspects of the Development of Race Relations in the Congo Independent State* (London and New York: Oxford University Press, 1962), 7.

33. A. Verbeken, *La première traversée du Katanga en 1806* (Brussels: Académie royale des sciences d'outre-mer, 1953).

34. R. Antsey, *Britain and the Congo in the Nineteenth Century* (Oxford: Clarendon Press, 1962), 7.

35. J. K. Tuckey, *Narrative of an Expedition to Explore the River Zaire, Usually Called the Congo, in South Africa, in 1816, Under the Direction of Captain J. K. Tuckey, R.N.* (1818; reprint, London: John Murray, 1967), xxxvii.

36. Ibid., 71.

37. Ibid., 187.

38. Simmons was sometimes referred to as Somme Simmons. The use of *Somme* is not explained.

39. Tuckey, op. cit., 300–301.

40. Ibid., 98.

41. Antsey, op. cit., 9.

42. Tuckey, op. cit., 361.

43. McLynn, op.cit., 278.

44. Ibid., 373.

45. Tuckey, op. cit., 225.

46. Antsey, op. cit., 12.

47. Ibid., 33.

48. Bentley, op. cit., p. 57.

49. J. Vansina, *The Children of Woot: A History of the Kuba Peoples* (Madison: University of Wisconsin Press, 1978), 3.
50. Ibid., 151.
51. Ibid., 145.
52. W. H. Sheppard, *Pioneers in Congo* (Louisville, Ky.: Pentecostal Publishing Co., 1917), 114.
53. Vansina, 1978, op. cit., 169.
54. Sheppard, op. cit., 215ff.
55. Ibid., 117.
56. W. J. Samarin, *The Black Man's Burden: African Colonial Labor on the Congo and Ubangi Rivers, 1880–1900* (Boulder, Colo.: Westview Press, 1989), 12–13.
57. L. Dieu, *Dans la brousse congolaise* (Liège: Maréchal, 1946), 76–77.
58. Bentley, op. cit., 2:68.
59. Ibid., 144.
60. Ward, op. cit., 200.
61. J. Listowel, *The Other Livingstone* (Lewes, U.K.: Julien Friedman, 1974), 93.
62. Ibid., 96–97.
63. Ibid., 100.
64. Ibid.
65. Axelson, op. cit., 191.
66. R. Burton, *Two Trips to Gorilla Land and the Cataracts of the Congo*, 2 vols. (London: Sampson Low, 1876), 2:318.
67. Ibid., 317.
68. Ibid., 149.
69. Ibid., 283.

2. EXPLORING THE CONGO

1. F. McLynn, *Stanley: The Making of an African Explorer* (Chelsea, Mich.: Scarborough House, 1990), 327.
2. Sometimes written *Matadi*. In Bantu languages, the *r* and *d* sounds are often indistinguishable.
3. McLynn, op.cit.
4. J. Bierman, *Dark Safari: The Life Behind the Legend of Henry Morton Stanley* (New York: A. A. Knopf, 1990), 8.
5. H. M. Stanley, *The Autobiography of Henry Morton Stanley,* ed. Dorothy Stanley (Boston: Houghton-Mifflin, 1909), 195.
6. Ibid., 219.
7. L. M. Jones and I. Wynne, *H. M. Stanley and Wales* (St. Asaph, Wales: H. M. Stanley Exhibition Committee; Hawarden, Flintshire County Record Office, 1972), 22.
8. McLynn, op. cit., 44.
9. Ibid.
10. Bierman, op. cit., 41.
11. Stanley, op. cit., 424.
12. Bierman, op. cit., 83.
13. H. M. Stanley, *Through the Dark Continent*, 2 vols. (New York: Harper & Brothers, 1878), 1:101.
14. McLynn, op. cit., 134–35.
15. *New York Herald,* August 9, 1872.

16. R. Stanley and A. Neame, eds., *The Exploration Diaries of H. M. Stanley* (London: William Kimber, 1961), 195.

17. McLynn, op. cit., 123.

18. Journal, June 2, 1876, Stanley Family Archives, British Library, London.

19. S. Weintraub, *Victoria: An Intimate Biography* (New York: Dutton, 1987), 513.

20. W. R. Foran, *African Odyssey: The Life of Verney Lovett Cameron* (London: Hutchinson & Co., 1937), 39.

21. V. L. Cameron, *Across Africa*, 2 vols. (London: Daldy, Isbister & Co., 1877), 1:10.

22. Ibid., 207.

23. Ibid., 350.

24. Ibid., 2:199.

25. Ibid., 1:357.

26. F. McLynn, *Stanley: Sorcerer's Apprentice* (London: Constable, 1991), 9.

27. Cameron, op. cit., 2:230.

28. Foran, op. cit., 362.

29. H. M. Stanley, *Coomassie and Magdala: The Story of Two British Campaigns in Africa* (New York: Harper, 1874), 18.

30. McLynn, 1990, op. cit., 240.

31. Stanley, 1878, op. cit., 85.

32. Journal, June 13, 1974, Stanley Family Archives.

33. Ibid., July 17, 1874.

34. P. Forbath, *The River Congo: The Discovery, Exploration, and Exploitation of the World's Most Dramatic River* (New York: Harper & Row, 1977), 276–77.

35. A few years later, de Bellefonds was killed in Sudan.

36. Bierman, op. cit., 182.

37. H. Brode, *Tippoo Tib: The Story of His Career in Central Africa*, trans. H. Havelock (London: Edward Arnold, 1907).

38. Stanley, 1909, op. cit., 325.

39. F. McLynn, *Hearts of Darkness: The European Exploration of Africa* (London: Hutchinson, 1992), 267–68.

40. Bierman, op. cit., 201–3.

41. Stanley, 1878, op. cit., 2:201.

42. Stanley and Neame, op. cit., 143.

43. L. Farrant, *Tippu Tip and the East African Slave Trade* (New York: St. Martin's Press, 1975), 87.

44. Stanley and Neames, op. cit., 177.

45. Forbath, op. cit., 315.

46. Stanley, 1878, op. cit., 2:447.

47. A. A. Serpa Pinto, *How I Crossed Africa: From the Atlantic Ocean, Through Unknown Countries: Discovery of the Great Zambesi Affluents, etc.*, trans. A. Elwes (London: Sampson, Low, Marston, Searle, & Rivington, 1881).

48. A. Hochschild, *King Leopold's Ghost: A Story of Greed, Terror, and Heroism in Colonial Africa* (Boston: Houghton Mifflin, 1998), 28.

49. Stanley, 1878, op. cit., 2:480.

50. Z. Nadjer, *Joseph Conrad: A Chronicle* (New Brunswick, N.J.: Rutgers University Press, 1983), 127.

51. R. West, *Congo* (New York: Holt, Rinehart and Winston, 1972), 74.

52. J. H. Franklin, *George Washington Williams: A Biography* (Chicago: University of Chicago Press, 1985), 244–45.

53. Forbath, op. cit., 357.

54. Journal, November 27, 1883, Stanley Family Archives.

55. L. H. Gann and P. Duignan, *The Rulers of Belgian Africa, 1884–1914* (Princeton: Princeton University Press, 1979), 35.

56. Nadjer, op. cit., 127.

57. J. Marchal, *L'État Libre du Congo: Paradis Perdu: L'Histoire du Congo, 1876–1900,* 2 vols. (Borgloon, Belgium: Éditions Paula Bellings, 1996b).

58. R. Cornet, *La Bataille du Rail* (Brussels: Éditions L. Cuypers, 1958).

59. I. R. Smith, *The Emin Pasha Relief Expedition, 1886–1890* (Oxford: The Clarendon Press, 1972), 14.

60. Ibid., 151.

61. Ibid., 45.

62. W. G. Stairs, *Victorian Explorer: The African Diaries of Captain William G. Stairs,* ed. J. M. Konczacki (Halifax, Nova Scotia: Nimbus, 1944), 15.

63. Hochschild, op. cit., 98.

64. Bierman, op. cit., 269.

65. R. Jones, *The Rescue of Emin Pasha* (London: Allison & Busby, 1910), 98.

66. Ibid.; and Smith, op. cit., 86.

67. H. R. Fox Bourne, *The Other Side of the Emin Pasha Relief Expedition* (London: Chatto & Windus, 1891), 46.

68. H. M. Stanley, *In Darkest Africa; or, The Quest, Rescue, and Retreat of Emin, Governor of Equatoria,* 2 vols. (New York: Charles Scribner's Sons, 1890), 1:73.

69. T. H. Parke, *My Personal Experiences in Equatorial Africa* (New York: Charles Scribner's Sons, 1891), 407.

70. Jones, op. cit., 186.

71. A. J. M. Jephson, *Emin Pasha and the Rebellion at the Equator* (London: Sampson, Low, Marston, Searle & Rivington, 1890), 917.

72. Parke, op. cit., 223.

73. Jones, op. cit., 208.

74. *Daily Telegraph,* October 28, 1890.

75. Jones, op. cit., 432.

76. Stanley, 1890, 1:471–73.

77. J. S. Jameson, *Story of the Rear Column of the Emin Pasha Relief Expedition,* ed. Mrs. J. S. Jameson (London: R. H. Porter, 1890), 291.

78. *Times* of London, November 10, 1890.

79. Bierman, op. cit., 327.

80. J. R. Troup, *With Stanley's Rear Column* (London: Chapman and Hall, 1890), 145.

81. H. Ward, *My Life with Stanley's Rear Guard* (London: Chatto & Windus, 1891), 157.

82. *Times* of London, November 16, 1990.

83. McLynn, 1991, op. cit., 235.

84. Ibid.

85. *New York Herald,* October 26, 1890.

86. Bierman, op. cit., 328.

87. Nadjer, op. cit., 526.

88. McLynn, 1991, op. cit., 270.

89. D. Middleton, ed., *The Diary of A. J. Mounteney Jephson: Emin Pasha Relief Expedition, 1887–1889* (Cambridge: Cambridge University Press, 1969), 413.

90. Bierman, op. cit., 317.

91. Stairs, op. cit., 170.

92. Jones, op. cit., 348.

93. Parke, op. cit., 504–5.

94. Bierman, op. cit., 320–23; and McLynn, 1991, op. cit., 325.

95. Jones, op. cit., 394.

3. CONQUERING THE CONGO

1. L. H. Gann and P. Duignan, *The Rulers of Belgian Africa, 1884–1914* (Princeton: Princeton University Press, 1979).

2. B. Emerson, *Leopold II of the Belgians, King of Colonialism* (London: Weidenfeld and Nicolson, 1979), 72.

3. Gann and Duignan, op. cit., 29.

4. R. Lemarchand, *Political Awakening in the Belgian Congo* (Berkeley: University of California Press, 1964).

5. D. Pipes, *Slave Soldiers and Islam: The Genesis of a Military System* (New Haven: Yale University Press, 1981).

6. J. W. Blassingame, *The Slave Community: Plantation Life in the Antebellum South* (Oxford: Oxford University Press, 1979); and D. B. Davis, "Slavery—White, Black, Muslim, Christian," *The New York Review of Books*, July 5, 2001.

7. D. B. Davis, *Slavery and Human Progress* (Oxford: Oxford University Press, 1984).

8. H. M. Stanley, *How I Found Livingstone*, 2 vols. (New York: Scribner, Armstrong & Co., 1872), 1:262.

9. E. D. Moore, *Ivory Scourge of Africa* (New York: Harper and Brothers, 1931).

10. Ibid., 66.

11. E. J. Glave, *Six Years of Adventure in Congo-Land* (with an introduction by H. M. Stanley) (London: Sampson, Low, Marston & Company, 1893), 329–30.

12. S. L. Hinde, *The Fall of the Congo Arabs* (1897; reprint, New York: Negro Universities Press, 1969), 7.

13. Ibid., 283.

14. Ibid., 62–64.

15. E. Torday, *On the Trail of the Bushongo* (London: Seeley, Service & Co., 1925), 70.

16. Hinde, op. cit., 53.

17. Ibid., 90.

18. M. W. Hilton-Simpson, *Land and the Peoples of the Kasai, Being a Narrative of a Two-Years' Journey Among the Cannibals of the Equatorial Forest and Other Savage Tribes of the South-Western Congo* (London: Constable and Company, 1911), 148–49.

19. H. Norden, *Fresh Tracks in the Belgian Congo: From the Uganda Border to the Mouth of the Congo* (Boston: Small, Maynard & Co., 1925), 277.

20. Torday, op. cit., 226–27.

21. A. B. Lloyd, *In Dwarf Land and Cannibal Country: A Record of Travel and Discovery in Central Africa* (London: T. Fischer Unwin, 1900), 358.

22. J. Bierman, *Dark Safari: The Life Behind the Legend of Henry Morton Stanley* (New York: A. A. Knopf, 1990), 304.

23. Hinde, op. cit., 63–64.

24. H. Ward, *A Voice from the Congo: Comprising Stories, Anecdotes, and Descriptive Notes* (London: William Heinemann, 1910), 276.

25. H. Ward, *Five Years with the Congo Cannibals* (London: Chatto & Windus, 1891), 134.

26. Ibid., 22.

27. P. Bourgoin, "Herbert Ward, 1863–1919: Explorer, Writer, Sculptor and Collector," *The World of Tribal Art,* spring 1996, 48–62.

28. Ibid., 26.

29. Ibid., 140.

30. Ibid., 155.

31. H. Marles, "Arrested Development: Race and Evolution in the Sculpture of Herbert Ward," *Oxford Art Journal* 19 (1996): 16–28. Although fifty-two years old when World War I broke out, Ward volunteered for duty as a lieutenant with the British Ambulance Committee on the western front in 1915, experiencing endless horrors and being badly injured himself. His oldest son, Charles, a boxing champion at Oxford, was killed in 1916 while on a patrol only thirty yards from German trenches. Ward's youngest son, Herbert, a British pilot, was shot down and badly wounded but nevertheless escaped from a German prison camp and safely returned to England. Ward was awarded the Croix de Guerre for his services before he died in 1919 at age fifty-six (S. S. Pawling, *Mr. Poilu: Notes and Sketches with the Fighting French* [London: Hodder and Stoughton, 1916]).

32. Ward, 1910, op. cit., 286.

33. Hinde, op. cit., 8.

34. H. Brode, *Tippoo Tib: The Story of His Career in Central Africa,* trans. H. Havelock (London: Edward Arnold, 1907), 41; and Moore, op. cit.

35. L. Farrant, *Tippu Tip and the East African Slave Trade* (New York: St. Martin's Press, 1975), 3.

36. Ibid.

37. Brode, op. cit.; Moore, op. cit.; M. P. Monahan, "The Sound of Guns: A Biography of Tippu Tip," (master's thesis, Department of History, San Francisco State College, 1972); and Farrant, op. cit.

38. Farrant, op. cit., 35.

39. Moore, op. cit., 114.

40. R. P. P. Ceulemans, *La question arabe et le Congo (1883–1892)* (Bruxelles: MARSC, 1959), 32.

41. A. J. Swann, *Fighting the Slave Hunters in Central Africa* (London: Seeley, 1910), 49.

42. Farrant, op. cit., 6–7.

43. Bierman, op. cit., 192–93.

44. F. McLynn, *Stanley: Sorcerer's Apprentice* (London: Constable, 1991), 153.

45. T. H. Parke, *My Personal Experiences in Equatorial Africa* (New York, Charles Scribner's Sons, 1891), 68.

46. Ward, 1910, op. cit., 73–74.

47. Moore, op. cit., 142.

48. W. J. Samarin, *The Black Man's Burden: African Colonial Labor on the Congo and Ubangi Rivers, 1880–1900* (Boulder, Colo.: Westview Press, 1989).

49. Ibid., 61.

50. Gann and Duignan, op. cit., 225.

51. Samarin, op. cit., 43.

52. B. P. Shaw, "Force Publique, Force Unique" (Ph.D. diss., Department of Psychology, University of Wisconsin, Madison, 1984), 286.

53. Ibid., 312.

54. Samarin, op. cit., 10.

55. Ibid., 51; Hinde, op. cit., 109.

56. A. Flament, *La Force Publique de sa naissance à 1914: Participations des militaires à l'histoire des premières années du Congo* (Brussels: Institut Royal Colonial Belge, 1952).

57. Hinde, op. cit., 23.

58. Captain Michaux, *Carnet de Campagne: Episodes & Impressions de 1889–1897* (Bruxelles: Librairie Falk, 1907), 97.

59. Hinde, op. cit.

60. Michaux, op. cit., 92.

61. Hinde, op. cit., 209.

62. Ceulemans, op. cit., 339.

63. Hinde, op. cit., 276; and T. Packenham, *The Scramble for Africa, 1876–1912* (New York: Random House, 1991).

64. Hinde, op. cit., 96.

65. Michaux, op. cit., 178.

66. Hinde, op. cit., 24.

67. Michaux, op. cit., 176–80.

68. Ibid., 116.

69. Ibid., 183.

70. Hinde, op. cit., 33.

71. Ibid., 32ff.

72. G. Burrows, *The Curse of Central Africa: With which is incorporated, A Campaign Amongst Cannibals,* by Edgar Canisius (London: R. A. Everett & Co., 1903), 107.

73. Ibid., 177.

74. Ibid., xxv, 252, 255.

75. Ibid., 43.

76. Hinde, op. cit., 125.

77. Ibid., 101–2.

78. Ibid., 112.

79. Ibid., 113.

80. Ibid., 184–85.

81. Ibid., 185.

82. Gann and Duignan, op. cit., 74.

83. Farrant, op. cit., 17.

84. Ibid., 143.

85. R. Jones, *The Rescue of Emin Pasha* (London: Allison & Bushy, 1910), 395.

86. Gann and Duignan, op. cit., 57.

87. Brode, op. cit.

88. R. M. Slade, *King Leopold's Congo: Aspects of the Development of Race Relations in the Congo Independent State* (London and New York: Oxford University Press, 1962), 116.

89. Ibid., 114.

90. Gann and Duignan, op. cit., 100.

91. Ibid., 107.

92. Viscount Mountmorres, *The Congo Independent State: A Report on a Voyage of Enquiry* (London: Williams and Norgate, 1906), 73.

93. Ibid., 78–79.

94. S. Axelson, *Culture Confrontation in the Lower Congo: From the Old Congo Kingdom to the Congo Independent State with Special Reference to the Swedish Missionaries in the 1880's and 1890's* (Falköping, Sweden: Gummessons, 1970), 260.

95. G. De Boeck, *Baoni: Les Révoltes de la Force Publique sous Léopold II, Congo, 1895–1908* (Brussels: Les Éditions EPO, 1987).

96. E. G. Ravenstein, ed., *The Strange Adventures of Andrew Battell of Leigh, in Angola and the Adjoining Regions* (London: The Hakluyt Society, 1901), 21.

97. Hinde, op. cit., 52–53.

98. Ibid., 135.

99. Ibid., 65.

100. J-P. Hallet, *Congo Kitabu* (New York: Random House, 1964), 64. In 1961 in Uganda, a man offered to sell me human fingers that had been smoked. When I declined in horror, he offered to return with a smoked slab of a young woman's buttocks, a truly "choice cut," as he put it.

101. H. H. Johnston, *The River Congo From Its Mouth to Bolobo* (London: Sampson, Low, Marston & Company, 1895), 127.

102. A. Chapaux, *Le Congo: Historique, Diplomatique, Physique, Politique, Économique, Humanitaire, et Colonial* (Brussels: Rozez, 1894), 510.

103. R. R. Stuart, *Kassai: The Story of Raoul de Prémorel, African Trader* (Stockton, Calif.: University of the Pacific, 1975), 63.

104. Ibid., 97.

105. Burrows, op. cit., 168.

106. W. H. Sheppard, *Pioneers in Congo* (Louisville, Ky.: Pentecostal Publishing Co., 1917), 65; and R. Benedetto, ed., *Presbyterian Reformers in Central Africa: A Documentary Account of the American Presbyterian Congo Mission and the Human Rights Struggle in the Congo, 1890–1918*, trans. Winifred K. Vass (Leiden: E. J. Brill, 1996), 123.

107. R. Anstey, *King Leopold's Legacy: The Congo Under Belgian Rule, 1908 1960* (London: Oxford University Press, 1966), 7.

108. A. Hochschild, *King Leopold's Ghost: A Story of Greed, Terror, and Heroism in Colonial Africa* (Boston: Houghton Mifflin, 1998).

4. SAVING THE CONGO

1. S. M. Jacobs, ed., *Black Americans and the Missionary Movement in Africa* (Westport, Conn.: Greenwood, 1982), 21.

2. Ibid., 23.

3. S. Axelson, *Culture Confrontation in the Lower Congo: From the Old Congo Kingdom to the Congo Independent State with Special Reference to the Swedish Missionaries in the 1880's and 1890's* (Falköping, Sweden: Gummessons, 1970), 229–31.

4. Ibid., 277.

5. Ibid., 288.

6. H. Ward, *A Voice from the Congo: Comprising Stories, Anecdotes, and Descriptive Notes* (London: William Heinemann, 1910), 51.

7. W. H. Bentley, *Pioneering on the Congo*, 2 vols. (Oxford: The Religious Tract Society, 1900).

8. W. E. Phipps, *The Sheppards and Lapsley: Pioneer Presbyterians in the Congo* (Louisville, Ky.: The Presbyterian Church, 1991), 2.

9. Ibid., 9.

10. W. H. Sheppard, *Pioneers in Congo* (Louisville, Ky.: Pentecostal Publishing Co., 1917), 20.

11. S. Shaloff, *Reform in Leopold's Congo* (Richmond, Va.: John Knox Press, 1970), 20.

12. J. W. Lapsley, ed., *Samuel Norvell Lapsley, Missionary to the Congo. Valley, West Africa, 1866–1892* (Richmond, Va.: Whittet and Shepperson, 1893), 55.

13. Shaloff, op. cit., 26.

14. Sheppard, op. cit., 40.

15. Lapsley, op. cit., 108.

16. Ibid., 115.

17. Ibid., 173, 192.

18. Ibid., 187.

19. Ibid., 189.

20. Jacobs, op. cit., 139.

21. J. H. Franklin, *George Washington Williams: A Biography* (Chicago: University of Chicago Press, 1985), 3.

22. Ibid., 10.

23. Ibid., 40.

24. Ibid., 115.

25. Ibid., 181.

26. Ibid., 182.

27. Ibid., 191.

28. Ibid., 202–3.

29. Ibid., 244–45.

30. Ibid., 206.

31. R. M. Slade, *English-Speaking Missions in the Congo Independent State (1878–1908)* (Brussels: Académie Royale des Sciences Coloniales, 1959), 244.

32. Lapsley, op. cit., 94.

33. Phipps, op. cit., 40–41.

34. J. Vansina, "Les Croyances Religieuses des Kuba," *Zaire* 12 (1958): 726.

35. Shaloff, op. cit., 34–35.

36. Phipps, op. cit., 53.

37. Jacobs, op. cit., 141.

38. J. L. Kellersberger, *Lucy Gantt Sheppard, Shepherdess of His Sheep on Two Continents* (Atlanta: Committee on Women's Work, Presbyterian Church in the United States, n.d.).

39. Ibid.

40. Jacobs, op. cit., 144.

41. Kellersberger, op. cit., 11.

42. W. L. Williams, "William Henry Sheppard, Afro-American Missionary in the Congo, 1890–1910," in S. M. Jacobs, ed., *Black Americans and the Missionary Movement in Africa* (Westport, Conn.: Greenwood, 1982).

43. *The Missionary,* July 26, 1898.

44. E. D. Morel, *Red Rubber: The Story of the Rubber Slave Trade Which Flourished on the Congo for Twenty Years, 1890–1910,* new and rev. ed. (1906; reprint, Manchester: National Labour Press, 1919), 43–44.

45. B. P. Shaw, "Force Publique, Force Unique" (Ph.D. diss., Department of Psychology, University of Wisconsin, Madison, 1984), 25.

46. C. Legum, *Congo Disaster* (Baltimore: Penguin Books, 1961), 32.

47. W. H. Sheppard, *Southern Workman,* December 1893, 182.
48. L. M. Schall, "William H. Sheppard: Fighter for African Rights," in K. L. Schall, ed., *Stony the Road: Chapters in the History of Hampton Institute* (Charlottesville: University Press of Virginia, 1977), 108.
49. Phipps, op. cit., 83.
50. Ibid.
51. Ibid.
52. Ibid., 84.
53. Ibid.
54. Shaloff, op. cit., 77.
55. Axelson, op. cit., 265.
56. Ibid., 264.
57. Ibid., 265.
58. Shaloff, op. cit., 79.
59. R. Benedetto, ed., *Presbyterian Reformers in Central Africa: A Documentary Account of the American Presbyterian Congo Mission and the Human Rights Struggle in the Congo, 1890–1918,* trans. Winifred K. Vass (Leiden: E. J. Brill, 1996), 108.
60. Morel, op. cit., 58.
61. Slade, op. cit.
62. Bentley, op. cit.
63. Slade, op. cit., 255.
64. G. Hawker, *The Life of George Grenfell: Congo Missionary and Explorer* (London: The Religious Tract Society, 1909), 542.
65. W. R. Louis and J. Stengers, *E. D. Morel's History of the Congo Reform Movement* (London: Oxford, 1968), 125–26.
66. C. A. Cline, *E. D. Morel, 1874–1924: The Strategies of Protest* (Dundonald, Belfast: Blackstaff Press, 1980), 34.
67. Slade, op. cit., 265.
68. Shaloff, op. cit., 90.
69. Slade, op. cit., 259.
70. W. R. Louis, "Roger Casement and the Congo," *Journal of African History* 5 (1964): 114.
71. Morel, op. cit., 47.
72. Ibid., xv.
73. Ibid., 304.
74. Shaloff, op. cit., 103.
75. Slade, op. cit., 330–31.
76. W. II. Sheppard, *Kasai Herald,* January 1, 1908, 12–13.
77. Phipps, op. cit., 106.
78. Benedetto, op. cit., 28–29.
79. H. G. Cureau, "William H. Sheppard: Missionary to the Congo, and Collector of African Art," *Journal of Negro History* 67 (1982): 340–52.
80. Shaloff, op. cit., 41.
81. P. V. Bradford and H. Blume, *Ota: The Pygmy in the Zoo* (New York: St. Martin's Press, 1992).
82. Benedetto, op. cit., 245–46.
83. Ibid., 244–45.
84. Ibid., 424–25.

Notes

85. Ibid.
86. Jacobs, op. cit., 156–57.
87. Ibid., 157.
88. S. L. V. Timmons, *Glorious Living: Informal Sketches of Seven Women Missionaries of the Presbyterian Church, U.S.* (Atlanta: Committee on Women's Work, Presbyterian Church, U.S., 1937).
89. Jacobs, op. cit., 161.
90. J. L. Kellersberger, *A Life for the Congo: The Story of Althea Brown Edmiston* (New York: Fleming H. Revell, 1947), 33.
91. Ibid., 57.
92. Ibid.
93. Ibid., 87.
94. C. Young, *Politics in the Congo: Decolonization and Independence* (Princeton: Princeton University Press, 1965), 12–13.
95. R. Lemarchand, *Political Awakening in the Belgian Congo* (Berkeley: University of California Press, 1964), 126.

5. THE BELGIAN CONGO

1. Baroness DeVaughan, with P. Faure, *A Commoner Married a King* (New York: Ives Washburn, 1937).
2. D. Northrup, *Beyond the Bend in the River: African Labor in Eastern Zaire, 1865–1940* (Athens: Ohio University Center for International Studies, 1988).
3. J. Stengers, *Belgique et Congo: L'élaboration de la charte coloniale* (Brussels: La Renaissance du Livre, 1963), 199.
4. G. Stinglhamber and P. Dresse, *Léopold II au Travail* (Brussels: Éditions du Sablon, 1945), 52–53.
5. E. Carton de Wiart, *Léopold II, souvenirs des dernières années, 1901–1909* (Brussels: Goemaere, 1944), 203.
6. J. Marchal, *E. Morel Contre Léopold II: L'Histoire du Congo, 1876–1900*, 2 vols. (Paris: Éditions L'Harmattan, 1996a), vol. 2.
7. Ibid.
8. R. Lemarchand, *Political Awakening in the Belgian Congo* (Berkeley: University of California Press, 1964), 118.
9. J. Vansina, introduction to D. Vangroenweghe, *Du Sang sur les Lianes* (Brussels: Didier Hatier, 1986).
10. R. Anstey, *King Leopold's Legacy: The Congo Under Belgian Rule, 1908–1960* (London: Oxford University Press, 1966), 38.
11. L. H. Gann and P. Duignan, *The Rulers of Belgian Africa, 1884–1914* (Princeton: Princeton University Press, 1979), 17.
12. Ibid., 184.
13. H. Norden, *Fresh Tracks in the Belgian Congo: From the Uganda Border to the Mouth of the Congo* (Boston: Small, Maynard & Co., 1925), 65.
14. Anstey, op. cit., 42.
15. A. P. Merriam, *Congo: Background of Conflict* (Evanston: Northwestern University Press, 1961), 37.
16. G. Martelli, *Leopold to Lumumba: A History of the Belgian Congo, 1877–1960* (London: Chapman & Hall, 1962).
17. Ibid., 45.

18. B. Fetter, *The Creation of Elisabethville, 1910–1940* (Stanford: Stanford University Press, 1976).
19. Ibid., 29.
20. Norden, op. cit., 173.
21. Fetter, op. cit., 35.
22. Ibid., 23.
23. Anstey, op. cit., 39.
24. Lemarchand, op. cit., 39.
25. J-P. Hallet, *Congo Kitabu* (New York: Random House, 1964).
26. Viscount Mountmorres, *The Congo Independent State: A Report on a Voyage of Enquiry* (London: Williams and Norgate, 1906), 99.
27. Anstey, op. cit., 53.
28. Gann and Duignan, op. cit., 107.
29. Anstey, op. cit., 9.
30. G. Van der Kerken, *Les Sociétés Bantoues du Congo Belge* (Brussels: Établissements Émile Bruylant, 1920), 356–57.
31. T. C. Vinson, *William McCutchan Morrison: Twenty Years in Central Africa* (Richmond: Va.: Presbyterian Committee on Publication, 1921), 136.
32. Anstey, op. cit., 54.
33. B. P. Shaw, "Force Publique, Force Unique" (Ph.D. diss., Department of Psychology, University of Wisconsin, Madison, 1984), 91.
34. Norden, op. cit.
35. C. Young, *Politics in the Congo: Decolonization and Independence* (Princeton: Princeton University Press, 1965), 11.
36. Ibid., 21.
37. H. H. Johnston, *The River Congo: From Its Mouth to Bolobo* (London: Sampson, Low, Marston & Company, 1895), 86.
38. Young, op. cit., 93–94.
39. Anstey, op. cit., 206–7.
40. Martelli, op. cit., 191.
41. E. Close, *A Woman Alone in Kenya, Uganda and the Belgian Congo* (London: Constable & Co., 1924), 226.
42. Fetter, op. cit., 31.
43. Ibid.
44. Ibid., 32–33.
45. M. Severn, *Congo Pilgrim* (London: The Travel Book Club, 1952), 26.
46. Close, op. cit., 241.
47. Gann and Duignan, op. cit., 204.
48. Ibid.
49. Merriam, op. cit., 36.
50. Young, op. cit., 63–64.
51. Anstey, op. cit., 108.
52. Severn, op. cit., 55–56.
53. Anstey, op. cit., 119.
54. Fetter, op. cit., 88.
55. Anstey, op. cit., 201.
56. Norden, op. cit., 70.
57. Martelli, op. cit., 198.

58. Lemarchand, op. cit., 104.
59. Ibid., 112.
60. Shaw, op. cit., 313.
61. Martelli, op. cit., 201.
62. C. M. Turnbull, *The Lonely African* (London: Chatto and Windus, 1963), 107.
63. Anstey, op. cit., 125.
64. E. Andersson, *Messianic Popular Movements in the Lower Congo* (Uppsala, Sweden: Almquist & Wiksells, 1958), 57.
65. Anstey, op. cit., 134–35.
66. Andersson, op. cit., 263.
67. Ibid., 67.
68. Anstey, op. cit., 134.
69. Merriam, op. cit., 97.
70. Martelli, op. cit., 207.
71. Lemarchand, op. cit., 139–41.
72. Merriam, op. cit., 47.
73. Anstey, op. cit., 207.
74. E. O'Ballance, *The Congo-Zaire Experience, 1960–98* (New York: St. Martin's Press, 2000), 3.
75. Hallet, op. cit., 56.
76. Young, op. cit., 44.
77. Lemarchand, op. cit., 159.
78. D. P. Dugauquier, *Congo Cauldron* (London: Jarrolds, 1961), 20.
79. Hallet, op. cit.
80. Norden, op. cit., 82–83.
81. Ibid., 195.
82. Ibid., 220.
83. Young, op. cit., 88.
84. C. Legum, *Congo Disaster* (Baltimore: Penguin Books, 1961), 44.
85. Merriam, op. cit., 57–58.
86. Young, op. cit., 84.
87. Legum, op. cit., 52.
88. Young, op. cit., 73.
89. Norden, op. cit., 287.
90. Dugauquier, op. cit., 37–38.
91. R. Laxalt, *A Private War: An American Code Officer in the Belgian Congo* (Reno: University of Nevada Press, 1998), 46.
92. Young, op. cit., 105.
93. Ibid., 104.
94. I. Kabongo, "The Catastrophe of Belgian Decolonization," in P. Gifford and W. R. Louis, eds., *Decolonization and African Independence: The Transfers of Power, 1960–1980* (New Haven: Yale University Press, 1988), 388.
95. Lemarchand, op. cit., 200.
96. Martelli, op. cit.
97. Legum, op. cit.
98. M. C. C. De Backer, *Notes pour servir à l'étude des "groupements politiques" à Léopoldville* (Léopoldville: Infor-Congo, 1959), 26.

99. Young, op. cit., 290.
100. Ibid.
101. Lemarchand, op. cit., 173.
102. Legum, op. cit., 76.
103. S. Kelly, *America's Tyrant: The CIA and Mobutu of Zaire* (Washington, D.C.: American University Press, 1993), 16.
104. P. De Vos, *Vie et mort de Lumumba* (Paris: Calmann-Lévy, 1961), 195–96.

6. Independence — The Dream and the Nightmare

1. C. Legum, *Congo Disaster* (Baltimore: Penguin Books, 1961), 111.
2. Ibid., 113.
3. L. Merchiers, *A Preliminary Report on the Atrocities Committed by the Congolese Army Against the White Population of the Republic of the Congo Before the Intervention of the Belgian Forces* (New York: Belgian Government Information Center, 1960).
4. Ibid., 11–12.
5. C. Young, *Politics in the Congo: Decolonization and Independence* (Princeton: Princeton University Press, 1965), 319.
6. R. Anstey, *King Leopold's Legacy: The Congo Under Belgian Rule, 1908–1960* (London: Oxford University Press, 1966), 170.
7. Young, op. cit., 309.
8. S. Kelly, *America's Tyrant: The CIA and Mobutu of Zaire* (Washington, D.C.: American University Press, 1993), 33; and B. Urquhart, "The Tragedy of Lumumba," *The New York Review*, October 4, 2001.
9. M. G. Kalb, *The Congo Cables* (New York: Macmillan, 1982), 26–29.
10. Kelly, op. cit., 35.
11. R. D. Mahoney, *JFK: Ordeal in Africa* (New York: Oxford, 1983), 39.
12. *Analytical Chronology of the Congo Crisis*, Department of State, January 25, 1961.
13. Kelly, op. cit., 36.
14. Mahoney, op. cit., 71.
15. D. Doyle, *True Men and Traitors: From the OSS to the CIA, My Life in the Shadows* (New York: John Wiley & Sons, 2001), 130.
16. Kelly, op. cit., 46–47.
17. Mahoney, op. cit., 47.
18. E. O'Ballance, *The Congo-Zaire Experience, 1960–98* (New York: St. Martin's Press, 2000), 33.
19. C. Young and T. Turner, *The Rise and Decline of the Zairian State* (Madison: University of Wisconsin Press, 1985), 61.
20. E. Packham, *Success or Failure: The UN Intervention in the Congo After Independence* (Commack, N.Y.: Nova Science Publishers, 1998), 48.
21. L. De Witte, *L'assassinat de Lumumba* (Paris: Éditions Karthala, 2000).
22. J. Stockwell, *In Search of Enemies: A CIA Story* (New York: W. W. Norton, 1978), 105.
23. De Witte, op. cit.
24. Mahoney, op. cit., 74.
25. D. N. Chatterjee, *Storm Over the Congo* (New Delhi: Vikas, 1980), 73.
26. M. G. Schatzberg, *Mobutu or Chaos? The United States and Zaire, 1960–1990* (New York: University Press of America, 1991), 81–82.
27. Mahoney, op. cit., 116.

28. Ibid., 93.
29. T. Vleurinck, ed., *46 Angry Men: The 46 Civilian Doctors of Elisabethville Denounce U.N.O. Violations in Katanga* (Brussels: Belgian Senate, 1962).
30. F. Monheim, *Mobutu, l'homme seul* (Brussels: Éditions Actuelles, 1963).
31. J. Chomé, *L'ascension de Mobutu: du Sergent Joseph Désiré au Général Sese Seko* (Brussels: Éditions Complexe, 1974).
32. Ibid., 72.
33. Monheim, op. cit., 31.
34. Ibid., 74.
35. Kelly, op. cit., 10.
36. Young and Turner, op. cit., 438.
37. Ibid.
38. P. Masson, *La Bataille pour Bukavu* (Brussels: Impresor, 1965).
39. O'Ballance, op. cit., 72.
40. T. P. Odom, *Dragon Operations: Hostage Rescues in the Congo; Leavenworth Papers No. 14* (Fort Leavenworth, Kans.: Combat Studies Institute, U.S. Army Command and General Staff College, 1988), 20.
41. D. Reed, *111 Days in Stanleyville* (New York: Harper & Row, 1965), 53.
42. Ibid., 77.
43. M. P. E. Hoyt, *Captive in the Congo: A Consul's Return to the Heart of Darkness* (Annapolis, Md.: Naval Institute Press, 2000).
44. Reed, op. cit., 69.
45. Odom, op. cit., 102.
46. Ibid., 135.
47. O'Ballance, op. cit., 81.
48. Ibid.
49. Odom, op. cit., 149.
50. D. James, *Che Guevara, a Biography* (New York: Stein and Day, 1969).
51. Kelly, op. cit., 169.
52. M. Wrong, *In the Footsteps of Mr. Kurtz: Living on the Brink of Disaster in the Congo* (London: Fourth Estate, 2000), 63.
53. Ibid., 201.
54. B. Harden, *Africa: Dispatches from a Dark Continent* (Boston: Houghton Mifflin, 1990), 196.
55. B. Harden, *Washington Post,* November 10, 1987.
56. Harden, 1990, op. cit., 49; and Nguz a Karl-i-Bond, *Mobutu, ou l'Incarnation du Mal Zairois* (London: Rex Collins, 1982).
57. H. Winternitz, *East Along the Equator: A Journey up the Congo and into Zaire* (New York: Atlantic Monthly Press, 1987), 18.
58. Young and Turner, op. cit., 63.
59. O'Ballance, op. cit., 110.
60. Kelly, op. cit., 205.
61. A. Almquist, "The Society and Its Environment," in S. W. Meditz and T. Merrill, eds., *Zaire, a Country Study* (Washington, D.C.: Federal Research Division, Library of Congress, 1994), 107.
62. Harden, 1990, op. cit., 38.
63. Wrong, op. cit., 92.

64. B. Berkeley, *The Graves Are Not Yet Full: Race, Tribe and Power in the Heart of Africa* (New York: Basic Books, 2001), 111.
65. Almquist, op. cit., 114.
66. Wrong, op. cit., 94.
67. Almquist, op. cit., 126.
68. Ibid., 115.
69. J. MacGaffey, ed., *The Real Economy of Zaire: The Contribution of Smuggling and Other Unofficial Activities to Nation Wealth* (Philadelphia: University of Pennsylvania Press, 1991).
70. O'Ballance, op. cit., 128.
71. Wrong, op. cit., 102.
72. Ibid., 224.
73. Ibid., 100.
74. P. Janssen, *À la Cour de Mobutu* (Paris: Michel Lafon, 1997).
75. Ibid.
76. L. Joris, *Back to the Congo*, trans. Stacey Knecht (New York: Atheneum, 1992), 141.
77. Wrong, op. cit., 220–21; and Janssen, op. cit.
78. O'Ballance, op. cit., 141.
79. K. B. Richburg, *Out of America: A Black Man Confronts Africa* (New York: Basic Books, 1997).
80. G. B. N. Ayittey, *Africa in Chaos* (New York: Pantheon Books, 1998), 61.
81. George Bush, June 29, 1989.
82. Kelly, op. cit., 252.
83. *Africa-Confidential*, June 15, 1990.
84. Kelly, op. cit., 253.
85. *New York Times*, December 9, 1991.
86. A. H. Gnamo, "The Rwandan Genocide and the Collapse of Mobutu's Kleptocracy," in H. Adelman and A. Suhrke, eds., *The Path of a Genocide: The Rwanda Crisis from Uganda to Zaire* (London: Transaction Publishers, 1999).
87. *Washington Post*, January 24, 1997.
88. Wrong, op. cit., 278–79.
89. O'Ballance, op. cit., 175.
90. Associated Press, June 1, 1997.
91. Reuters, May 25, 1997.
92. *Time*, May 26, 1997, 22.

7. The Congo and Kabila—Father and Son

1. G. B. N. Ayittey, *Africa in Chaos* (New York: Pantheon Books, 1998), 68.
2. M. Wrong, *In the Footsteps of Mr. Kurtz: Living on the Brink of Disaster in the Congo* (London: Fourth Estate, 2000), 31.
3. K. Maier, *Into the House of Our Ancestors: Inside the New Africa* (New York: John Wiley & Sons, 1998).
4. Reuters, May 15, 1998.
5. Wrong, op. cit., 290.
6. *New York Times*, November 27, 1996.
7. H. Winternitz, *East Along the Equator: A Journey up the Congo and into Zaire* (New York: Atlantic Monthly Press, 1987).

8. *Washington Post,* January 23, 2001.
9. Ayittey, op. cit., 65.
10. *Washington Post,* July 6, 1997.
11. Ibid., July 9, 1997.
12. *African Business,* March 2001.
13. Wrong, op. cit., 300.
14. M. G. Schatzberg, *The Dialectics of Oppression in Zaire* (Bloomington: Indiana University Press, 1988).
15. B. Verhaegen, *Rebéllions au Congo,* 2 vols. (Brussels: CRISP, 1966).
16. E. Boissonade, *Kabila Clone de Mobutu?* (Paris: Éditions Moveux, 1998).
17. Ibid., 78.
18. *The African Observer,* June 5–11, 1997.
19. *Economist,* January 20, 2001.
20. J. Kwitney, *Endless Enemies: The Making of an Unfriendly World* (New York: Congdon & Weed, 1984); and J. C. McKinley, "Mobutu's Nemesis Keeps His Plans to Himself," *New York Times,* April 1, 1997, A1.
21. C. Braekman, "One Disaster After Another," *Index on Censorship* 1 (2001): 148.
22. B. Harden, "A Black Mud from Africa Helps Power the New Economy," *New York Times,* August 12, 2001.
23. B. Berkeley, *The Graves Are Not Yet Full: Race, Tribe and Power in the Heart of Africa* (New York: Basic Books, 2001), 239.
24. *African Business,* March 9, 2001.
25. Deutsche Press-Agentur, September 14, 2001.
26. *African Business,* March 2001.
27. UN Integrated Regional Information Network, September 25, 2001.
28. A. M. Simmons, "Kabila's Funeral Held Amid Tight Security," *Los Angeles Times,* January 24, 2001, A10.
29. *African Business,* March 2001.
30. *Los Angeles Times,* January 27, 2001.
31. *New York Times,* April 15, 2001.
32. *Washington Post,* January 21, 2001.
33. Ibid.
34. F. Misser, "Democratic Republic of Congo: Lessons in Statecraft," *African Business,* April 2001, 45–46.
35. *World Press Review,* April 2001, 25.
36. *Europe,* May 2001.
37. Ibid.
38. *Time International,* April 23, 2001.
39. *Economist,* May 5, 2001.
40. *Africa-Confidential,* July 13, 2001.
41. *Christian Science Monitor,* May 7, 2001.
42. BBC News, August 10, 2001.
43. *Los Angeles Times,* July 5, 2001.
44. *The Guardian,* July 31, 2001.
45. Harden, op. cit.
46. *New York Times,* August 10, 2001.
47. BBC News, November 28, 2001.
48. Ibid., August 11, 2001.

49. Ibid., November 23, 2001.
50. Harden, op. cit.
51. Ibid.
52. *The Post* (Lusaka), August 6, 2001.
53. *Los Angeles Times,* October 17, 2001.
54. *Addis Tribune,* October 19, 2001.
55. BBC News, November 17, 2001.
56. *Los Angeles Times,* January 20, 2002, A3.
57. Ibid., January 24, 2002.
58. Agence France Presse, March 15, 2002.
59. Reuters, July 30, 2002.

Bibliography

Achebe, C. "An Image of Africa: Racism in Conrad's *Heart of Darkness.*" *The Massachusetts Review* 18(1977): 782 89.

Almquist, A. "The Society and Its Environment." In S. W. Meditz and T. Merrill, eds., *Zaire, a Country Study*, 64–133. Washington, D.C.: Federal Research Division, Library of Congress, 1994.

An Analytical Chronology of the Congo Crisis. Department of State, January 25, 1961.

Andersson, E. *Messianic Popular Movements in the Lower Congo.* Uppsala, Sweden: Almquist & Wiksells, 1958.

Anstey, R. *Britain and the Congo in the Nineteenth Century.* Oxford: Clarendon Press, 1962.

———. *King Leopold's Legacy: The Congo Under Belgian Rule, 1908–1960.* London: Oxford University Press, 1966.

Axelson, S. *Culture Confrontation in the Lower Congo: From the Old Congo Kingdom to the Congo Independent State with Special Reference to the Swedish Missionaries in the 1880's and 1890's.* Falköping, Sweden: Gummessons, 1970.

Ayittey, G. B. N. *Africa in Chaos.* New York: Pantheon Books, 1998.

Balandier, G. *Daily Life in the Kingdom of the Kongo from the Sixteenth to the Eighteenth Century.* Translated by Helen Weaver. New York: Pantheon Books, 1968.

Boll, U. R. V. *Portugal and the Quest for the Indies.* London: Constable, 1974.

Benedetto, R., ed. *Presbyterian Reformers in Central Africa: A Documentary Account of the American Presbyterian Congo Mission and the Human Rights Struggle in the Congo, 1890–1918.* Translated by Winifred K. Vass. Leiden: E. J. Brill, 1996.

Bentley, W. H. *Pioneering on the Congo.* 2 vols. Oxford: The Religious Tract Society, 1900.

Berkeley, B. *The Graves Are Not Yet Full: Race, Tribe and Power in the Heart of Africa.* New York: Basic Books, 2001.

Bierman, J. *Dark Safari: The Life Behind the Legend of Henry Morton Stanley.* New York: A. A. Knopf, 1990.

Blassingame, J. W. *The Slave Community: Plantation Life in the Antebellum South.* Oxford: Oxford University Press, 1979.

Boissonade, E. *Kabila, Clone de Mobutu?* Paris: Éditions Moreux, 1998.

Bourgoin, P. "Herbert Ward, 1863–1919: Explorer, Writer, Sculptor and Collector." *The World of Tribal Art,* spring 1996, 48–62.

Bradford, P. V., and H. Blume. *Ota: The Pygmy in the Zoo.* New York: St. Martin's Press, 1992.

Braekman, C. "One Disaster After Another." *Index on Censorship* 1 (2001): 138–49.

Brode, H. *Tippoo Tib: The Story of His Career in Central Africa.* Translated by H. Havelock. London: Edward Arnold, 1907.

Burrows, G. *The Land of the Pigmies.* New York: Thomas Y. Crowell, 1898.

————. *The Curse of Central Africa: With which is incorporated, A Campaign Amongst Cannibals,* by Edgar Canisius. London: R. A. Everett & Co., 1903.

Burton, R. *Two Trips to Gorilla Land and the Cataracts of the Congo.* 2 vols. London: Sampson Low, 1876.

Caldwell, D. *Thinking Black: 22 Years Without a Break in the Long Grass of Central Africa.* London: Morgan and Scott, 1912.

Cameron, V. L. *Across Africa.* 2 vols. London: Daldy, Isbister & Co., 1877.

Carton de Wiart, E. *Léopold II, souvenirs des dernières années 1901–1909.* Brussels: Goemaere, 1944.

Casati, G. *Ten Years in Equatoria and the Return of Emin Pasha.* 2 vols. London: Frederick Warne, 1891.

Ceulemans, R. P. P. *La question arabe et le Congo (1883–1892).* Bruxelles: MARSC, 1959.

Chabal, P., and J-P. Daloz, eds. *Africa Works: Disorder as Political Instrument.* Oxford: The International African Institute, James Currey, 1999.

Chapaux, A. *Le Congo: Historique, Diplomatique, Physique, Politique, Économique, Humanitaire, et Colonial.* Brussels: Rozez, 1894.

Chatterjee, D. N. *Storm Over the Congo.* New Delhi: Vikas, 1980.

Chomé, J. *L'ascension de Mobutu: du Sergent Joseph Désiré au Général Sese Seko.* Brussels: Éditions Complexe, 1974.

Clark, J. F. "Mobutu Sese Seko of Zaire as a Nondemocratic Presidential Leader." In L. Graybill and K. W. Thompson, eds., *Africa's Second Wave of Freedom: Development, Democracy and Rights,* 43–64. Landham, Va.: University Press of America, 1998.

Cline, C. A. *E. D. Morel, 1874–1924: The Strategies of Protest.* Dundonald, Belfast: Blackstaff Press, 1980.

Close, E. *A Woman Alone in Kenya, Uganda and the Belgian Congo.* London: Constable & Co., 1924.

Clozel, F. J. "Les Banziris." *Revue Scientifique* 52 (1893): 295–99.

Colvin, I. *The Rise and Fall of Moishe Tshombe.* London: Leslie Frewin, 1968.

Cornet, R. *La Bataille du Rail.* Brussels: Éditions L. Cuypers, 1958.

Cornevin, R. *Histoire du Congo, Léopoldville-Kinshasa, des Origines Préhistoriques à la République Démocratique du Congo.* 3rd ed. Paris: Berger-Levrault, 1970.

Cureau, H. G. "William H. Sheppard: Missionary to the Congo, and Collector of African Art." *Journal of Negro History* 67 (1982): 340–52.

Davis, D. B. *Slavery and Human Progress.* Oxford: Oxford University Press, 1984.

———. "Slavery—White, Black, Muslim, Christian." *The New York Review of Books,* July 5, 2001.

Davis, R. H. *The Congo and Coasts of Africa.* New York: Charles Scribner's Sons, 1907.

De Backer, M. C. C. *Notes pour servir à l'étude des "groupements politiques" à Léopoldville.* Léopoldville: Infor-Congo, 1959.

De Boeck, G. *Baoni: Les Révoltes de la Force Publique sous Léopold II, Congo, 1895–1908.* Brussels: Les Éditions EPO, 1987.

De Bouveignes, O. "Jérôme de Montesarchio et la découverte du Stanley-Pool." *Zaire* 2 (1948): 989–1013.

DeVaughan, Baroness, with P. Faure. *A Commoner Married a King.* New York: Ives Washburn, 1937.

De Vos, P. *Vie et mort de Lumumba.* Paris: Calmann-Lévy, 1961.

De Witte, L. *L'assassinat de Lumumba.* Paris: Éditions Karthala, 2000.

Diène, D., ed. *From Chains to Bonds: The Slave Trade Revisited.* New York: Berghahn, 2001.

Dieu, L. *Dans la brousse congolaise.* Liège: Maréchal, 1946.

Donny, A., ed. *Renseignements Pratiques.* Brussels: A. Lesigne, 1896.

Dorman, M. R. P. *A Journal of a Tour in the Congo Free State.* London: Kegan Paul, Trench, Trübner & Co., 1905.

Dos Passos, J. *The Portugal Story: Three Centuries of Exploration and Discovery.* Garden City, N.Y.: Doubleday & Company, 1969.

Doyle, D. *True Men and Traitors: From the OSS to the CIA, My Life in the Shadows.* New York: John Wiley & Sons, 2001.

Dugauquier, D. P. *Congo Cauldron.* London: Jarrolds, 1961.

Duncan, S., and P. Duncan. *Bonganga: Experiences of a Missionary Doctor.* New York: William Morrow, 1960.

Elliot, J. M., and M. M. Dymally. *Voices of Zaire: Rhetoric or Reality.* Washington: Washington Institute Press, 1990.

Emerson, B. *Leopold II of the Belgians, King of Colonialism.* London: Weidenfeld and Nicolson, 1979.

Emizet, K. N. F. "Explaining the Rise and Fall of Military Regimes: Civil-Military Relations in the Congo." *Armed Forces and Society* 26 (2000): 203–20.

Farrant, L. *Tippu Tip and the East African Slave Trade.* New York: St. Martin's Press, 1975.

Fetter, B. *The Creation of Elisabethville, 1910–1940.* Stanford: Stanford University Press, 1976.

Flament, A. *La Force Publique de sa naissance à 1914: Participations des militaires à l'histoire des premières années du Congo.* Brussels: Institut Royal Colonial Belge, 1952.

Foran, W. R. *African Odyssey: The Life of Verney Lovett Cameron.* London: Hutchinson & Co., 1937.

Bibliography

Forbath, P. *The River Congo: The Discovery, Exploration and Exploitation of the World's Most Dramatic River.* New York: Harper & Row, 1977.

Fox Bourne, H. R. *The Other Side of the Emin Pasha Relief Expedition.* London: Chatto & Windus, 1891.

Franklin, J. H. *George Washington Williams: A Biography.* Chicago: University of Chicago Press, 1985.

Gann, L. H., and P. Duignan. *The Rulers of Belgian Africa, 1884–1914.* Princeton: Princeton University Press, 1979.

Glave, E. J. *Six Years of Adventure in Congo-land* (with an introduction by H. M. Stanley). London: Sampson Low, Marston & Company, 1893.

Gnamo, A. H. "The Rwandan Genocide and the Collapse of Mobutu's Kleptocracy." In H. Adelman and A. Suhrke, eds., *The Path of a Genocide: The Rwanda Crisis from Uganda to Zaire,* 321–49. London: Transaction Publishers, 1999.

Grévisse, F. *La Grande pitié des juridictions indigènes.* Brussels: I.R.C.B., 1949.

Hallet, J-P. *Congo Kitabu.* New York: Random House, 1964.

Harden, B. *Washington Post,* November 10, 1987.

———. *Africa: Dispatches from a Dark Continent.* Boston: Houghton Mifflin, 1990.

———. "A Black Mud from Africa Helps Power the New Economy." *New York Times,* August 12, 2001.

Harms, R. W. *River of Wealth, River of Sorrow: The Central Zaire Basin in the Era of the Slave and Ivory Trade.* New Haven: Yale University Press, 1981.

Hawker, G. *The Life of George Grenfell: Congo Missionary and Explorer.* London: The Religious Tract Society, 1909.

Hays, H. R. *From Ape to Angel: An Informal History of Social Anthropology.* New York: Capricorn Books, 1958.

Hibbert, C. *Africa Explored: Europeans in the Dark Continent, 1769–1889.* New York: W. W. Norton, 1982.

Hilton-Simpson, M. W. *Land and the Peoples of the Kasai, Being a Narrative of a Two-Years' Journey Among the Cannibals of the Equatorial Forest and Other Savage Tribes of the South-Western Congo.* London: Constable and Company, 1911.

Hinde, S. L. *The Fall of the Congo Arabs.* 1897. Reprint, New York: Negro Universities Press, 1969.

Hochschild, A. *King Leopold's Ghost: A Story of Greed, Terror, and Heroism in Colonial Africa.* Boston: Houghton Mifflin, 1998.

Hoyt, M. P. E. *Captive in the Congo: A Consul's Return to the Heart of Darkness.* Annapolis, Md.: Naval Institute Press, 2000.

Hyland, P. *The Black Heart: A Voyage to Central Africa.* London: Victor Gollancz, 1988.

Jacobs, S. M. "Their 'Special Mission': Afro-American Women as Missionaries to the Congo, 1894–1937." In S. M. Jacobs, ed., *Black Americans and the Missionary Movement in Africa,* 5–29. Westport, Conn.: Greenwood, 1982.

Jacobs, S. M., ed. *Black Americans and the Missionary Movement in Africa.* Westport, Conn.: Greenwood, 1982.

James, D. *Che Guevara, a Biography*. New York: Stein and Day, 1969.

Jameson, J. S. *Story of the Rear Column of the Emin Pasha Relief Expedition*. Edited by Mrs. J. S. Jameson. London: R. H. Porter, 1890.

Janssen, P. *À la Cour de Mobutu*. Paris: Michel Lafon, 1997.

Jephson, A. J. M. *Emin Pasha and the Rebellion at the Equator*. London: Sampson, Low, Marston, Searle & Rivington, 1890.

Johnston, H. H. "A Visit to Mr. Stanley's Stations on the River Congo." *Proceedings of the Royal Geographical Society* 5, no. 10 (1883): 569–81.

———. *The River Congo: From Its Mouth to Bolobo*. London: Sampson, Low, Marston & Company, 1895.

Jones, L. M., and I. Wynne. *H. M. Stanley and Wales*. St. Asaph, Wales: H. M. Stanley Exhibition Committee; Hawarden, Flintshire County Record Office, 1972.

Jones, R. *The Rescue of Emin Pasha*. London: Allison & Busby, 1910.

Joris, L. *Back to the Congo*. Translated by Stacey Knecht. New York: Atheneum, 1992.

Kabongo, I. "The Catastrophe of Belgian Decolonization." In P. Gifford and W. R. Louis, eds. *Decolonization and African Independence: The Transfers of Power, 1960–1980*, 381–400. New Haven: Yale University Press, 1988.

Kalb, M. G. *The Congo Cables*. New York: Macmillan, 1982.

Kellersberger, J. L. *A Life for the Congo: The Story of Althea Brown Edmiston*. New York: Fleming H. Revell, 1947.

———. *Lucy Gantt Sheppard, Shepherdess of His Sheep on Two Continents*. Atlanta: Committee on Women's Work, Presbyterian Church in the United States, n.d.

Kelly, S. *America's Tyrant: The CIA and Mobutu of Zaire*. Washington, D.C.: American University Press, 1993.

Kwitney, J. *Endless Enemies: The Making of an Unfriendly World*. New York: Congdon & Weed, 1984.

Lapsley, J. W., ed. *Samuel Norvell Lapsley, Missionary to the Congo Valley, West Africa, 1866–1892*. Richmond, Va.: Whittet and Shepperson, 1893.

Laxalt, R. *A Private War: An American Code Officer in the Belgian Congo*. Reno: University of Nevada Press, 1998.

Legum, C. *Congo Disaster*. Baltimore: Penguin Books, 1961.

Lemarchand, R. *Political Awakening in the Belgian Congo*. Berkeley: University of California Press, 1964.

Leslie, W. J. *Zaire: Continuity and Political Change in an Oppressive State*. Boulder: Westview Press, 1993.

Lindqvist, S. *"Exterminate the Brutes."* Translated by Joan Tate. New York: The New Press, 1996.

Listowel, J. *The Other Livingstone*. Lewes, U.K.: Julien Friedman, 1974.

Liveing, É. *Across the Congo: The Story of Norden's Pioneer Journey in 1923*. London: H. F. & G. Witherby, 1962.

Livingstone, D. *Missionary Travels and Researches in South Africa*. New York: Harper & Brothers, 1858.

————. *The Last Journals of David Livingstone in Central Africa, from 1865 to his Death.* 2 vols. London: John Murray, 1874.

Lloyd, A. B. *In Dwarf Land and Cannibal Country: A Record of Travel and Discovery in Central Africa.* London: T. Fischer Unwin, 1900.

Louis, W. R. "Roger Casement and the Congo." *Journal of African History* 5 (1964): 99–120.

Louis, W. R., and J. Stengers. *E. D. Morel's History of the Congo Reform Movement.* London: Oxford, 1968.

Lovell, M. S. *A Rage to Live: A Biography of Richard and Isabel Burton.* New York: W. W. Norton, 1998.

Mabie, C. L. *Congo Cameos.* Philadelphia: The Judson Press, 1952.

MacGaffey, J., ed. *The Real Economy of Zaire: The Contribution of Smuggling and Other Unofficial Activities to Nation Wealth.* Philadelphia: University of Pennsylvania Press, 1991.

MacGaffey, W. "Economic and Social Dimensions of Kongo Slavery." In S. Miers and I. Kopytoff, eds. *Slavery in Africa: Historical and Anthropological Perspectives,* 235–57. Madison: University of Wisconsin Press, 1977.

Mahoney, R. D. *JFK: Ordeal in Africa.* New York: Oxford, 1983.

Maier, K. *Into the House of Our Ancestors: Inside the New Africa.* New York: John Wiley and Sons, 1998.

Malengreau, G. *Vers un paysannat indigène. Les lotissements agricoles au Congo belge.* Brussels: I. R. C. B., 1949.

Mamdani, M. *When Victims Become Killers: Colonialism, Nativism, and the Genocide in Rwanda.* Princeton: Princeton University Press, 2001.

Marchal, J. *E. Morel contre Léopold II: L'Histoire du Congo, 1900–1910.* 2 vols. Paris: Éditions L'Harmattan, 1996a.

————. *L'État Libre du Congo: Paradis Perdu: L'Histoire du Congo, 1876–1900.* 2 vols. Borgloon, Belgium: Éditions Paula Bellings, 1996b.

Marles, H. "Arrested Development: Race and Evolution in the Sculpture of Herbert Ward." *The Oxford Art Journal* 19 (1996): 16–28.

Martelli, G. *Leopold to Lumumba: A History of the Belgian Congo, 1877–1960.* London: Chapman & Hall, 1962.

Masson, P. *La Bataille pour Bukavu.* Brussels: Impresor, 1965.

Maurice, A., ed. *H. M. Stanley: Unpublished Letters.* London: W. & R. Chambers, 1955.

Mbenge, D. M. *Histoire secrète du Zaire: l'autopsie de la barbarie au service du monde.* Brussels: Éditions de l'espérance, 1977.

McKinley, J. C. "Mobutu's Nemesis Keeps His Plans to Himself." *New York Times,* April 1, 1997, A1.

McLynn, F. *Stanley: The Making of an African Explorer.* Chelsea, Mich.: Scarborough House, 1990.

————. *Stanley: Sorcerer's Apprentice.* London: Constable, 1991.

————. *Hearts of Darkness: The European Exploration of Africa.* London: Hutchinson, 1992.

Meditz, S. W., and T. Merrill, eds. *Zaire, a Country Study*. Washington, D.C.: American University Press, 1994.

Merchiers, L. *A Preliminary Report on the Atrocities Committed by the Congolese Army Against the White Population of the Republic of the Congo Before the Intervention of the Belgian Forces*. New York: Belgian Government Information Center, 1960.

Merriam, A. P. *Congo: Background of Conflict*. Evanston: Northwestern University Press, 1961.

Michaux, Captain. *Carnet de Campagne: Episodes & Impressions de 1889–1897*. Bruxelles: Librairie Falk, 1907.

Middleton, D., ed. *The Diary of A. J. Mounteney Jephson: Emin Pasha Relief Expedition, 1887–1889*. Cambridge: Cambridge University Press, 1969.

Misser, F. "Democratic Republic of Congo: Lessons in Statecraft." *African Business*, April, 2001, 45–46.

Monahan, M. P. *"The Sound of Guns: A Biography of Tippu Tip."* Master's thesis, Department of History, San Francisco State College, 1972.

Monheim, F. *Mobutu, l'homme seul*. Brussels: Éditions Actuelles, 1963.

Moore, E. D. *Ivory Scourge of Africa*. New York: Harper and Brothers, 1931.

Morel, E. D. *Red Rubber: The Story of the Rubber Slave Trade Which Flourished on the Congo for Twenty Years, 1890–1910*. New and rev. ed. 1906. Reprint, Manchester: National Labour Press, 1919.

Mountmorres, Viscount. *The Congo Independent State: A Report on a Voyage of Enquiry*. London: Williams and Norgate, 1906.

Murdock, G. P. *Africa: Its Peoples and Their Culture History*. New York: McGraw-Hill, 1959.

Nadjer, Z. *Joseph Conrad: A Chronicle*. New Brunswick, N.J.: Rutgers University Press, 1983.

Ngolet, F. "African and American Connivance in Congo-Zaire." *Africa Today* 47 (2000): 64–80.

Nguz a Karl-i-Bond. *Mobutu, ou l'Incarnation du Mal Zairois*. London: Rex Collins, 1982.

Norden, H. *Fresh Tracks in the Belgian Congo: From the Uganda Border to the Mouth of the Congo*. Boston: Small, Maynard & Co., 1925.

Northrup, D. *Beyond the Bend in the River: African Labor in Eastern Zaire, 1865–1940*. Athens: Ohio University Center for International Studies, 1988.

O'Ballance, E. *The Congo-Zaire Experience, 1960–98*. New York: St. Martin's Press, 2000.

Odom, T. P. *Dragon Operations: Hostage Rescues in the Congo; Leavenworth Papers No.14*. Fort Leavenworth, Kans.: Combat Studies Institute, U.S. Army Command and General Staff College, 1988.

Packenham, T. *The Scramble for Africa, 1876–1912*. New York: Random House, 1991.

Packham, E. *Success or Failure: The UN Intervention in the Congo After Independence*. Commack, N.Y.: Nova Science Publishers, 1998.

Parke, T. H. *My Personal Experiences in Equatorial Africa*. New York: Charles Scribner's Sons, 1891.

Pawling, S. S. *Mr. Poilu: Notes and Sketches with the Fighting French*. London: Hodder and Stoughton, 1916.

Phipps, W. E. *The Sheppards and Lapsley: Pioneer Presbyterians in the Congo.* Louisville, Ky.: The Presbyterian Church, 1991.

Pigafetta, F. *A Report of the Kingdom of Congo and of the Surrounding Countries; Drawn out of the Writings and Discourses of the Portuguese, Duarte Lopez.* Translated by M. Hutchinson. 1591. Reprint, London: John Murray, 1881.

Pipes, D. *Slave Soldiers and Islam: The Genesis of a Military System.* New Haven: Yale University Press, 1981.

Pons, V. *Stanleyville: An African Urban Community Under Belgian Administration.* London: Oxford University Press, 1969.

Ravenstein, E. G., ed. *The Strange Adventures of Andrew Battell of Leigh, in Angola and the Adjoining Regions.* London: The Hakluyt Society, 1901.

Reed, D. *111 Days in Stanleyville.* New York: Harper & Row, 1965.

Richburg, K. B. *Out of America: A Black Man Confronts Africa.* New York: Basic Books, 1997.

Roth, D. F. "The 'Black Man's Burden': The Racial Background of Afro-American Missionaries and Africa." In S. M. Jacobs, ed., *Black Americans and the Missionary Movement in Africa,* 31–38. Westport, Conn.: Greenwood, 1982.

Samarin, W. J. *The Black Man's Burden: African Colonial Labor on the Congo and Ubangi Rivers, 1880–1900.* Boulder, Colo.: Westview Press, 1989.

Schall, L. M. "William H. Sheppard: Fighter for African Rights." In K. L. Schall, ed., *Stony the Road: Chapters in the History of Hampton Institute,* 105–24. Charlottesville, University Press of Virginia, 1977.

Schatzberg, M. G. "Beyond Mobutu: Kabila and the Congo." *Journal of Democracy* 8 (1977): 70–84.

———. *The Dialectics of Oppression in Zaire.* Bloomington: Indiana University Press, 1988.

———. *Mobutu or Chaos? The United States and Zaire, 1960–1990.* New York: University Press of America, 1991.

Schweitzer, G. *Emin Pasha: His Life and Work.* 2 vols. London: Archibald Constable and Co., 1898.

Segal, R. *African Profiles.* Baltimore, Md.: Penguin Books, 1962.

Serpa Pinto, A. A. *How I Crossed Africa: From the Atlantic Ocean, Through Unknown Countries; Discovery of the Great Zambesi Affluents, etc.* Translated by A. Elwes. London: Sampson, Low, Marston, Searle, & Rivington, 1881.

Severn, M. *Congo Pilgrim.* London: The Travel Book Club, 1952.

Shaloff, S. *Reform in Leopold's Congo.* Richmond, Va.: John Knox Press, 1970.

Shaw, B. P. "Force Publique, Force Unique." Ph.D. diss. Department of Psychology, University of Wisconsin, Madison, 1984.

Sheppard, W. H. *Southern Workman,* December 1893, 182.

———. *Kasai Herald,* January 1, 1908.

———. *Pioneers in Congo.* Louisville, KY.: Pentecostal Publishing Co., 1917.

Simmons, A. M. "Kabila's Funeral Held Amid Tight Security." *Los Angeles Times,* January 24, 2001, A10.

Singleton-Gates, P., and M. Girodias. *The Black Diaries: An Account of Casement's Life and Times, with a Collection of His Diaries and Public Writings.* New York: Grove Press, 1959.

Slade, R. M. *English-Speaking Missions in the Congo Independent State (1878–1908).* Brussels: Académie Royale des Sciences Coloniales, 1959.

———. *The Belgian Congo: Some Recent Changes.* London: Institute of Race Relations, Oxford University Press, 1960.

———. *King Leopold's Congo: Aspects of the Development of Race Relations in the Congo Independent State.* London and New York: Oxford University Press, 1962.

Smith, I. R. *The Emin Pasha Relief Expedition, 1886–1890.* Oxford: The Clarendon Press, 1972.

Springer, J. M. *Pioneering in the Congo.* New York: Katanga Press, 1916.

Stairs, W. G. *Victorian Explorer: The African Diaries of Captain William G. Stairs.* Edited by J. M. Konczacki. Halifax, Nova Scotia: Nimbus, 1994.

Stanley, H. M. *How I Found Livingstone.* 2 vols. New York: Scribner, Armstrong & Co., 1872.

———. *Coomassie and Magdala: The Story of Two British Campaigns in Africa.* New York: Harper, 1874.

———. *Through the Dark Continent.* 2 vols. New York: Harper & Brothers, 1878.

———. *In Darkest Africa; or, The Quest, Rescue and Retreat of Emin, Governor of Equatoria.* 2 vols. New York: Charles Scribner's Sons, 1890.

———. *The Autobiography of Henry Morton Stanley.* Edited by Dorothy Stanley. Boston: Houghton-Mifflin, 1909.

Stanley, R., and A. Neame, eds. *The Exploration Diaries of H. M. Stanley.* London: William Kimber, 1961.

Stanley Family Archives. British Library, London.

Stengers, J. *Belgique et Congo; l'élaboration de la charte coloniale.* Brussels: La Renaissance du Livre, 1963.

Stinglhamber, G., and P. Dresse. *Léopold II au Travail.* Brussels: Éditions du Sablon, 1945.

Stockwell, J. *In Search of Enemies: A CIA Story.* New York: W. W. Norton, 1978.

Stuart, R. R. *Kassai: The Story of Raoul de Prémorel, African Trader.* Stockton, Calif.: University of the Pacific, 1975.

Swann, A. J. *Fighting the Slave Hunters in Central Africa.* London: Seeley, 1910.

Tayler, J. *Facing the Congo.* St. Paul, Minn.: Ruminator Books, 2000.

Taylor, J. V., and D. Lehmann. *Christians of the Copperbelt.* London: S. C. M. Press, 1961.

Timmons, S. L. V. *Glorious Living: Informal Sketches of Seven Women Missionaries of the Presbyterian Church, U.S.* Atlanta: Committee on Women's Work, Presbyterian Church, U.S., 1937.

Torday, E. *On the Trail of the Bushongo.* London: Seeley, Service & Co., 1925.

Troup, J. R. *With Stanley's Rear Column.* London: Chapman and Hall, 1890.

Tuckey, J. K. *Narrative of an Expedition to Explore the River Zaire, Usually Called the Congo, in South Africa, in 1816, Under the Direction of Captain J. K. Tuckey, R.N.* 1818. Reprint, London: John Murray, 1967.

Turnbull, C. M. *The Lonely African.* London: Chatto and Windus, 1963.

Twain, M. *King Leopold's Soliloquy: A Defense of His Congo Rule.* Boston: P. R. Warren, 1905.

Urquhart, B. "The Tragedy of Lumumba." *The New York Review,* October 4, 2001.

Van der Kerken, G. *Les Sociétés Bantoues du Congo Belge.* Brussels: Établissements Émile Bruylant, 1920.

Vansina, J. "Les Croyances Religieuses des Kuba." *Zaire* 12 (1958): 725–58.

———. *Introduction à l'Ethnographie du Congo.* Brussels: Éditions Universitaires du Congo, 1965.

———. *Kingdoms of the Savanna.* Madison: University of Wisconsin Press, 1966.

———. "Du royaume kuba an 'territoire des Bakubo.' " *Études Congolaises* 12 (1969): 3–54.

———. *The Children of Woot: A History of the Kuba Peoples.* Madison: University of Wisconsin Press, 1978.

———. Introduction to D. Vangroenweghe. *Du Sang sur les Lianes.* Brussels: Didier Hatier, 1986.

———. *Paths in the Rainforests: Toward a History of Political Tradition in Equatorial Africa.* Madison: University of Wisconsin Press, 1990.

Verbeken, A., and M. Walraet. *La première traversée du Katanga en 1806.* Brussels: Académie Royale des Sciences d'Outre Mer, 1953.

Verhaegen, B. *Rébellions au Congo.* 2 vols. Brussels: CRISP, 1966.

Vinson, T. C. *William McCutchan Morrison: Twenty Years in Central Africa.* Richmond, Va.: Presbyterian Committee on Publication, 1921.

Vleurinck, T., ed. *46 Angry Men: The 46 Civilian Doctors of Elisabethville Denounce U.N.O. Violations in Katanga.* Brussels: Belgian Senate, 1962.

Ward, H. *Five Years with the Congo Cannibals.* London: Chatto & Windus, 1891a.

———. *My Life with Stanley's Rear Guard.* London: Chatto & Windus, 1891b.

———. *A Voice from the Congo: Comprising Stories, Anecdotes, and Descriptive Notes.* London: William Heinemann, 1910.

———. *Mr. Poilu: Notes and Sketches with the Fighting French.* London: Hodder and Stoughton, 1916.

Ward, S. *A Valiant Gentleman, Being the Biography of Herbert Ward, Artist and Man of Action.* London: Chapman and Hall, 1927.

Weeks, J. H. *Among the Primitive Bakongo.* London: Seeley, Service & Co., 1914.

Weintraub, S. *Victoria: An Intimate Biography.* New York: Dutton, 1987.

West, R. *Congo.* New York: Holt, Rinehart and Winston, 1972.

Williame, J-C. *L'Odyssée: Trajectoire pour un Congo Nouveau?* Paris: Éditions Karthala, 1999.

Williams, W. L. "William Henry Sheppard, Afro-American Missionary in the Congo, 1890–1910." In S. M. Jacobs, ed. *Black Americans and the Missionary Movement in Africa,* 135–53. Westport, Conn.: Greenwood, 1982.

Winternitz, H. *East Along the Equator: A Journey up the Congo and into Zaire.* New York: Atlantic Monthly Press, 1987.

Wissmann, H. von. *My Second Journey Through Equatorial Africa from the Congo to the Zambezi in the Years 1886 and 1887*. London: Chatto & Windus, 1891.

Wrong, M. *In the Footsteps of Mr. Kurtz: Living on the Brink of Disaster in the Congo*. London: Fourth Estate, 2000.

Young, C. *Politics in the Congo: Decolonization and Independence*. Princeton: Princeton University Press, 1965.

———. "Rebellion and the Congo." In R. I. Rotberg and A. A. Mazrui eds. *Protest and Power in Black Africa*, 969–1011. New York: Oxford University Press, 1970.

Young, C., and T. Turner. *The Rise and Decline of the Zairian State*. Madison: University of Wisconsin Press, 1985.

Index

Index